ADULT PSYCHOLOGICAL PROBLEMS

Adult psychological problems
An introduction
(Second Edition)

edited by

Lorna Champion
Department of Clinical Psychology,
Royal Edinburgh Hospital, UK

Mick Power
Department of Psychiatry,
University of Edinburgh, UK

PSYCHOLOGY PRESS
ALERE FLAMMAM
Taylor & Francis Group

First published 2000 by Psychology Press Ltd
27 Church Road, Hove, East Sussex, BN3 2FA

http://www.psypress.co.uk

Simultaneously published in the USA and Canada
by Taylor & Francis Inc
325 Chestnut Street, Suite 800, Philadelphia, PA 19106

Reprinted 2002 by Psychology Press
27 Church Road, Hove, East Sussex, BN3 2FA
29 West 35th Street, New York, NY 10001

Psychology Press is part of the Taylor & Francis Group

British Library Cataloguing in Publication Data
A catalogue record for this book is available from the British Library

ISBN 0–86377–641–8 (hbk)
ISBN 0–86377–642–6 (pbk)

ISSN: 1368–9207 (Contemporary Psychology Series)

Cover design by Leigh Hurlock
Typeset by Graphicraft Ltd, Hong Kong
Printed and bound in Great Britain by
Biddles Ltd, Guildford and King's Lynn

Contents

List of contributors

Margie Callanan, Clinical Psychology Training Scheme, Salomons, Centre for Applied Social and Psychological Development, Broomhill Road, Southborough, Tunbridge Wells, Kent, TN3 0TG, UK

Lorna Champion, Department of Clinical Psychology, Royal Edinburgh Hospital, 40 Colinton Road, Edinburgh, EH10 5HF, UK

Patricia d'Ardenne, Department of Clinical Psychology, The City & Hackney Community NHS Trust, 52 Clifden Road, London, E5 0LJ, UK

Padmal de Silva, Department of Psychology, Institute of Psychiatry, De Crespigny Park, Denmark Hill, London, SE5 8AF, UK

Tony Lavender, Clinical Psychology Training Scheme, Salomons, Centre for Applied Social and Psychological Development, Broomhill Road, Southborough, Tunbridge Wells, Kent, TN3 0TG, UK

Helen McCarthy, Department of Clinical Psychology, Gwent Community NHS Trust, 12 Park Square, Newport, Gwent, NP9 4EL, UK

Jean Mitchell, Anglian Harbours NHS Trust, 3 Moores Cottages, Upper Holton, Halesworth, Suffolk, IP19 8QP, UK

Karen Partridge, Department of Psychology and Counselling, Kingston District Community NHS Trust, Richmond Healthcare Hamlet, Kew Foot Road, Richmond, London, TW9 2TE, UK

Jane Powell, Department of Psychology, Goldsmiths College, New Cross, London, SE14 6NW, UK

Michael Power, Department of Psychiatry, Royal Edinburgh Hospital, University of Edinburgh, Edinburgh, EH10 5HF, UK

Contemporary Psychology Series

Series Editor: Professor Raymond Cochrane
School of Psychology
The University of Birmingham
Birmingham B15 2TT, UK

This series of books on contemporary psychological issues is aimed primarily at 'A' Level students and those beginning their undergraduate degree. All of these volumes are introductory in the sense that they assume no, or very little, previous acquaintance with the subject, while aiming to take the reader through to the end of his or her course on the topic they cover. For this reason the series will also appeal to those who encounter psychology in the course of their professional work: nurses, social workers, police and probation officers, speech therapists and medical students. Written in a clear and jargon-free style, each book generally includes a full (and in some cases annotated) bibliography and points the way explicitly to further reading on the subject covered.

Series preface

The aim of this book is to introduce the reader to the study of adult psychological problems. Lorna Champion and Mick Power begin with a balanced overview of the main approaches that are currently in use in abnormal psychology and allied disciplines. The historical background to each approach is sketched out in order to provide a sense of the context in which the approach developed. A number of the controversies that surround the area as a whole are also outlined. Champion and Power set the scene in the hope that the reader will feel sufficiently enthused to follow up some of the recommended reading and pursue his or her own study of the area.

All of the contributors to the book are practising clinicians in addition to their academic and research interests. The aim of each chapter is to provide the reader with a sense of the particular disorder described and how it manifests itself, before going on to discuss the ways in which the disorder may be understood and treated.

It is inevitable that contributors have preferences for some approaches rather than others and that the individual chapters should reflect these preferences. For example, the chapter on alcohol and drugs and on obsessive-compulsive disorders are strongest on cognitive and behavioural approaches, whereas the chapter on family problems focuses on systems models. These emphases, however, not only reflect the authors' preferences but also indicate current trends in how these disorders are most commonly treated.

Many students come to psychology because of a desire to understand the nature and origins of psychological problems, and this book provides an ideal introduction to the topic which has been written to be accessible to the beginning student, but also goes into sufficient depth to satisfy the person seriously considering a career in clinical psychology.

Ray Cochrane

CHAPTER ONE

Models of psychological problems: An overview

Mick Power
Department of Psychiatry, University of Edinburgh, UK

Lorna Champion
Department of Clinical Psychology, Royal Edinburgh Hospital, UK

INTRODUCTION

What is "psychology"? Not only is it a difficult word to spell, but it is also a difficult word to define. The problem, as we shall see, is that the definition depends on the view of psychology to which you subscribe. For example, the behavioural approach might define psychology as the "study of behaviour" whereas, in contrast, a cognitive psychologist might define psychology as "the science of mental life". It is possible of course that a full definition might have to incorporate all of these elements such as in the definition "the science of behaviour and mental life . . .". Although the focus of the present book is on adult psychological problems, the different views about psychology are reflected in the different approaches to and models of these disorders. However, for most disorders it seems likely that no particular model is sufficient in itself, but a number of models may need to be integrated together in order to provide a full account of the problem.

So why are you interested in psychology? When asked this question early in their studies, most psychology students do not report a burning interest in visual perception in the frog, or a fascination for vestibular balance mechanisms in the guinea pig. Instead, they say that they may have read something about Freud and found it interesting, or that a friend or relative had psychological problems, or even, in the more honest and insightful cases, that they were aware of personal problems that they hoped psychology would address. Catch the same students a few years later, however, and either they will tell you that Freud is not worth a jot because he is not a scientist and that their heroes are now people with strange

1

names whom nobody has ever heard of but who are doing wonderful things with the caudate nucleus (wherever that is!), or, alternatively, they will say that psychology had nothing to offer them personally, which is why they are now joining a leading advertising firm in The City. Between these extremes, however, we believe that psychology *does* have something to offer on both a personal and a scientific level. The purpose of this book is to demonstrate both of these sides of psychology—the personal and the scientific—and to show how the various theories and therapies can contribute to our understanding of the problems that can beset us all during our adult lives.

Psychology is a very strange subject. Like politics and religion there are as many opposing views as there are psychologists. Unlike politics and religion, no wars have yet been started in the name of psychology. Nevertheless, battles are waged daily throughout the civilised psychological world in books, academic journals, lecture rooms, and conference halls between the supporters of opposing approaches to psychology. As will be evident from the contents of their chapters, some of the contributors to this volume have clearly identified which side they are on, Cavalier or Roundhead, the righteous or the infidel. We believe, however, that each approach has something to offer, has something of value, has good theoretical constructs and bad theoretical constructs, has good practitioners and bad practitioners.

To return to the question of what psychology is, the student who comes from a scientific background will be shocked, even disturbed, by the lack of incontrovertible fact, by the contradictory nature of the theories, and by the importance of opinion and choice. The student from an arts background will be thrown by numbers and statistics, the use of computers and animals. In order to examine the question therefore of "What is psychology?", we must first examine the question "What is science?" in order to understand some of the disagreements. In so doing, we will see that two views of science can be identified: first, the traditional view taught in schools, which emphasises fact, experiment and measurement and which has had a strong influence on behavioural psychology, and, second, a modern view of science, which emphasises subjectivity, unpredictability, and non-deterministic processes. This modern view is more compatible with Cognitive Psychology.

WHAT IS SCIENCE?

The traditional view of science emphasises a number of basic principles, which have proven of great value in the history and development of science. In fact, 19th-century scientists thought that they had answered all of the major problems of science and that only the details were left to be filled in: witness the achievements of Newton's mechanics, thermodynamics, Darwin's theory of evolution, and so on. The basic principles on which these developments were considered to depend are outlined in the following points.

Observation and fact. Facts are observable measurable properties of the world: Tigers are indigenous to India; the eye is sensitive to light: water freezes at 0 degrees centigrade. A large part of any science therefore is the routine accumulation of facts and observations; thus, the modern computer can store a vast number of facts about weather conditions, star positions, activity in a bubble chamber, or amino acid sequences in proteins. Of course, even traditional science was aware that "facts" do not always turn out to be what they appear to be. The earth was originally thought to be flat because it looked flat, besides which if it wasn't flat you would fall off the edge; then astronomers discovered that the earth was round. Later on we learned that the earth was not perfectly round but flattened at the poles; finally, science told us that in fact the earth is geoid-shaped (i.e. the fact is the earth turns out to have been "earth-shaped" all along!).

Description and classification.   If science only consisted of observation and fact, it would turn out to be like one long boring gossip session with little meaning or use. "Have you heard that water consists of hydrogen and oxygen?" "No, really!" "Two parts hydrogen, what's more!" "Get away." Instead, the next step is finding the appropriate level of description which can be meaningfully included in a classification system. For example, Linnaeus' classification of living things provided a magnificent taxonomy that helped to advance biology; the appropriate level of description seems relatively straightforward in that individual plants or animals provide the lowest level of description, which, in turn, can be grouped together at more general levels (species, phyla, etc.). Classification systems may nevertheless contain surprises that are counter to common sense: Whales are animals, tomatoes are fruit.

A second example of a classification system that had powerful predictive properties was Mendeleev's periodic table which provides a meaningful classification of chemical elements. The original Greek classification of the four "elements"—earth, air, fire, and water—proved to be an inappropriate one for science in that each of these so-called "elements" was divisible into more basic elements in the way that salt is divisible into the elements sodium and chlorine. The power of Mendeleev's system, which classified elements by atomic weight, was that it revealed gaps or missing elements which had not been discovered at that time, but which have subsequently been discovered.

Theory and hypothesis.   Theories group together facts and descriptions in a way that provides an overall working model relevant to the domain in question. A good theory, in the philosopher Karl Popper's terms, is both useful and falsifiable; thus, a good theory should generate hypotheses that may be novel and surprising and that can be tested in artificial or "natural" experiments. For example, Einstein's theory of relativity predicted that light would bend in a gravitational field, a prediction that was dramatically upheld when the light from a distant source was shown to bend as it passed the sun.

Popper and others used his notion of falsifiability to argue that certain "theories" such as psychoanalysis are not scientific theories at all because they are not falsifiable. Whatever happens in the rest of science, theories in psychology are rarely if ever rejected because of evidence to the contrary, but rather they go out of fashion. We will return however to Popper's allegations about psychoanalysis later in the chapter.

Experiment. Hypotheses derived from scientific theories may be tested in artificial and natural experiments in order to decide whether or not the experimental outcome is that predicted by the hypothesis. Experiments have to be carefully designed in order to be sure that the variable that the experimenter manipulates is truly the one that leads to differences in the variable that is measured. If the experimental outcome is due to some other confounding variable rather than the one that is manipulated, then the experiment is invalid. Psychology experiments on human subjects are notoriously difficult because what the *subject* thinks the experiment is about can be more important that what the *experimenter* thinks the experiment is about. In addition, many of the advances in psychology and medicine come not from experiments in which the experimenter manipulates one or more variables, but rather from "experiments of nature" such as road traffic accidents, strokes, life events, and natural disasters, the tragic consequences of which can provide insights into how the mind works.

The modern view of science (see Penrose, 1989) does not reject the role of facts, measurement, observation, hypothesis, classification, and experiment, but it does point to some severe limitations which draw modern science and modern psychology closer together. To begin with, let us take the building blocks of science, that is, "facts" or "observations". These holy objects have the status of absolute truths in traditional science, but modern science has emphasised their possible subjective nature and the role that inference as well as observation plays in making a fact a fact. For example, our sensory experience tells us the "fact" that the sun rises in the East and sinks in the West. The fact is, however, that it is not the sun that rises and falls, but the earth that rotates on its axis. Every schoolchild knows about the existence of electrons, protons, and neutrons, but nobody has ever observed these particles directly. Instead, it is both useful and necessary to infer their existence from other observations such as pathways in a bubble chamber.

Traditional science has emphasised prediction and control in deterministic systems, that is, the idea that outcomes are always knowable if all of the initial conditions are known. In contrast, modern science emphasises unpredictability and non-deterministic systems. Even at the atomic level, Heisenberg's uncertainty principle tells us that we cannot know both the position of an electron and its momentum, because the measurement of one affects the other; at best all we can do is make probabilistic statements about what might or might not happen.

In a similar manner in psychology we can study the rules that people use to construct sentences and participate in conversations but we can never determine what any speaker will say on any particular occasion. Meteorologists face similar problems even for short-term weather predictions and may gain public notoriety for the extent of their inaccuracy, as when the British meteorologist Michael Fish's immortal words "there will not be a hurricane tonight" were followed by the worst storm in 200 years! The problem faced by the complex systems that meteorologists and psychologists study is that very small differences in initial conditions can make a considerable difference to outcome: The developments in so-called "chaos" or "catastrophe theory" in the physical sciences demonstrate vividly how even simple systems can have unpredictable outcomes (see e.g. Gleick, 1988).

The moral of this tale for psychology is that both the traditional and the modern views of science have their advantages and disadvantages. Behavioural and experimental psychologists have focused on observation and measurement and, as we shall see, have made considerable contributions to our understanding of the laws of learning and the acquisition and treatment of a range of behavioural disorders. However, many psychoanalytic and cognitive psychologists have come to emphasise the importance of subjective factors and how they influence an individual's thoughts and actions. The focus in psychoanalysis on factors that are both subjective and unobservable does not imply that psychoanalysis is unscientific, contrary to what some psychologists and philosophers would have us believe. The aim of this book is to demonstrate how each approach to psychology has something to offer for our understanding of psychological disorders. In the next section, therefore, the basic principles of psychoanalysis, behaviourism, and cognitive psychology will be outlined, and in a subsequent section the relationship between psychology and biological and social models will also be examined.

THREE APPROACHES TO PSYCHOLOGY

In this section three key approaches to psychology will be outlined each of which has had a general impact on the theory and treatment of adult psychological disorders. These three areas are psychoanalysis, behaviourism, and cognitive psychology. The purpose of the section is to provide the key concepts for each approach without covering too much detail about specific applications. The specific applications of these and other approaches will be provided in subsequent chapters.

Psychoanalysis

The key figure in the development of psychoanalysis was Sigmund Freud (1856–1939). Freud's early career was as a neurologist; he invented the gold chloride method of staining nervous tissue, he was almost the first to discover the use of cocaine as a local anaesthetic, he published a book on aphasia and coined the term "agnosia" (the inability to name objects), and was one of the world's leading authorities on childhood paralyses, all before the age of 40! He even at the age of 21 spent a summer dissecting male eels in order to search for their apparently elusive gonads, an early sign perhaps of his later interests. The general point, however, is that Freud was very much a scientist working in a scientific tradition and it was this scientific rigour that he brought to psychoanalysis. In fact, one of his early unpublished works called "Project for a Scientific Psychology" (1895/1966) outlined a set of scientific principles which in many ways provided the basis for the subsequent developments in psychoanalysis. Unfortunately, he became disillusioned with the Project, left the manuscript with his friend Wilhelm Fliess, and never asked for it back.

In order to understand the basic concepts that underpin psychoanalysis, an outline of the following will be provided: the unconscious, psychic energy, repression, developmental stages, transference and countertransference, and the free association technique. Although these are only a few of the basic concepts, they should be sufficient to understand the psychoanalytic accounts presented in later chapters.

The unconscious.   Freud was by no means the first to suggest that the greater part of our psychic life occurs outside of conscious awareness (see Power, 1997), but his major contribution was his emphasis on the *dynamic* aspects of the unconscious. That is, Freud did not simply see the unconscious as an inactive storehouse of past memories, but rather as a system of wishes, fantasies, impulses, and memories that actively influenced our thoughts, actions, symptoms, dreams, mistakes, accidents, and emotions. He proposed that the unconscious was derived from innate drives of which we could never become directly conscious, and repressed material which was typically of an unpleasant personal nature. In his earlier writings he saw the unconscious as a system in itself, though later on in "The Ego and the Id" (1923/1984) he proposed an alternative system that consisted of Id, Ego, and Superego. Different aspects of these three structures were then viewed as unconscious.

One of the key points Freud proposed about the unconscious was that it defied time and logic and was not constrained by reality. For example, painful memories could be recalled from many years past as if they were happening now and had lost none of their emotional impact. In a similar manner, opposite and contradictory thoughts and impulses can be held in the unconscious; the same person can be both loved and hated at the same time.

Psychic energy.   Freud believed that the mind was fuelled by psychic energy very much in the way that physical energy is needed to fuel a physical machine. This energy, or "libido" as it was called, he initially considered to be derived from the life-preserving drives, "Eros". However, following the First World War and the loss of his favourite daughter (see Gay, 1988), he added a second set of life-destroying drives, "Thanatos", which typically manifested themselves as aggression towards the self or towards others. A number of subsequent analysts have disagreed with the concept of destructive drives, though one notable exception can be found in the work of Melanie Klein and her followers.

The comparison that Freud made between psychic energy and physical energy led to him adopting the so-called Principle of Constancy; namely, that by analogy with the laws of thermodynamics, *psychic* energy can never be created nor destroyed, but can only be changed from one form to another. For example, if sexual energy is blocked from being expressed through the normal channels, then it has to be expressed in other forms. In milder cases these forms could be disguised in dreams, in symptoms such as headaches or in teenage spots (!), in excessive intellectual activity, and so on. However, in more extreme cases Freud suggested that severe psychological disorders including anxiety, depression, and obsessional disorders resulted from the blocking of sexual energy.

Repression.   Freud used the term "repression" in various ways in his writings in order to refer to either the conscious or the unconscious avoidance of painful or unwanted information, in particular, information about the self or the self in relation to significant others. Freud used repression as a general term therefore to refer to almost any defence mechanism, though his daughter, Anna Freud, in 1937 provided a systematic list that, along with repression (in the specific sense of an *unconscious* avoidance of an unacceptable impulse or idea), included a number of other defence mechanisms such as reaction formation, sublimation, and projection.

In order to illustrate the actions of repression we can consider two different models of anxiety that Freud considered during his lifetime. In the early study carried out in collaboration with his mentor Josef Breuer, "Studies on Hysteria" (1895/1974), Freud argued that anxiety occurred as a consequence of repressed energy that was directly transformed into anxiety. However, in his later work, "Inhibitions, Symptoms and Anxiety" (1926/1979) he reversed this equation and proposed that anxiety can be a warning state of the ego that signals the necessity for repression, and thereby defends the ego against internal danger arising from forbidden wishes and impulses. Freud likened the warning state to immunisation, in that immunisation works through experiencing a mild dose of the illness in order to protect the individual from a more lethal dose.

Developmental stages.   Freud is normally credited with the concept of developmental sexual stages through which the child passes. In fact, the idea for such stages came from colleagues, such as Karl Abraham, based on their clinical observations. The proposal is that the child passes through a series of developmental stages labelled the oral, anal, phallic, latency, and genital phases. The main sources of pleasure in the oral, anal, and phallic stages are the mouth, the anus, and the genitals, respectively.

One of the additional proposals is that fixation can occur at different stages of development, which can either be apparent as personality traits, or revealed at times of stress. Typical oral characteristics are talkativeness, greed, gullibility, and generosity, whereas typical anal characteristics include obstinacy, orderliness, and miserliness.

A significant extension of the notion of developmental stages was provided by Erik Erikson (1963), who focused on more general psychosocial development rather than just sexual development, and also proposed that development does not stop in childhood or adolescence but continues through into adulthood. The adult stages emphasise the interpersonal roles that individuals take on and their productivity within those roles.

Transference.   Freud's early collaborator, Josef Breuer, found that one of his hysterical patients, Anna O, developed very strong feelings towards him in the course of his treatment of her. Breuer was unable to cope with the strength of her feelings (and presumably his own) and terminated her treatment. The feelings that the patient has for the therapist are called transference. Originally, therefore, transference was seen as a nuisance that got in the way of therapy, but Freud eventually came to encourage the development of transference, because he believed that transference was a re-enactment in the relationship with the therapist of earlier significant relationships and provided an opportunity to examine their nature via the exploration of fantasies and feelings in the transference relationship. In fact, the exploration of transference is considered to be the key therapeutic tool in psychoanalytic work, because it provides insight into past and present relationships and allows the working through of related conflicts and problems. The intimate situation in which the therapist and patient are placed and the fact that the psychoanalyst sits behind the patient is one way in which transference is encouraged; the technique of free association, whereby the patient is meant to say whatever comes into his or her mind, also allows the patient to dwell on fantasies about the therapist which the more directive therapies such as behaviour therapy and cognitive therapy (to be described later) would typically steer the patient away from.

The fact that patients have strong reactions to their therapists does not preclude the fact that therapists may have strong reactions, both positive and negative, to their patients. Such reactions are called countertransference and again can either be seen as nuisance phenomena that have no relevance to the treatment process or can be used in the course of therapy as a source of important information about the therapeutic relationship (see Casement, 1985).

Is psychoanalysis scientific?

The philosopher Karl Popper and the psychologist Hans Eysenck were two of the most vehement critics of psychoanalysis, both claiming that psychoanalysis was not scientific. We hope that the discussion so far has highlighted that science must in its modern form address both the "objective" and the "subjective", but in so doing changes the very nature of science itself. Popper's accusation that psychoanalysis is not falsifiable has been rejected by more recent philosophers of science (Grunbaum, 1984). In fact, many of the specific proposals outlined in this section are both testable and falsifiable. Whether or not believers and practitioners choose to ignore such empirical evidence is another matter, but we would note that this problem applies equally to behaviour therapists as to psychoanalytic therapists!

Behaviourism

The American psychologist J.B. Watson was the early champion of the behavioural approach to psychology. Watson reacted against the then dominant "introspectionist" approach to psychology, in which armchair psychologists who were specially trained and selected sat and recorded their own mental processes. Not surprisingly, despite careful selection, the occasional disagreement arose. Watson's reaction was to dismiss the study of mind as of scientific irrelevance because it is unobservable and, indeed, he subsequently focused solely on the environment. He argued that only behaviour is observable and therefore that a science of psychology must be a science of behaviour. Watson, by the way, was subsequently caught out by his own environment, when, following a scandalous affair with a graduate student, he left psychology and, like all the best psychologists, went into advertising.

One of the key areas of research that the behaviourists drew on was the work of the Russian physiologist Ivan Pavlov. Pavlov was awarded the Nobel Prize for his work on the physiology of digestion. In the course of subsequent work on salivation in the dog, he noticed that the dogs began to salivate before food was presented to them, if they simply noticed the attendant who normally fed them. A lesser scientist than Pavlov would probably have carried on regardless, or perhaps told the attendants off, but Pavlov made those observations the basis for his subsequent study of the conditioned reflex (or "conditional reflex" in Pavlov's own terms). His most famous studies were of bell-ringing and salivation in dogs. Perhaps it is no surprise that the scientist who became famous for studies of bell-ringing was the son of a priest.

Two other significant figures in behavioural psychology were Edward Thorndike and B.F. Skinner. Thorndike became famous for locking cats in puzzle boxes; over a number of trials the cats were found through trial-and-error learning to escape more quickly from the boxes. Thorndike's so-called "law of effect' stated that responses were either more likely or less likely to occur according to the consequences that they produced. B.F. Skinner was, by his own account, a failed novelist, a claim that he eventually proved when, at the height of his fame as a psychologist, he published one of the world's worst Utopian novels, *Walden Two* (1948). His work in psychology however had more impact, and it was in his continuation of Thorndike's study of learning based on the consequences of behaviour that he provided his greatest contribution. Many behaviourists accepted that thoughts and feelings had a causal role to play in our behaviour, but because they were unobservable were not the proper stuff of science. In contrast to these "methodological behaviourists", Skinner espoused a so-called "radical behaviourist" philosophy which stated that although such private events existed, they played no causal role in behaviour but were merely by-products of internal physiological processes. Skinner stated that the true determinants of behaviour were the environment and the organism's genetics and learning history, which were both represented neurophysiologically.

In parallel to the discussion of psychoanalysis, a number of key concepts that are crucial to the understanding of behaviourism will now be outlined. The concepts to be presented include classical conditioning, operant conditioning, and escape/avoidance, following which an outline of their application in behaviour therapy will be given.

Classical conditioning.   This type of learning is the one originally identified by Pavlov, therefore it is also known as Pavlovian conditioning. The basic paradigm is shown in Fig. 1.1. It shows that an unconditioned stimulus (UCS) such as food leads to an unconditioned response (UCR) such as salivation. The pairing of an initially neutral stimulus such as a bell with the UCS eventually leads the bell to become a conditioned stimulus (CS) for the conditioned response (CR) of salivation. Pavlov demonstrated that conditioning occurs optimally if the CS occurs just prior to the UCS, that conditioning will generalise to other stimuli that are similar to the original CS, and that the CR will gradually extinguish over a number of trials if the CS is presented on its own without the UCS. Pavlov originally thought that any stimulus could be paired with any other stimulus, though subsequent research has questioned this idea. For example, Seligman (1971) suggested that certain evolutionarily significant stimuli or "prepared stimuli" may be more conditionable than others in fear reactions; thus, it is far more common for people to develop snake phobias than to develop kitchen sink phobias even though they may never have had any direct experience with a snake, but have unpleasant experiences with kitchen sinks every day. However, the evidence for Seligman's proposal is still unclear (Rachman, 1990).

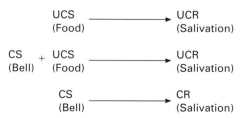

FIG. 1.1   An outline of classical (Pavlovian) conditioning.

One of the main applications of classical conditioning to adult psychological disorders has been through an analysis of "conditioned emotional responses". The idea is that the pairing of a neutral stimulus with an aversive or traumatic UCS that produces an unpleasant emotional response will lead the neutral stimulus to produce conditioned emotional responses. A famous early demonstration of this sequence was carried out by Watson and Rayner (1920) with a 1-year-old child named Little Albert. The child was happily playing with a white rat (the CS) when a loud noise (the UCS) behind him produced a startle reaction and considerable distress (the UCR). After a few such pairings of the white rat and the noise, the white rat eventually produced an unpleasant emotional reaction (the CR) on its own. This reaction generalised to other similar objects such as white rabbits. We shall see later that this traumatic conditioning demonstration was taken as the account of the onset of many anxiety disorders.

Operant conditioning.   Both Skinner and Thorndike emphasised that classical conditioning was one type of learning that applied in the main to more reflex-like or autonomic nervous system behaviour. In contrast, they argued that voluntary behaviour is dependent on its consequences for whether or not it is likely to be repeated. More formally, Skinner stated that operant (or "instrumental") conditioning is based on the three-term contingency of *discriminative stimulus*, *response*, and *outcome*. A discriminative stimulus indicates whether or not a particular contingency applies, for example, a green light might indicate that any pressing of a lever in a Skinner box would lead to a food reward. The notion of a response is defined functionally in the sense that it is not how the rat presses the bar that is important, but, rather the fact that the bar is pressed, whether with its paw or its nose, or whatever. The outcome can be positive (e.g. food) and therefore the likelihood of the response increases, that is, it is positively reinforcing, or it can be negative (e.g. electric shock) in which case the response is punished and is less likely to occur again under those stimulus conditions.

Other key concepts in operant conditioning are *negative reinforcement, schedules of reinforcement*, and *shaping*. In contrast to the punishment procedure described earlier in which a response is less likely to occur because the outcome is unpleasant, in negative reinforcement the response is *more* likely to occur because it switches off an aversive stimulus such as shock or loud noise. The term "schedule of reinforcement" refers to the fact that in many situations not every response is reinforced; for example, people are typically rewarded with money for their work once a week or once a month (a "fixed-interval" schedule), though some individuals on piecework are rewarded for the amount that they produce (normally a "fixed-ratio" schedule). One of the properties of these partial rather than continuous reinforcement schedules is that the behaviour is more resistant to extinction; thus, if reinforcement is no longer presented, an individual who has been rewarded for every response will normally stop responding sooner than someone who has received partial reinforcement. The term "shaping" refers to the technique whereby the organism is initially rewarded for responses that only vaguely resemble the desired response, but gradually the reinforced response approximates closer to the final response. For example, a pigeon is unlikely to pirouette three times and then curtsy straight-off, but through *shaping by successive approximations* to the desired behaviour could be trained to do so.

Escape and avoidance   are two further important types of operant conditioning. In escape learning, the organism receives an aversive stimulus such as an electric shock, which a particular response such as pressing a lever will remove. In avoidance learning, an initial discriminative stimulus signals that if the appropriate response does not occur, then the aversive stimulus will be presented. One well-known variant on escape/avoidance learning is Seligman's (1975) "learned helplessness". In learned helplessness tasks, the organism initially receives non-contingent punishment, that is, the aversive stimulus is received whatever response the animal makes. The contingency is then changed such that a response would lead to escape from the aversive stimulus, but the typical finding is that the animal remains helpless and does not find the escape response. Seligman proposed that learned helplessness could provide a model for the acquisition and maintenance of depression in humans, though as will be evident from Chapter 2, the theory has subsequently undergone a number of major revisions.

Behaviour therapy

A classic demonstration of behaviour therapy was carried out by Mary Cover Jones (1924). Following in the Little Albert tradition, she successfully treated a young boy's fear of rabbits by having him eat in the presence of a rabbit, while gradually bringing the rabbit closer to him over a number of occasions. The basic idea of the encouragement of a response such as eating which is incompatible with fear was further elaborated by Joseph Wolpe (1958). Wolpe first taught phobic adults a muscle relaxation technique, which they then used whilst imagining increasingly fearful stimuli; a technique that Wolpe called *systematic desensitisation*. Although sometimes still used, behaviour therapists now prefer actual exposure to the feared object or situation when this is possible rather than just working in imagination.

One of the classic theories on which behaviour therapy was based was Mowrer's (1939) two-factor theory of the acquisition and maintenance of fear. Mowrer proposed that both classical and operant conditioning were involved. The first step was that an originally neutral stimulus acquired fearful properties by being paired with a frightening or painful event, that is, through a classical conditioning procedure. The second step is that through a process of operant conditioning, the individual learns to reduce the fear by avoidance of the relevant object or situation. Much of the focus of behavioural interventions in anxiety (see Chapter 3) and obsessional disorders (see Chapter 6) has therefore included exposure to the feared object or situation, a procedure that is repeated until the fear response drops substantially. However, it is now well-recognised that not all fears are acquired in accordance with the two-factor theory (e.g. Rachman, 1990) and that not all so-called fears or phobias are based on anxiety but that some are based on disgust reactions (Power & Dalgleish, 1997). For example, most people with a fear of flying have never actually flown, so their fear could not have been acquired by classical conditioning in the situation itself. Conversely, not everybody who has experienced a traumatic event while flying (e.g. a hijack or plane crash) develops a phobia. Instead, the observation of someone else (e.g. a parent) being fearful about an object or situation (known as "vicarious" or "observational" learning) is also a common source of fears and phobias.

There have, of course, been a large number of behavioural techniques that have been adopted for use with clinical conditions, but we will leave these for subsequent chapters, which will examine specific adult disorders and the types of theories and therapies that have been developed to deal with them.

Cognitive psychology

In contrast to the great heroes of psychoanalysis and behaviourism, the recent heroes of cognitive psychology can hardly be described as household names. These lesser deities include individuals such as George Miller, Noam Chomsky, Jerome Bruner, Allan Newell, and Herbert Simon. Bruner (1983) suggests that the birth of modern cognitive psychology was on 11 September 1956, with the delivery taking place during a symposium at the Massachusetts Institute of Technology.

The general area of cognitive psychology is a broad one that overlaps with other disciplines such as linguistics, philosophy, artificial intelligence, and anthropology and, indeed, a new discipline of "cognitive science" has emerged from this overlap. Rather than attempt to cover everything, however, the focus will be on those issues that have some bearing on adult psychological problems. There is as yet no one grand theory in cognitive psychology, nor even one that can be said to be more dominant than others. Instead, there is a general agreement that, whatever form they might take, internal mental states play important causal roles in the generation of action. Beyond this, there is agreement that the system must process information from a range of sensory inputs, that this information needs to be transformed in various ways so that, for example, meaningless sequences of sounds can be interpreted meaningfully, and that there must be an overall system that co-ordinates these multiple functions. Most of this information processing of necessity occurs outside of our awareness, and we only become aware of the extent to which it is automatic when we put shaving cream on our toothbrush, or drive home to the flat that we used to live in rather than the one that we've just moved to. In the remainder of this section an outline will be provided of a number of key areas from cognitive psychology that are relevant to adult psychological disorders. Included in this list will be perception and attention, memory, reasoning, and emotion. We will then look at cognitive therapy and how it might relate to cognitive psychology in general.

Perception and attention.   The German physicist and physiologist Hermann von Helmholtz is considered to be the father of perception. Long before Freud had developed his ideas on the dynamic unconscious, Helmholtz, in the 1860s, had argued that perception must be based on "unconscious inferences" (Power, 1997). For example, when we look at an object at different distances it looks the same size, even though the physical size of the object on the retina is very different (known as "object constancy"); the same object can be looked at from different angles yet appears to preserve its shape ("shape constancy"); and an object can be viewed under different lighting conditions and appear the same colour ("colour constancy"). Although the unconscious perceptual processes that give rise to these constancies have clear advantages, the fact that processing necessarily distorts the incoming information can under other circumstances lead to disadvantages that, at one extreme can be mildly amusing perceptual illusions, and at the other extreme can lead the individual to perceive life-threatening danger where there is none.

One of the central questions in the perception and attention literature has been the extent to which sensory information is analysed prior to conscious awareness. Broadbent (1958) argued that this input is analysed at a superficial physical level and that only input that reaches awareness is analysed for its meaning. Subsequent work however has suggested that the sensory input can be analysed for meaning without the individual having to be aware of the input; in the so-called "cocktail party phenomenon" an individual can be attending to one conversation, but suddenly become aware of his or her name being taken in vain in another conversation. The phenomenon demonstrates that the unattended information must have been analysed for meaning for this switch of attention to occur. The relevance of the area of perception and attention will become clearer in the section on cognitive therapy and also in the chapters on anxiety (see Chapter 3) and schizophrenia (see Chapter 9).

Memory.   One of the questions that cognitive psychology has addressed is the form that internal representation of the world takes. Do we remember visual scenes as if they were video-recorded sequences? or conversations as if they were tape-recorded? Given the arguments that couples have about who said what to whom and when (see Chapter 7), it might seem unlikely that memory is veridical in the manner of tape and video-recorders. The question then is to what extent memory is a reconstruction, one part truth to nine parts fiction? In his classic book on cognitive psychology, Ulric Neisser (1967) took an extreme constructivist view that the process of remembering is like the palaeontologist who, on the basis of a couple of small bones, constructs an awesome dinosaur.

More recently, Neisser has stepped back from this extreme view in the recognition that, although as every storyteller will verify, it is occasionally necessary to exaggerate, memory can also be surprisingly accurate. We must recognise too that in the development of childhood vulnerability for later adult disorders (e.g. see Chapter 2 on depression), the child may be given conflicting information that is difficult to integrate in memory; for example, a mother may repeatedly insist to the child that she loves him above all else, though her actions may clearly contradict her statements. There is no reason, of course, why there could not be more than one memory (or group of memories) of a particular event or person; a number of current views of memory would be consistent with such a possibility. In such cases some of the aims of therapy may be to help the adult identify such discrepancies, to work through the consequent emotions, and to reintegrate the memories into a more realistic overall representation of the person or the event (e.g. Power & Dalgleish, 1997).

A further question that cognitive psychologists ask about memory is what the basic psychological units are. To this question there have been numerous answers and few if any conclusions. One of the types of internal representation that has played a significant role, from the work of Bartlett earlier in the 20th century onwards, is the "schema". Piaget also used the term schema in his studies of child development, and Beck in his account of cognitive therapy. Although there is considerable variation in the use of the term (see Power & Champion, 1986), schemata refer to unitary representations of regularly encountered objects, events, and situations, and activation of one part of a schema leads automatically to activation of all other parts. To give a simple example, if subjects are shown a picture of a car that does not show the wheels, they may make the schematic error later in recall and include wheels that were not originally shown, because cars normally have wheels. Schema theory therefore predicts that processes such as memory and perception are prone to schema-congruent errors. It must be noted that in certain clinical conditions these schemata are less than benign and may, for example, lead the depressed individual to perceive or to recall loss (see Chapter 2), or the anxious person to perceive or to recall life-endangering threat (see Chapter 3). It must be remembered that despite their widespread use, schemata are one of a whole panoply of units that have been used for knowledge representation.

Reasoning.   An assumption made by many philosophers and psychologists is that people use formal logical rules in reasoning. Perhaps the clearest account of such a system was provided by Jean Piaget in his studies of child development. However, there is now a considerable body of research that demonstrates the limits of the adult capacity for reasoning, though the debate still continues over whether errors are the result of performance limitations (e.g. working memory being limited in processing capacity) or whether they genuinely exclude a mental logic.

Three main types of reasoning task are *deduction*, *induction*, and *probability judgement*. Deduction is the drawing of a conclusion from a set of premises; induction is the drawing of a general rule on the basis of one or a limited number of instances; and probability judgements involve a statement about the likelihood of an event occurring. As an example of deductive reasoning, for the premises:

> If I pass my exams I'll study psychology at university.
> If I fail my exams I'll go into politics and become Prime Minister.
> I've passed my exams.

the valid and perhaps fortunate conclusion is that I will study psychology at university.

As an example of the problems that can arise with inductive reasoning, Wason and Johnson-Laird (e.g. see Johnson-Laird, 1988) presented subjects with the series of digits "2 4 6" and asked them to discover the underlying rule through the production of additional examples. Most subjects set about *confirming* the possible rule "even numbers increasing by two" by generating large numbers of positive instances of the rule, instead of attempting to *disconfirm* the rule by generating negative instances such as "7 8 9". Had they done so, they would have eventually discovered that the rule was "any three increasing numbers". This confirmatory bias is one of the many biases that are evident from studies of reasoning. Other biases have been examined in an elegant series of studies by Kahneman and Tversky (e.g. Kahneman, Slovic, & Tversky, 1982). For example, the availability bias leads subjects to say that more words begin with the letter "R" than have "R" as the third letter, because it is easier to generate words beginning with "R". In a similar manner to the biases introduced by schemata in memory, these reasoning biases can be quite benign in their effects and even on occasion lead us to be blissfully ignorant of our faults. However, under other circumstances the same biases can lead depressed individuals to conclude that they are insignificant and that life is not worth living (see later section on Cognitive Therapy and Chapter 2).

Emotion.   Cognitive psychologists were long accused of ignoring the question of emotion, a problem that probably arose because of a view that emotion is somehow more primitive than cognition, given that it was long thought that it was language and reasoning that distinguishes us from the beasts (see Power & Dalgleish, 1997). In fact, the full range of our emotional reactions requires the full range of the cognitive apparatus; although there may be undifferentiated states of a positive or negative emotional tone, the further interpretation of such a state depends on the range of cognitive and social factors available to the individual. Following a number of other theorists, Oatley and Johnson-Laird (1987) have argued that there is a set of "basic emotions" such as sadness, anxiety, anger, happiness, and disgust. These emotions typically arise at different points in our working towards particular goals and plans; for example, happiness can arise if sub-goals towards a main goal are achieved, whereas sadness can arise if an important goal or role is lost or has to be abandoned.

One of the crucial questions that many of the chapters in this book will address is what the relationship is between the range of normal experience of emotion and the emotional disorders. The answers are, of course, many and varied. For example, the same affect-laden thought or impulse can be experienced as perfectly normal by one individual or be experienced as a desperately unwanted intrusion in an obsessional-compulsive individual (see Chapter 6); the individual prone to depression may have lost the only role or goal that really mattered and life feels meaningless as a consequence (see Chapter 2); or an individual who has learned to repress anger as a child may have problems in developing intimate adult relationships because of problems in expressing hostility (see Chapter 7).

Cognitive therapy

The relationship between cognitive psychology and cognitive therapy is minimal when compared to theory and therapy in psychoanalysis and behaviourism. Theory and therapy in psychoanalysis and behaviourism are very closely connected, whereas cognitive therapy and cognitive psychology have developed almost independently of each other; thus, it would be feasible to derive a cognitive-based therapy from current cognitive science that contrasted with cognitive therapy on most points, or, more optimistically, it may be possible to bring cognitive therapy closer to cognitive science (Power, 1989).

The details of cognitive therapy will be spelt out in subsequent chapters so they will only be summarised here. The theory has been developed by Beck (e.g. 1976) and is based on the idea that dysfunctional schemata arise in childhood typically in problematic parental relationships. These schemata normally remain dormant until later in life when a negative life event or stress occurs that activates the schemata. For example, if the schemata focus on the need to feel loved by everybody and the first serious relationship goes wrong, the individual is vulnerable to becoming depressed. As a consequence of these activated schemata, the individual becomes overwhelmed with negative automatic thoughts (see Fig. 1.2) such as "I am unlovable", "Nobody has ever really loved me", and so on, thoughts which lead the individual into a state of depression.

The therapy itself has four main components:

(1) *Education*. The depressed or anxious individual may have little information about depression or anxiety, or may have mistaken information such as a belief that a panic attack is the same as a heart attack (see Chapter 3). One of the useful features of cognitive therapy is the fact that individuals are provided

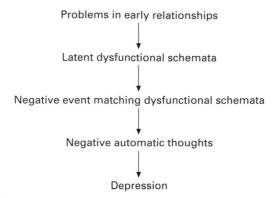

Problems in early relationships

Latent dysfunctional schemata

Negative event matching dysfunctional schemata

Negative automatic thoughts

Depression

FIG. 1.2   An outline of Beck's cognitive theory of depression.

with information about the condition they are experiencing and about the procedures used in cognitive therapy.

(2) *Goal-setting and graded activities.* Many depressed individuals withdraw from their normal activities, and the resultant inactivity may help to maintain the state of depression (see Chapter 2). One of the key strategies of both cognitive therapy and behaviour therapy is the identification of what these activities might be, and then setting activities or homework to be carried out between clinical sessions. The activities typically begin with easier ones and then gradually build up to more difficult ones in order to lessen the chance of failure early on in therapy.

(3) *The identification of negative automatic thoughts.* A key step in cognitive therapy is helping the individual to identify the negative automatic thoughts that are intimately connected with feelings of depression and anxiety (see Fig. 1.2). These may be identified in the clinical sessions themselves, for example, by asking the individual to role-play a difficult encounter, or they can be identified as homework by asking the individual to keep a diary of such thoughts in the situations in which they arise. Once identified, the individual is then encouraged to test their validity, to question them, and to check for the evidence for and against them.

(4) *Challenging dysfunctional schemata.* The identification and challenging of negative automatic thoughts leads into the final phase of cognitive therapy, which is challenging the dysfunctional schemata that underlie the negative thoughts. In depression, these core beliefs typically centre around the need to be loved or the need to do well at all costs. The depressed individual tends to take a one-sided view of past achievements in love and work and may feel hopeless about the possibility of any future success; although some of these views may well be realistic, the problem for the therapist is to disentangle the genuine failures from the imagined ones, so that individuals can take a more balanced view of themselves and their future (see Chapter 2).

PSYCHOANALYSIS, BEHAVIOURISM, AND COGNITIVE PSYCHOLOGY

The purpose of the previous section was to outline some of the basic principles of psychoanalysis, behaviourism, and cognitive psychology, and to give a sense of the therapies that are associated with them. It will be evident from the presentation that often the area addressed by one approach is very different from that of the other approaches; thus, does the demonstration of classical conditioning in the dog necessarily have any bearing on the existence of a dynamic unconscious, or on the occurrence of perceptual biases in *Homo sapiens*? The purpose of this section is to offer some points of comparison and contrast on both the theoretical and the therapeutic levels.

The first question that can be asked is whether there is a basic analogy that underlies each of the three approaches. Table 1.1 shows that the original analogy that Freud used for psychoanalysis was based on the laws of thermodynamics (see Power, 1997). These laws were one of the mainstays of 19th-century science; they relate to the fact that energy can neither be gained nor destroyed in a system, though it can be transformed from one type to another. By analogy, Freud considered that psychic energy should follow the same rules as physical energy, and the Principle of Constancy (see earlier) was one such rule. The underlying analogy for behaviourism is that of the telephone exchange; dial the right input and you get the desired output. In contrast, the analogy for cognitive psychology is that of the computer; thus, the computer consists of hardware (the actual cogs, valves, transistors, microchips, or whatever the computer is built from), software (the programs that can be run on the hardware), and the implementation rules for how a particular piece of software runs on a particular piece of hardware. Whereas the telephone exchange should give a consistent input–output relationship because the relationship is defined by the hardware, the relationship for the computer is more complex because the action taken by the computer depends on the software or program that is currently running; thus,

TABLE 1.1
Some comparisons between psychoanalysis, behaviourism, and cognitive science

	Psychoanalysis	*Behaviourism*	*Cognitive science*
Main analogy	Thermodynamic laws	Telephone exchange	Computer
Philosophy	Associationism	Associationism	Constructivism + Neo-associationism
Role of unconscious	Dynamic	None	Cognitive
Role of environment	Low	High	Medium
Developmental stages	Yes	No	Yes
Focus on relationship in therapy	Yes	No	Some (recently)

dialling "999" on a British telephone exchange should normally connect with the emergency services, but typing in "999" on a computer could lead to the number "999" being entered in a word-processing file, or to a connection being made with another terminal, or the Starship Enterprise moving into Inter-Galactic Space. Cognitive science emphasises therefore that it is not the stimulus *per se* but the interpretation of the stimulus that is important.

Related to the question of the basic analogy is the question of the underlying philosophy of the three approaches (see Table 1.1). Both behaviourism and psychoanalysis share similarities in their philosophical roots, in particular, in their origins in associationism. The basic laws of learning by association were adumbrated by the British Empiricist philosophers from the 17th century onwards, who outlined many of the basic principles long before behaviourism. The main question was under what conditions might two "Ideas" become linked together, and spatial contiguity, temporal contiguity, and similarity or resemblance were considered the main ingredients. Freud also adapted these laws for psychoanalysis, and the free association technique is explicitly derived from this philosophical basis. The emphasis in cognitive science (see Table 1.1) is partly on the mind being much more active or "constructive" in mental processes, in contrast to the passive mechanistic associations that are considered in behaviourism and psychoanalysis. Nevertheless, as Table 1.1 expresses, cognitive science also has a strong influence of associationism and some of the latest computer modelling incorporates a recent version of associationism (see Johnson-Laird, 1988, for an excellent introduction to these issues).

The other comparisons presented in Table 1.1 summarise some of the points detailed in the earlier discussion of each approach. The role of the unconscious in psychoanalysis and cognitive science is seen very differently; psychoanalysis emphasises the motivating force of the unconscious in relation to drives and drive-related impulses, whereas cognitive science follows a different tradition derived from Helmholtz's work on perceptual processes. In Skinner's radical behaviourism there is no role for a psychological unconscious, because it is the organism's internal physiology that plays a causal role in behaviour; in methodological behaviourism (which accepts that there could be internal mental states that play a causal role in behaviour) the question of the conscious or unconscious status of such states would be seen as a scientific red herring, because neither type would be seen as the proper study of science. This emphasis in behaviourism on the observable and the measurable and its rejection of unobservable mental states is summed up in the following joke recounted by Phil Johnson-Laird (1988, p. 18): Did you hear the one about the two behaviourists making love? Afterwards one of them turned to the other and said "That was fine for *you*, but how was it for *me*?"

Further points in Table 1.1 show that environmental factors play a greater role in behaviourism than in either cognitive science or psychoanalysis. Obviously, the details differ from theory to theory, but current environmental factors on average play a lower role in psychoanalytic theories. Both psychoanalysis and cognitive science consider that there may be stages in development, even though the focus in psychoanalysis is on psychosexual and emotional development, whereas the focus in cognitive science is on conceptual development, for example, in relation to language and reasoning ability. Because behaviourism focuses on laws of learning that are seen to be general both across species and throughout individual development, behaviourists have rejected the need for models that include developmental stages.

A final contrast in Table 1.1 is on the role of the therapist–patient relationship in therapy. At one extreme, psychoanalysis would see the whole therapeutic relationship and in particular the transference relationship (see earlier) as central to therapeutic change. At the other extreme, there are behaviour therapists who say that therapy can be done as effectively by a computer or a self-help manual as by a therapist (e.g. Marks, 1987). Cognitive therapy seems to be in a grey area in between; in its earlier short-term form it de-emphasised the therapeutic relationship, but in its recent extension to more difficult problems, the therapeutic relationship is being seen to play a more important role (e.g. Beck & Freeman, 1990).

The points presented in Table 1.1 emphasise that in many ways the three main approaches in clinical psychology contrast with each other in terms of theory and therapy. However, we believe that although these differences exist, there is considerable scope for theoretical and practical integration between the three approaches. As an illustration of the potential for integration consider the two mainstays of psychoanalysis and behaviour therapy, transference and exposure treatment respectively. Surely such different ways of working could not be integrated? In fact, the mechanisms of both seem to be very similar; both involve the arousal of intense emotion in the patient, the emotion derives from prior learning particularly in childhood, and the emotion needs to be worked through so that the patient responds more appropriately in the critical situations. As discrepant therefore as the different approaches seem, we hope that this book will illustrate that often similar conclusions are reached even though the starting points are very different. In addition to the considerations of theory and technique, there is the issue of "horses for courses"; thus, different approaches will appeal to different people be they clients or therapists, and a host of social and individual characteristics will influence such appeal.

In Table 1.2 we have attempted to present an alternative way of comparing the three approaches. For example, although behaviourism has proven itself to

TABLE 1.2
Further comparisons between psychoanalysis, behaviourism,
and cognitive science

	Psychoanalysis	Behaviourism	Cognitive science
Theoretical adequacy	Medium	Low	Medium/High
Empirical usefulness	Low	High	Medium/High
Clinical usefulness	High	High	Medium

be of high clinical and empirical use, its theoretical adequacy is now known to be low. In contrast, psychoanalysis has proven to be of high clinical usefulness for some groups in some settings, but of low empirical usefulness.

ADDITIONAL MODELS IN PSYCHOLOGY

There are many approaches other than those falling under the umbrellas of psychoanalysis, behaviourism, and cognitive science that must be considered in the understanding of adult psychological disorders. Two such approaches that will be repeatedly encountered throughout this book are the *biological/medical* and the *social* approaches. Brief introductions therefore will be given to these approaches. A third approach, that of *humanism*, has had a considerable impact in the area of counselling and a number of its principles have filtered through into the practice of other therapies. However, there has been little theoretical development in this area to account for the origins and development of specific adult problems; this will be evident from a reading of the remaining chapters. We will not attempt therefore to provide an introduction to this approach (the interested reader should see for example, Mearns & Thorne, 1988).

Biological/medical models

The basic tenet for the biomedical approach is that disorders result from patho-genic physical processes of external or internal origin in relation to the organ-ism. External pathogens include invasive agents such as harmful organisms and toxins which when introduced into the body can cause disease and temporary or permanent physical damage. Typical invasive agents include viruses, bacteria, and fungi, which cause a wide range of common and not-so-common illnesses. Physical trauma may also cause temporary or permanent damage to the organism. Pathogenic processes of internal origin can, for example, result from genetic defects and natural ageing processes; thus, in the condition phenylketonuria (PKE) a simple genetic defect leads to the inability to metabolise a particular amino acid found in certain food products and can lead to the death of a new-born if not diagnosed. At the other end of the lifecycle, normal ageing processes also lead to the death of the organism due to the physical deterioration of a range of tissues and internal organs.

A number of psychiatric conditions are the result of pathogenic physical processes of external or internal origin. For example, in so-called multi-infarct dementia an internal series of strokes lead to the increased death of brain matter and consequent general intellectual and personality impairments in the sufferer. Psychoactive drugs taken either deliberately or accidentally can lead to a range of psychological problems (see e.g. Chapters 4 and 9). And there are a number of harmful organisms that can also lead to psychiatric problems; one of the classic historical examples being tertiary syphilis, which was originally called General Paralysis of the Insane (GPI) but was subsequently found to result from spirochaetal infection. The recognition of conditions such as GPI to be of infectious origin led to the development of effective treatment methods, so that unlike the Victorian asylum whose wards contained many such individuals our present-day mental health facilities rarely if ever see such individuals. However, these specific successes can sometimes lead to wild goose chases, for example, for *the* virus or *the* gene that causes schizophrenia (see Chapter 9) and the proposal of simplistic biomedical models for complex psychological disorders.

A more sophisticated type of biomedical approach is provided by so-called diathesis–stress models. The diathesis part of the model refers to a permanent physical vulnerability of the body which makes it more vulnerable to particular diseases, for example of invasive origin (the "stress"). A classic example in the history of medicine was the recognition that tuberculosis arose from an interaction between an inherited vulnerability and the tubercule bacillus; thus, not everybody who is infected with the bacillus develops tuberculosis, only those with an inherited vulnerability. In relation to psychiatric disorder, diathesis–stress models have been proposed for a number of conditions that have included psychosomatic disorders such as gastric ulcer, myocardial infarctions, and eczema, and conditions such as schizophrenia (see Chapter 9) and certain types of severe depression (see Chapter 2). In these disorders, the interaction between a permanent physical vulnerability and some form of physical or psychosocial stress forms the central part of the model. In fact, diathesis–stress models are now commonplace, not only in the biomedical approach, but in a range of psychological and social models also, though the diathesis or vulnerability factor is expressed at a psychological (e.g. sensitivity to the experience of loss) or social level (e.g. a lack of social support from other individuals) rather than at a physical level.

One health warning that must be added to this discussion of biomedical models is that they provide reductionistic accounts of psychological disorders, in the sense that psychological phenomena are seen to be caused by physical pathogenic processes. For example, in the case of depression negative thoughts would be treated as symptoms caused by an underlying physical process or illness, in contrast to Beck's cognitive therapy (see earlier) in which such thoughts are considered to be the cause rather than consequence of depression. Suffice it to say that although some psychological problems may be reducible to physical levels of explanation (with GPI, discussed earlier, one such success), the general cognitive approach to psychology emphasises that many psychological processes are not reducible to solely physical terms. In other words, your chemistry might be perfectly okay but that doesn't necessarily stop you from having a hard time.

Social models

Throughout the remaining chapters contributors will refer to a wide range of social factors that can influence the onset and course of psychological disorders (see Goldberg & Huxley, 1992, for an overview of the social approach and its integration with other models); factors such as the size of the individual's social network, the amount of support available, paid employment, criticism of the individual by significant others, and the presence of problems in significant others. Typically, one or two such social factors may be included in many examples of essentially psychological models. In some instances more complex models are presented which are primarily social; in these examples specific social factors may be seen in the context of the individual's culture and lifestyle (see Chapter 2); thus the effect of the presence or absence of paid employment, for example, varies according to a number of interacting factors that include social class, cultural values, lifestage, and gender, therefore a model that considered employment independently of such factors can be regarded as overly simplistic. When the usefulness of psychological approaches to treatment is assessed, social factors need to be considered. Thus psychological approaches can often be improved by an integration with a social approach, though this is rarely achieved.

The application of a different type of social model to psychological disorders is illustrated by a number of family therapy approaches (see Chapter 8). The extension of general systems theory to social groups such as families and organisations demonstrates the potential for pathogenic processes at a social level, processes which cannot be simply reduced to a psychological level of explanation. Dramatic examples are presented in the family therapy literature in which the "ill" member of the family is "cured" only for another member of the family to become "ill" in turn (see Chapter 8). Although the focus of this book is on the psychological level of explanation, we hope that the chapters on family and marital problems (Chapters 8 and 7, respectively) will serve as a reminder that no person is a "psychological island" immune from the effects of others, and that there may be pathogenic social systems for which the appropriate intervention is social rather than psychological.

FINAL REMARKS

This chapter stands as a basic introduction to the broad range of psychological disorders that will be discussed in subsequent chapters. Many of the basic concepts will of necessity be repeated in order to illustrate their application to the psychological problem in question. We must reiterate, however, that different problems have come to be dominated by different approaches; for example, simple phobias and obsessive-compulsive disorders are dominated by the behavioural approach, anxiety and depression by the cognitive approach, and it is no surprise that family problems have become dominated by family-systems approaches. In addition to the type of problems being considered, therapists and researchers also have their own preferences according to their own personalities—preferences that will be evident in a number of the chapters. Nevertheless, most practising clinicians subscribe to a pragmatism that adapts the type of approach they take according to a mixture of problem type, therapist and patient factors, and available resources. Our understanding of what constitutes good theory and good therapy for psychological problems is far too impoverished for any one approach to claim that it presents a complete answer; as the history of psychology shows, such claims fall flat on their face far too often!

RECOMMENDED READING

General

Atkinson, R.L., Atkinson, R.C., Smith, E.E., & Bem, D.J. (1993). *Introduction to psychology* (11th ed.). New York: Harcourt Brace Jovanovich.

Generations of psychology students have grown up on this classic introductory text which has plenty of editions left in the old horse yet. But will subsequent generations remember Hilgard, who after 40 years disappears?

Specific

Brown, D., & Pedder, J. (1991). *Introduction to psychotherapy: An outline of psychodynamic principles and practice* (2nd ed.). London: Tavistock.

Probably the best introduction still to psychoanalytic principles and to the practice of psychotherapy in general.

Goldberg, D., & Huxley, P. (1992). *Common mental disorders: A bio-social model*. London: Tavistock/Routledge.

An appetising cocktail of social and biological factors in an easy-to-read text.

Johnson-Laird, P.N. (1988). *The computer and the mind*. London: Fontana.

One of the best introductions to cognitive science written by one of its leaders.

Johnstone, E.C., Freeman, C., & Zealley, A.K. (1998). *Companion to psychiatric studies* (6th ed.). Edinburgh, UK: Churchill Livingstone.

Miss Jean Brodie's Morningside guide to psychiatry. Crème de la crème!

Pearce, J.M. (1997). *Animal learning and cognition: An introduction* (2nd ed.). Hove, UK: Psychology Press.

A genuinely *modern* introduction to *classical* and other types of learning.

Power, M.J., & Dalgleish, T. (1997). *Cognition and emotion: From order to disorder.* Hove, UK: Psychology Press.

Well, you have to expect some positive bias!

REFERENCES

Beck, A.T. (1976). *Cognitive therapy and the emotional disorders.* New York: Meridian.
Beck, A.T., & Freeman, A. (1990). *Cognitive therapy of personality disorders.* New York: Guilford Press.
Breuer, J., & Freud, S. (1974). Studies on hysteria. In A. Richards (Ed.), *The Pelican Freud Library, Vol. 3.* Harmondsworth, UK: Penguin. (Original work published 1895)
Broadbent, D.E. (1958). *Perception and communication.* New York: Pergamon Press.
Bruner, J. (1983). *In search of mind: Essays in autobiography.* New York: Harper & Row.
Casement, P. (1985). *On learning from the patient.* London: Tavistock.
Erikson, E.H. (1963). *Childhood and society* (2nd ed.). Harmondsworth, UK: Penguin.
Freud, A. (1937). *The ego and the mechanisms of defence.* London: Hogarth Press.
Freud, S. (1966). Project for a scientific psychology. In *Standard Edition of the Complete Psychological Works of Sigmund Freud, Vol. 1.* London: Hogarth Press. (Original work written 1895)
Freud, S. (1979). Inhibitions, symptoms and anxiety. In A. Richards (Ed.), *The Pelican Freud Library, Vol. 10.* Harmondsworth, UK: Penguin. (Original work published 1926)
Freud, S. (1984). The ego and the id. In A. Richards (Ed.), *The Pelican Freud Library, Vol. 2.* Harmondsworth, UK: Penguin. (Original work published 1923)
Gay, P. (1988). *Freud: A life for our time.* London: Dent.
Gleick, J. (1988). *Chaos: Making a new science.* London: Heinemann.
Grunbaum, A. (1984). *The foundations of psychoanalysis.* Berkeley, CA: University of California Press.
Johnson-Laird, P.N. (1988). *The computer and the mind: An introduction to cognitive science.* London: Fontana.
Jones, M.C. (1924). A laboratory study of fears: The case of Peter. *Pediatric Seminary, 31,* 308–315.
Kahneman, D., Slovic, P., & Tversky, A. (1982). *Judgement under uncertainty: Heuristics and biases.* Cambridge, UK: Cambridge University Press.
Marks, I. (1987). *Fears, phobias and rituals.* Oxford, UK: Oxford University Press.
Mearns, D., & Thorne, B. (1988). *Person-centred counselling in action.* London: Sage.
Mowrer, O.H. (1939). A stimulus-response analysis of anxiety and its role as a reinforcing agent. *Psychological Review, 46,* 553–565.
Neisser, U. (1967). *Cognitive psychology.* New York: Appleton-Century-Crofts.
Oatley, K., & Johnson-Laird, P.N. (1987). Towards a cognitive theory of emotions. *Cognition and Emotion, 1,* 29–50.
Penrose, R. (1989). *The emperor's new mind: Concerning computers, minds and the laws of physics.* London: Vintage.
Power, M.J. (1989). Cognitive therapy: An outline of theory, practice and problems. *British Journal of Psychotherapy, 5,* 544–556.
Power, M.J. (1997). Conscious and unconscious representations of meaning. In M.J. Power & C.R. Brewin (Eds.), *The transformation of meaning in psychological therapies: Integrating theory and practice.* Chichester, UK: Wiley.
Power, M.J., & Champion, L.A. (1986). Cognitive approaches to depression: A theoretical critique. *British Journal of Clinical Psychology, 25,* 201–212.
Power, M.J., & Dalgleish, T. (1997). *Cognition and emotion: From order to disorder.* Hove, UK: Psychology Press.

Rachman, S.J. (1990). *Fear and courage* (2nd ed.). New York: W.H. Freeman.

Seligman, M.E.P. (1971). Phobias and preparedness. *Behavior Therapy*, *2*, 307–320.

Seligman, M.E.P. (1975). *Helplessness*. San Francisco, CA: W.H. Freeman.

Skinner, B.F. (1948). *Walden Two*. New York: Macmillan.

Watson, J.B., & Rayner, R. (1920). Conditioned emotional reactions. *Journal of Experimental Psychology*, *3*, 1–14.

Wolpe, J. (1958). *Psychotherapy by reciprocal inhibition*. Stanford, CA: Stanford University Press.

CHAPTER TWO

Depression

Lorna Champion
Department of Clinical Psychology, Royal Edinburgh Hospital, UK

Everyone at some time in his or her life experiences low moods. These low points are often described by using words such as sorrow, sadness, and despair, or by words that mean the absence of something good, such as hopeless, restless, uneasy, and unhappy. Low points in mood often occur when an experience threatens or results in the loss of some valued person, object, or idea. The pervasiveness of depression when used in this everyday sense is clear. However, depression also refers to a serious disorder that can disrupt all areas of a person's life so that he or she cannot work or maintain relationships. In some cases depression can be life threatening because of the risk of suicide. Of those people diagnosed as clearly suffering from clinical depression in a psychiatric context, about 15% will eventually commit suicide, and a higher proportion (up to 40%) will make suicide attempts (see Paykel, 1989).

Clinical depression is regarded by some approaches to psychopathology as a disease. However, there is no consensus regarding exactly how depression should be distinguished from unhappiness, and many regard the so-called clinical state as the extreme end of a continuum (see Gilbert, 1992; Kendell, 1976). Little attention has been given to the study of unhappiness or sadness as opposed to depression (see Power, 1999). It is clear that most depressed people are unhappy, but it is not the case that most unhappy people are depressed. In this chapter on depression as a psychological problem in adult life, the focus is on a disorder that involves depressed mood and a range of other symptoms which, taken together, will have an adverse effect on the person's ability to function in important areas of his or her life.

DEFINING DEPRESSION AS A DISORDER

Depression is the most commonly presented psychiatric disorder and has been of great interest to the medical profession since Hippocrates first described melancholy over 2000 years ago (Gilbert, 1992). The classification of depressive disorder into various types has received a great deal of attention from psychiatry. The emphasis on classification is important, because different causal factors have been proposed for the different types of depression. These different causal factors have implications for the type of model used to explain and treat the disorder in clinical practice. Before however we consider the main classification systems, the key symptoms of depression will be outlined.

The symptoms

Depressed mood is the most central symptom to the definition of depression and it is a prerequisite for diagnosis. In addition some or all of the following main symptoms are normally found to be present:

- sleep disturbance—usually insomnia, particularly with a tendency to wake much earlier than desired in the morning
- appetite disturbance—usually a loss of the desire to eat and/or weight loss
- excessive tiredness
- decrease in sexual interest
- loss of interest in usual activities
- slowness in thinking and, in more severe cases, in movement
- feelings of self-condemnation, shame, guilt, and self-disgust
- thoughts of suicide and suicide attempts.

In addition to the main symptoms just outlined, depression often includes variation in mood throughout the day (diurnal variation), with mood usually being lowest in the morning.

Guilt and shame are common experiences, as noted earlier; these feelings may be intense and to others will seem out of proportion with the "crimes" that depressed people believe they have committed. Often minor misdeeds that occurred long ago will become a focus for intense feelings of shame. Anxiety often exists with depression and can include panic symptoms. Fear of losing one's mind or going mad can be a consequence of the self-perceived deficits in the depressed person's performance. These deficits may be in sharp contrast to the often highly efficient performance of the depression-prone person when he or she is not depressed (see section on depressive personality). Having outlined the main symptoms, those classification issues that have implications for the usefulness of the various treatment models will be described.

THE CLASSIFICATION OF DEPRESSION

We will begin this section with a discussion of previous attempts at the classification of depression, because it is informative to see how careful research has rejected some of the earlier diagnostic approaches. Much attention was given previously to the distinction between endogenous or psychotic depression and reactive or neurotic depression. From a practical point of view these two sets of complex terms can be understood as a way of distinguishing between the most severe disabling depressive states and the usually milder but often more chronic depressions. A diagnosis of endogenous or psychotic depression was usually made where the symptoms were more severe, especially sleep and appetite disturbances. Endogenous depression was defined as having an onset unrelated to upsetting or unpleasant events, the cause supposedly coming from within the person. This proposed lack of reaction to external stress was in stark contrast to the neurotic/reactive type where the onset of disorder was defined to be linked to a stressful or upsetting event. The preponderance of more physical disturbance in those depressions labelled as endogenous, such as the severe disruption of sleep and appetite, often with serious weight loss and many somatic symptoms, made this more severe type of depression a focus for biological theories of causation and treatment.

Investigators who have gone to some length to find out if those patients who were previously classified as endogenously depressed had experienced an event, have almost always found that they have (e.g. Brown & Harris, 1978). Endogenous depression, therefore, can no longer be defined by the absence of external events, but can only be defined by the presence of more severe symptomatology.

The inaccessibility of the severely depressed person to attempts at communication is one reason that this type of depression was more often considered unrelated to events in the person's life. Such a person is simply less likely to tell others about what has happened or to be able to think in a meaningful way about what may cause his or her distress. A case example of this was a very severely depressed man in his 70s. He had been highly successful in his work and family life prior to the onset of his disorder. He was hospitalised for depression and was suffering from a host of severe physical symptoms. He could give no reason for his state of despair and seemed to present a classic picture of endogenous depression. After several weeks of attempting to talk to this man, he mentioned that his only son, who had had a glowing career and young family, had died quite suddenly from cancer. Following this event, but some time before the onset of the depression, the patient had sold his large family home, because he thought it too great a burden for him and his wife to manage. Just before the onset of his depression he had learned that this house was to become a nursing home for the elderly. He said he could not bear the thought that so many others would spend their last years in his beautiful house while he would have to end his days in a small flat which he now felt it had been a mistake to buy. He did not connect these events with his depression; he felt that because he had been so fortunate in life, he had no justification for feeling so bad, either about the loss of his son, or his regret about his home. He had never mentioned any of these problems to the staff who had cared for him, because he said he could see no point in doing so.

Those depressions that were previously given the label of neurotic/reactive, although often milder in terms of symptoms, were not always so. The sufferer is likely to be aware of what may have contributed to the depression, often an event involving some kind of significant loss, or the threat of loss. Common examples may include the ending of a love relationship, or the loss of a valued job. Sometimes depression will occur in the context of more chronic stress; there may have been no major event, but instead a minor incident that triggers a feeling of hopelessness about the situation. Examples of this more chronic stress would be: an unhappy, conflict-ridden marriage, caring for several very young children in inadequate housing, or an unsatisfactory work situation where there seems to be no hope of improvement. The work of Brown and Harris (e.g. 1978) provides a host of such examples in their now classic study of women living in the community.

To return to the issue of the current diagnosis of depression, the two main classification systems in use (the American Psychiatric Association's DSM-IV [APA, 1994], which is short for Diagnostic and Statistical Manual 4th edition, and the World Health Organisation's ICD-10 [WHO, 1992], which is short for International Classification of Diseases 10th edition) now agree on two important distinctions in the classification of depression. The first distinction is that between *unipolar* and *bipolar* depressions, and the second follows the distinction based on severity considered earlier and distinguishes *major depressive episodes* (which are severe with most of the symptoms noted previously) versus less severe *dysthymic disorders* (which have fewer symptoms but which are of a more chronic nature).

The one type of depressive disorder that does seem to be distinct and which will undoubtedly survive future changes in classification is that of *bipolar disorders* (as they are known in the DSM-IV system) or *manic depressive disorders* (as they are still known in the UK). The truth is that neither term captures the disorder accurately, though we will use the term bipolar disorder because of its current more widespread applicability. The term bipolar distinguishes it from all the other types of depression which are unipolar in nature; in bipolar disorder there are two extremes of mood as opposed to only one. Mood can be excessively high or excessively low. Severe bipolar disorders include periods of being manic. Mania can be regarded as the opposite of depression: There will be feelings of elation, usually a great deal of activity, sometimes to the point of exhaustion or collapse. The person will feel powerful, grand, on top of the world. Although mania may sound a pleasant state to be in, it is not generally so except sometimes in the milder variant known as *hypomania*. There can be a loss of contact with reality in mania; sometimes when this occurs the person can run up huge debts from spending sprees and make major decisions which, in a more normal mood, would be regarded as disastrous.

Bipolar depression is clearly distinguished from other types of depression by the presence of manic episodes. Research has shown that there is likely to be a clear genetic contribution to its development, evidence for which is lacking in other types of depression (see McGuffin & Katz, 1989). The relative importance of biological factors, including genetic factors in the causation of depression, is a highly complex and a much researched area. In general, the more severe types of depression are considered to have a greater degree of biological causation than the milder more neurotic types. Current thinking and research does not point towards any one clear factor to be the cause, but, instead, sees the biological contribution as one of various vulnerabilities, which if they come together will then result in an episode of depression in the at-risk person (see Chapter 1). This idea of multiple causal factors applies to the genetic contribution too; depression does tend to run in families, but it is most important to remember that this does not mean the cause is genetic. Families usually have many things in common aside from their genes: the way they relate to others, the way they cope with stress, the kind of environment they live in, and so on. (The interested reader is referred to the following references: Goodwin, 1998; Hammen, 1997.)

THE PREVALENCE OF DEPRESSION

Depression is one of the most common adult psychological problems. Carefully conducted community surveys, which attempt to assess the rate of clinically significant depression, reveal rates of between 3 and 7% of the general population (see Paykel, 1989). Approximately 3% of the general population are treated by their GPs for depression, but it is generally thought that about half of the cases presenting depression to a GP are not recognised as such (Goldberg & Huxley, 1992). About 1 per 1000 of the general population are admitted to hospital annually with depression, while about 3 per 1000 are referred to a psychiatrist. A large community survey conducted in inner London estimated that seven out of ten women and four out of ten men will have at least one clinically significant episode of depression by the time they are 65 years of age (Bebbington Katz, McGuffin, Tennant, & Hurry, 1989). This last figure raises the important issue of the difference between men and women regarding rates of depression. Overall, women are about twice as likely as men to suffer from depression, though there is recent evidence that depression and suicide may be increasing in younger men (e.g. see Hammen, 1997). The general overall ratio however applies regardless of how prevalence is assessed; it applies to both rates in the community and hospital admissions (see Nolen-Hoeksema, 1990). Depression is also more common amongst those in the lower social class groups, and amongst the unmarried as compared to the married. The study of the prevalence of depression in different social groups has made important contributions to our understanding of the disorder. Explaining these differences is an important challenge for the various models and theories of depression that have been developed. Differences in the rates of depression in various social groups are discussed in more detail in the later section on social models.

Finally, it is necessary to consider depression in relation to life stage. Depression can occur in childhood and in adolescence. It is of interest that before the age of 15 boys are more likely to be treated for depression than girls (Harrington, 1993). A first episode of depression can occur at any age in adult life; the milder depressions tend to begin earlier, usually between the ages of 20 and 40. The onset of these disorders may be gradual and often occurs in those with a vulnerable personality. Early adult life is a demanding period during which many transitions need to be negotiated: for example, gaining independence from family, establishing oneself in the domains of work, love relationships, and child rearing. Each of these transitions will place considerable demands on the person who may be susceptible to depression in the face of stress (see Maughan & Champion, 1990). The course of a disorder that begins early in adult life may be chronic, with fluctuations occurring in severity of symptoms according to the demands placed upon the individual. The more severe types of depression tend to have an onset later in life, usually around mid-life or later and may often occur in individuals who have apparently coped well with their lives. When thinking about the onset of depression, it is important to consider the major transitions that are likely to characterise each life-stage. Negotiating major transitions may put a person at an increased risk for depression. Hammen (1997) states that on average a depressive episode lasts between 4 and 6 months, although obviously the length of an episode will be affected by whether treatment is received and how successful this is.

Having outlined some of the main issues to consider about the various models and theories of depression, we can now go on the consider each main approach in turn.

COGNITIVE MODELS

Cognitive approaches to both the understanding and treatment of depression represent the most recent major development in the area from a psychological perspective. The work of Aaron Beck (e.g. Beck, Rush, Shaw, & Emery, 1979) has been the most influential; his ideas will therefore be considered in some detail. This approach regards the main causal factor in depression as a disorder of cognition; this means that there is a problem with the person's perception and thinking (see Chapter 1). Beck regards the depressed person's thinking as excessively negative. Such individuals view themselves, the world, and the future in a negative way. The theory proposes that, in the course of development, people acquire knowledge about themselves and the world in general; this knowledge is stored in the form of stable mental structures called schemas. It is these schemas, which can also be regarded as beliefs or assumptions, that form the basic structures a person uses to perceive, understand, and think about the world (see Chapter 1). The schemas of the depressed person are constructed in such a way that they generate a negative bias when interpreting experience. One feature of these schemas is that they generate what Beck terms negative automatic thoughts. It is these automatic thoughts that can cause depressed mood. The thoughts are called automatic because the person does not make a conscious decision to think them, but they come into the person's mind and may even go unnoticed by the person; the truthfulness of the content of these thoughts is not questioned. Because the meaning of the thought is negative, it has an adverse effect on the person's performance or enjoyment of experience.

The original theory proposes the following sequence: A critical incident will occur in a person's life, which will often be an event involving loss; this critical incident will activate the dysfunctional assumptions (schemas) and will generate negative automatic thoughts which in turn produce depression (see Fig. 1.2 in Chapter 1).

An example of this process can be demonstrated in the case of someone we shall call Ann. Ann had been brought up by caring, but highly critical parents. Her attempts to please her parents always seemed unsatisfactory in some way. She frequently experienced feelings of being unloved and rejected. Ann found that trying hard at her work led to success, and approval by her parents. Work came to seem more controllable and rewarding for Ann than relationships did.

Experiences such as those are likely to lead to a dysfunctional assumption of the form "unless I am successful in my work, I am worthless and unlovable". This assumption was of little trouble to Ann while she was being highly successful in her work. However, a disagreement led to a loss of a hoped-for major promotion. Following this experience, Ann came to feel she was unable to cope with responsibility; she could not find the energy to apply for other jobs, even though she knew this might help to improve her situation. It was at this stage that she became depressed. She was not particularly aware of what she was thinking, but when asked to reflect, she reported thinking such automatic thoughts as "I know I'm no good" and "I'm useless, I'm a failure". Ann did not question the truthfulness of these thoughts, but was only aware of being unable to do anything to make herself feel better.

This model of depression has generated a form of treatment called cognitive therapy (see also Chapter 1). An important assumption made by the model is that people are capable of examining their thinking in a logical, rational, scientific way. This means that they can be objective in their assessment of themselves and the world around them. The cognitive therapist sets out to help the depressed person by explaining the general model and then works with the client to demonstrate exactly how, in his or her particular case, excessively negative thinking contributes to being depressed. Clients are asked to describe in great detail the events of their day (this is often done by diary keeping); at each point a recording is made, the automatic negative thoughts are identified, and the client's belief in these thoughts is assessed. The therapist works with the client to help him or her to challenge or question the truthfulness of the thoughts, carefully weighing up the evidence on the basis of what the client knows and has previously told them. The aim of this process is to enable the clients to begin to think about themselves, the world, and their future in a less distorted way, and replace the negative bias with a more realistic, logical, rational assessment.

This brief account does not do full justice to cognitive therapy for depression, which involves a whole range of other techniques for helping the depressed person to change. Many of these techniques are aimed at directly recording and changing the person's behaviour, particularly increasing the amount of rewarding experiences the person has on a daily basis. These techniques and the theory behind them are more accurately termed behavioural than cognitive. Although there is a definite cognitive element to them, they are not unique to cognitive therapy. The interested reader is referred to Beck et al. (1979) for a complete account of cognitive therapy and its techniques and to Weishaar's (1993) interesting biography of Beck and summary of developments in cognitive therapy.

The unique contributions of Beck's cognitive model can be summarised as follows: A disorder of cognition is a primary causal factor in depression. This disorder of cognition includes an excessively negative bias in processing information about the self, the world, and the future. People are capable of logical assessment of their thoughts and can be trained to think in a more rational, less biased way. Therapy is regarded as a collaborative process between therapist and client. The therapist shares his or her model of the disorder with the client and therefore the client's understanding and acceptance of the model is important.

This account has concentrated on Beck's model. However, a number of other models and theories of depression could also be regarded as cognitive because they place considerable emphasis on the role of processes such as perception and thinking. Examples of these theories include those with a strong developmental element and basis in psychoanalytic ideas (e.g. Arieti & Bemporad, 1978) and those models originally based on strict behavioural principles, for example, the learned helplessness model (discussed later). When the latter model was applied to depression in humans it was necessary to expand the theory to take into account how individuals perceived their helplessness. It was found that it was the person's perception of his or her helpless state in a given situation that resulted in depression rather than the helpless situation *per se*.

Beck's model and its therapy have been criticised on a number of grounds, for example on the adequacy of the cognitive theory on which it is based (see Power & Champion, 1986; Power & Dalgleish, 1997) and through its insufficient emphasis on social factors (Champion & Power, 1995).

THE BEHAVIOURAL MODEL

Behavioural psychology and behaviour therapy have produced models of depression and methods of treatment. There is a wide range of different approaches within this school of thought and the interested reader is referred to Gilbert (1992) for a full account of these. In this section, the main principles of the behavioural approach to depression will be outlined, concentrating on its unique contribution.

In general, behavioural models claim that depression occurs because the person is receiving inadequate or insufficient positive reinforcement or reward from his or her environment. If the person's behaviour is changed so that an increase in the amount of positive reinforcement or reward is received, the depression will decrease. So the focus of this approach is on behaviour change. Some models, for example Ferster's (1973) operant model, argue that a careful analysis needs to be carried out to determine the function of the depressed person's behaviour. Such an analysis involves assessing what the person is obtaining from behaving in the way he or she does. For example, the passive behaviour of the depressive may be a way of avoiding punishment or criticism. Such passive behaviour may have been learned because it was more reinforcing than active behaviour which was experienced as punishing; thus, a depressed person may have ceased to talk to his wife because he has learned from experience that talking to her elicited a critical response. It is not difficult to see how this process can gradually generalise to produce a very impoverished environment in which the depressed person engages in less and less activity that has the potential of providing any positive reinforcement.

In behavioural terms, the behaviour of the depressed person has been learned (see Chapter 1); therefore, the task of treatment is to provide an environment in which more adaptive, non-depressed behaviour can be learned by ensuring that such behaviour receives optimum reinforcement. The example of the husband and wife is a social one; other theorists, for example Lewinsohn (1974) have proposed that the main problem in depression is a lack of response-contingent positive social reinforcement. In ordinary language this means that the person's actions in social situations do not produce rewards. This problem might occur because the person never enters into social situations in the first place, or because the depressed person's behaviour in social situations is such that it fails to produce a rewarding response from those with whom he or she interacts. Lewinsohn proposes that in treatment the therapist needs to establish:

- the number of activities or experiences that are potentially reinforcing for that person
- the availability of resources in the person's environment to make reinforcing activity possible
- the extent to which the person has the skills to elicit those behaviours that will be reinforcing; this usually means social skills.

As with many other originally purely behavioural theorists, Lewinsohn has since gone on to propose a much broader theory encompassing cognitive and biological ideas (see Lewinsohn, Hoberman, Teri, & Hautzinger, 1985). The clearest example of how the behavioural approach to depression can be useful, but inadequate as a complete explanation of the disorder in humans, is shown by the model termed *learned helplessness*.

Learned helplessness

The theory of learned helplessness (see Seligman, 1975) was developed following a series of laboratory experiments in which dogs were given inescapable electric shocks. The behaviour of these dogs was compared to another group who were given the chance to learn how to avoid the shocks. The dogs in the first group showed severe learning deficits on subsequent learning tasks. The behaviour of the dogs in the inescapable shock group showed a pattern not unlike depression; they were lethargic and did not make attempts to learn. The essential causal factor in producing this state of helplessness was the uncontrollability of the stimulus, in this case shock. In other words, there was no contingency between the animal's response and the outcome the animal achieved; no matter what they did to try to avoid the shock, they still received it. This state of helplessness was thought to be similar to depression, and a considerable amount of research was conducted to assess the validity of the theory in humans. The learning tasks used to induce helplessness in humans typically involved some form of impossible reasoning problems and, fortunately, not inescapable electric shock! (See Abramson, Seligman, & Teasdale, 1978.)

The results of this research showed that it was possible to induce a state of dysphoria by exposing people to helplessness experiences in a laboratory setting. However, it became clear that in order for depression to occur, how the person perceived the negative experience was crucial. Therefore, Abramson et al. (1978) proposed a new model which they termed reformulated learned helplessness. This reformulation involved the addition of a cognitive level of explanation that included an analysis of the attributions a person makes for his or her experience of failure. This model can be summarised as follows:

(1) The model does not account for all types of depression; it is therefore a sufficient but not a necessary condition for depression.
(2) The person learns to expect that a highly aversive state of affairs is likely to occur and that a positive state of affairs is unlikely.
(3) The person expects that he or she will be able to do nothing about the likelihood of this aversive state of affairs occurring.
(4) The person possesses a maladaptive attributional style.

A maladaptive attributional style in this sense means that when a negative event is experienced, it is attributed to factors that are internal, stable, and global to the individual. When a positive event is experienced, it is attributed to external, unstable, specific factors. So if we take the event of failing an exam, for example, the attribution the person makes for this failure will determine whether or not he or she becomes depressed. An example of an internal, stable, global factor is intelligence; intelligence is internal to the person, stable in that it will not change over time, and global in that it is likely to affect most tasks the person performs. If the failure of the exam is attributed to lack of intelligence, this will more likely lead to depression than if the failure is attributed to a particularly difficult set of questions that the person had not been taught how to answer. In this latter case the attribution is made to an external factor, namely the difficulty of the paper; this attribution is also unstable in that another exam paper is unlikely to be as difficult; it is specific because the problem of difficulty in this case concerns only exam papers and not all of life's challenges.

The reformulated model of learned helplessness has been further developed and refined and is now called the hopelessness theory; the interested reader is referred to Abramson, Metalsky, and Alloy (1989) for further details.

PSYCHODYNAMIC MODELS

As an approach to depression, psychoanalysis presents a range of models or theories rather than just one unitary view (see Arieti & Bemporad, 1978; Coyne, 1985). Salient features of the approach are that it places emphasis on unconscious factors and has a great deal to say about early development and how this can create vulnerability to depression in adult life. A good place to begin is Freud's (1917) paper "Mourning and Melancholia". In this paper Freud made the link between mourning and depression. He argued that in both states something is lost, but in depression what is lost is often less clear. The loss in depression may be a more abstract concept, such as the failure of a valued plan or the loss of a cherished idea or ideal. Because this approach places great emphasis on the importance of the unconscious and on defence mechanisms that prevent painful or unacceptable thoughts and ideas from entering consciousness, it is possible that a person may not be consciously aware of loss, but, instead he or she is aware of feeling hopeless and depressed.

Freud states that a major difference between mourning and depression is that the latter involves a lowering of self-regard and self-denigration; this can be seen as an attack on the self. In mourning it is the world which has become poor and empty, but in depression it is the ego itself. Freud proposed the following sequence to explain one common way in which depression can develop:

(1) The person experiences a disappointment, for example with a loved one.
(2) The loved one cannot be abandoned as worthless and the affection transferred to someone else, perhaps because the loved one is felt to be essential in the way that a child needs a mother.

(3) Instead of abandonment, the person identifies with the other and internalises him/her. In psychoanalytic terms this would be described as the introjection of the object as part of the ego.
(4) Because the loved one is now felt to be a part of the self or ego, the attacks on the self can be understood as denigration and attacks against the lost or disappointing person.

This sequence of events presents an early psychoanalytic formulation of depression which has been both expanded on and criticised by a number of more recent psychoanalytic theorists (e.g. Bibring, 1953). However, before moving on to consider more recent ideas, Freud's formulation is important in drawing attention to the following. First, the difficulty depressed individuals have in giving up what they have lost. There appears to be an intense need to maintain the ideal situation, whether this is a loved person, a goal, aspiration, or quality of the self. It is as if the person cannot survive without his/her cherished ideal; there is little or no intrinsic sense of self-worth or value aside from the attainment of the ideal (see Arieti & Bemporad, 1978).

Second, there is the idea of repressed hostility in depression, a phenomenon that will be apparent to anyone who has been exposed to a severely depressed person. Indeed depression itself can be seen as an indirect and unconscious way of expressing hostility. This aspect of the account could be considered to solve the riddle of suicide in depression. The depressive really wants to kill or attack the person who has caused his or her sense of disappointment or abandonment. Because this person is now felt to be a part of the self, by killing the self, the depressive kills the person who has caused the hurt.

Third, the loss of energy in depression and the withdrawal of interest from the external world can be explained by the absorbing and exhausting nature of the conflict set up in the person's inner world. This conflict being brought about by the perceived discrepancy between the actual situation and the wished for situation which cannot be abandoned.

More recent psychoanalytic formulations (see Bibring, 1953) have emphasised the importance of the helplessness of the ego as the central mechanism in causing depression. It is argued that depression is the emotional expression of a state of powerlessness of the self to achieve or live up to the strongly held wishes. Such wishes may include the following; the need to be worthy and loved, to be strong and secure, and to be good and not aggressive or destructive. Bibring states that depression results from the tension between these aspirations, which are felt to be essential for the survival of the self, and the ego's acute awareness of its perceived (but not necessarily real) helplessness and incapacity to live up to them. The person becomes tired of the struggle and gives up, withdrawing from the external world and in extreme cases wishes to die. In contrast to Freud's formulation, Bibring argues that it is the ego's awareness of its helplessness which in some cases forces it to turn the aggression away from what has caused its suffering onto the self. In other words, the turning of the aggressive impulses against the self is secondary to the breakdown in self-esteem.

All psychoanalytic theorists see the origin of this situation to be in a developmental context. Particular emphasis is placed on the earliest experiences of feeding in the infant because it is at this stage in development that the organism really is quite helpless without the adequate care of another person (usually a mother). At this early stage of development the infant does not have the necessary understanding of the world to know that food will come soon or that the lack of comfort is not a permanent state but only a temporary one. How much deprivation and frustration an infant has to experience, how this is handled by the infant's care-takers, and how well the infant can tolerate these experiences will all contribute to how helpless the infant feels. In situations of loss in adult life, psychoanalytic theory argues that there is a temporary regression in which the feelings of these much earlier experiences of loss and helplessness are experienced again. Therefore, how individuals cope with loss, whether or not they become helpless and depressed, will depend to some extent on how they coped with these earlier losses and disappointments. How such resilience is conceptualised varies according to the particular psychodynamic theory, but to put it very simply, resilience will depend on the extent to which a person was able to internalise good experiences; good experience should enable a person to tolerate or withstand the inevitable bad experiences of loss and disappointment without feeling helpless. However, it is important to emphasise that the needs for love and care and the meeting of basic needs extend well beyond earliest infancy, and it is likely that any experiences of extreme helplessness may well contribute to later vulnerability to depression (see Bowlby, 1988). Conversely, the experience of a positive loving relationship later on in development may lead to greater resilience to depression by the suggested process of internalisation (Bowlby, 1988). Indeed, one way in which psychoanalytic psychotherapy may work is through the provision of a form of repetition of the parent–child relationship with the hope that the patient can internalise a better experience of a caring and understanding other than he or she had done previously. This internalisation of the therapeutic relationship should have a beneficial effect on self-esteem and so increase resilience to depression.

There is insufficient space here to provide a detailed account of psychoanalytic approaches to the treatment of depression. The unique features of this approach are that emphasis is placed on the therapeutic relationship and on working in the transference (see Chapter 1). In contrast to Beck's cognitive therapy, the psychoanalytic therapist would not talk directly about distortions in perception. Instead, distortions in perception would be drawn to the patient's attention using interpretation of material that the patient presented. Indeed, many interpretations would address how such distortions influenced the patient's perception of the therapist. In this way, the psychoanalytic therapist helps the patient to work through difficulties and conflicts in the here and now of the therapeutic situation. Links would also be made with the patient's past experiences of significant others, relating to both conscious and unconscious memories or conflicts. Psychoanalytic theory provides a framework which informs the therapist about the possible nature of unconscious conflicts in depression together with a framework in which to view the development of depression across the lifespan.

THE DEPRESSIVE PERSONALITY

The idea of vulnerability has already been briefly considered in relation to genetic and social factors. The cognitive model also suggests a type of cognitive vulnerability and indicates how that may have developed. It is clear to some therapists and researchers who have worked extensively with depressed people that many have a certain type of personality. This sort of personality can be seen as providing a kind of fertile "soil" in which, given the necessary conditions, the "seed" of depressive disorder will be more likely to grow.

Psychoanalytic approaches to depression have gone to great lengths to describe the personality type of the depression-prone person; attention is paid to what may have contributed to the development of this vulnerability from birth onwards. In contrast, other approaches, particularly the behavioural approach, have given very little attention to this area. The idea of personality is important because biological and social factors interact with the personality and influence if, when, and how depressive disorder develops. Only a very brief account can be given here of the main characteristics of the depressive personality. A clear and useful account is given by Anthony Storr (1990).

A central feature of the depressive personality is the absence of a secure sense of self-worth or built-in sense of self-esteem. This characteristic may not be at all obvious to an observer when the person is not depressed. What may be more obvious in many cases is that the person is compliant and reticent in stating opinions. Because the depressive does not have a built-in sense of self-esteem, he or she needs constantly to obtain it from the external world. This need will be manifested in over-anxiety to please, to fit in, and to be successful and achieve. Popularity and achievement are essential requirements because this is the only way any confirmation can be obtained. Storr (1979, p. 99) states "It is impossible for the depressive to be indifferent to what others think of him, since repeated assurance of their good opinion is as necessary to his psychic health as are repeated feeds of milk to the physical well-being of infants." To be in such a position, makes a person excessively vulnerable to criticism and makes being assertive in the face of opposition a very risky enterprise. For these reasons, those with depressive personalities may be regarded as "nice", but often will not gain the respect that they deserve or feel is due to them for the considerable efforts they make on other's behalf. They are likely to feel resentment and hostility because of this, but be unable to express these feelings for fear of rejection and loss of the other's good opinion. It is not difficult to see how this state of affairs can lead to a vicious circle of overcompliance, leading to more resentment and then increased attempts to conceal resentment by more over-compliance, and so on.

This picture of the depressive personality presents a view of the more passive type. However, the same basic lack of self-esteem can manifest itself as far from passive. Some individuals will reach a point in development when they come to see that success can relieve feelings of worthlessness. In this case ceaseless striving will replace passivity. In many capable individuals, such striving can lead to considerable success and acclaim in the external world. Winston Church-ill provides an excellent example of someone who was prone to depression and who suffered at times from severe depressive disorder, but for most of his life presented as anything but passive and helpless. This picture can be seen as a kind of overcompensation for feelings of inadequacy. All is well for such a person if the external world provides a focus for what may otherwise remain inner conflicts. Such a person is particularly prone to a depressive disorder following a success as well as a failure, because success can be felt to be a loss; that is, loss of a goal or something to strive for. Once the goal is obtained, the person returns to a basic feeling of being worthless and empty.

BIOLOGICAL MODELS

This book is primarily about psychological models of adult disorders and does not attempt to cover biological explanations. However, no consideration of the causes and treatment of depression would be complete without some mention of biochemistry and the action of anti-depressant drugs.

Drugs to treat depression entered the public arena in the late 1950s and have been the focus of much publicity since that time. Increasing numbers of people have gone to their general practitioner expecting effective drug treatment for de-pression, especially since the introduction of a new generation of anti-depressants such as Prozac. Indeed for most people anti-depressant medication will be the first treatment received. It is only usually after this has been initiated that psy-chological treatments will be offered either in conjunction with drugs or because, for one reason or another, the drug treatment has proved unsatisfactory (WHO, 1989).

A brief summary of the action of anti-depressant drugs

In the late 1950s, evidence gradually came together to suggest that there was a link between mood disorder and the level of monoamines in the central nervous system. The main substances implicated were noradrenaline (NA) also called norepinephrine (NE), dopamine (DA) and 5-Hydroxytryptamine (5-HT), also called serotonin. Noradrenaline and dopamine are both catecholamines. Serotonin is an indolamine. Two pieces of evidence implicated this link. First, reserpine, a drug used to treat hypertension, was found to produce a lowering of mood and symptoms similar to depression in a small proportion of patients treated. It was known that reserpine produced a lowering of the levels of NA, DA, and 5-HT in the central nervous system. In contrast, another drug, iproniazid, which was used to treat tuberculosis, sometimes produced a raising of mood, or symptoms opposite and incompatible with depression. Iproniazid was known to increase levels of NA, DA, and 5-HT in the brain. A vast amount of research has been conducted to establish the validity of this hypothesis and to establish exactly how these neurotransmitters are regulated leading to levels being raised or lowered. Other neurotransmitters such as acetylcholine have also been implicated. No attempt will be made here to consider the mechanisms involved in the action of these neurotransmitters; the interested reader is referred to the following references: Cunningham-Owens (1998), Goodwin (1998).

The main groups of anti-depressant drugs, namely the monoamine oxidase inhibitors (MAOIs), the tricyclic anti-depressants, and the latest group of select-ive serotonin reuptake inhibitors (SSRIs) such as Prozac, work on the basic hypothesis that increasing the levels of NA, DA, and 5-HT will alleviate the symptoms of depression. These three main groups of drugs together with lithium, which is the most widely used treatment for bipolar disorders, all have different mechanisms of action for achieving an increase in the levels of these neuro-transmitters in the central nervous system. Attempts have been made to establish if certain amines are more important than others in the production of specific symptoms. For example, DA has been associated with a lack of pleasure, whereas 5-HT has been especially linked with sleep disturbance. Overall, this search for specificity has not as yet proved successful, which may in part be because improvement in mood can be achieved by many different routes, with improve-ment in one symptom having a beneficial effect more generally.

The most widely used anti-depressant drugs are those from the tricyclic groups such as imipramine and amitriptyline, and the more recent group of SSRIs such as fluoxetine (Prozac) and sertraline. These anti-depressants are generally pre-ferred to the MAOIs, which can be more dangerous because they can produce a hypertensive crisis if certain common foods like cheese, which contain tyramine, are consumed. Bipolar disorders are almost always treated with lithium, or, because of the toxicity of lithium, with one of the newer mood stabilisers such as carbamazepine or sodium valproate. This treatment is usually continuous once the diagnosis is made, though patients on such lithium prophylactic treat-ment are required to have blood levels of the drug checked every two months or so. It is important to note from a psychological perspective that anti-depressant drugs do not have an immediate action, but need to be taken in the correct dosage over many days or sometimes weeks before they have a therapeutic effect. Side-effects are common and these may be very unpleasant and reduce compliance in many patients. Although drug treatment is usually the first treatment offered to those presenting with depression, it is not effective for everyone; this is due, at least in part, to the problems with compliance in taking the drugs correctly over a long period of time and due to problems with the side-effects that some people experience. In addition to these considerations, many people do not consider a chemical solution to their depression is desirable and taking drugs can increase a feeling of helplessness or being trapped in a dependence which they do not like nor fully understand. Current approaches to anti-depressant medication suggest that drugs should be continued for at least six months after recovery from depression and that only after this time should the medication be reduced gradually. For those with a recurrent disorder where there has been more than one episode of depression in the past five years, long term or permanent medication is often considered (WHO, 1989).

Considering this information, practitioners using psychological treatments for depression will often be working with people who are on medication for depression. In this case, and for those who have received apparently unsuccessful drug treatments for depression, it is often important to know about the side-effects anti-depressant drugs produce; sometimes these effects can be a source of distress and mistaken for symptoms of the disorder. In addition, the patients' attitude to the drugs, their understanding of how they may work and why they have to take them, may need to be integrated into a psychological approach to treatment.

Finally, drug treatments and other physical treatments such as electroconvulsive therapy (ECT) are often the treatment of choice, and sometimes the only reasonable option in cases of very severe depression, where the person is not capable of entering into any kind of relationship with a therapist or complying with any treatment regime which requires the person's understanding or active participation. The desirability of drug treatment is likely to be influenced by many factors including life-stage and the attitudes of the person concerned. Very elderly patients who are severely depressed may find many of the psychological treatments unacceptably demanding and so be more appropriately treated with drugs. In cases of very severe depression, physical treatments are often used as a first stage, helping to reduce the severity of symptoms, so that more demanding treatment approaches can be used once there has been some improvement. Simple behavioural techniques can often be used with quite severely depressed patients with a view to gradually helping them to increase their range of activities. Again, after some progress has been made, more demanding cognitive approaches can be attempted. Psychotherapy using an analytic approach is likely to be a long-term treatment; generally this type of treatment will have to be modified during the most severe phases of a major depression and the therapist needs to be much more active than he or she would normally be.

SOCIAL MODELS

So far in this chapter we have considered models of depression that focus on behaviour, cognition, biology, and early experience. Most of these models have mentioned the experience of loss as a precipitant of depression. However, none of these models have said much about the contribution of social factors in the person's environment, or about the broad influences of sex, class, race, culture, and life stage.

Social models of depression consider the cause of the disorder to be primarily of social origin (see Brown, 1989; Brown & Harris, 1978). In other words, depression can be caused by upsetting or unpleasant experiences in the person's social world. These experiences may be acute life events, such as the loss of a valued friend or partner, or more long-term experiences of adversity, such as living in damp, crowded housing conditions for a long period of time with no obvious hope of ever being able to move. The models considered so far have emphasised the experience of helplessness and the lack of a sense of control over one's environment as a major cause of depression. It is not difficult to see how certain social conditions or certain social roles can produce a greater likelihood of this experience than others.

Before moving on to consider a specific social model for depression, it is important to point out that the rates of unipolar depression differ between certain social groups, differences that are not found with the bipolar disorders. First, there is a dramatic sex difference in the rates of depression; adult women are about twice as likely as men to be diagnosed as having major depression (Nolen-Hoeksema, 1990; Weissman & Klerman, 1985). There is insufficient space here to go into all the possible explanations that have been proposed for this difference. Many of these explanations are biological, including endocrine or genetic factors. However, biological explanations are undermined by the finding that the sex difference is not consistently found when other, more social, comparisons are made. To give one example, divorced and widowed men have higher rates of depression than single or married women. It is, in fact, only amongst those who are married that the large excess of women over men is to be found (Cochrane, 1983).

Some research has suggested that having children may be the crucial factor in accounting for the higher rate of depression in women (e.g. Gater, Dean, & Morris, 1989). It is important to point out that the excess of depression in women who have had children is not adequately explained by the occurrence of the mild dysphoria (the "maternity blues") that occurs immediately after childbirth in about 50% of women across cultures, nor is it explained by the more severe postpartum psychosis. The severe and relatively rare disorder of postpartum psychosis occurs soon after childbirth and appears to have a distinct aetiology linked to biological changes (see Kumar & Brockington, 1988). Indeed, recent research suggests that there is little evidence that women are at increased risk for the more commonly occurring types of depression immediately following child-birth (Bhugra & Gregoire, 1993). It is important to point out that, in general, women with children are at increased risk for depression when compared to those without children, though the problems of selecting an appropriate control group with which to make comparisons are considerable.

In order to explain the sex difference in rates of depression, it is necessary to look at social explanations, including those that relate to women's social roles and the stress these roles may cause (see Champion & Power, 1995). Various social explanations have been put forward; these include sex discrimination, the early role socialisation of girls to be more helpless and powerless than boys, and the greater acceptability for women in our society to express depression. Some sociologists have argued that women's greater vulnerability to depression lies in the types of roles women are expected to fulfill (see Gove & Tudor, 1973); roles such as being the carer for young children, cleaner, housewife, working mother, etc. The work that these roles demand is not highly valued in our society; it is often unpaid or poorly paid; there are no fixed hours and generally very poor conditions of service. For many women, especially those who are poor and have few material or social resources, the experience may produce the feelings of being trapped and helpless that are so characteristic of depression.

A well-developed and influential social approach to depression has been pre-sented by Brown and his colleagues (Brown, 1989; Brown & Harris, 1978). Over the past three decades, this research on the social origins of depression has proposed increasingly complex models of the cause of depression and has also implicated the role of social factors in recovery. The approach has many sim-ilarities with the other approaches already outlined; for example, the role of early experience is emphasised; a range of vulnerability factors are identified; and specific events are defined that immediately precede or trigger the onset of disorder. The unique contribution of this approach is that all the aspects men-tioned are defined in social terms. Adversity in the social world is seen as the cause of the internal changes in biology, cognition and behaviour which are characteristic of depression.

The work of Brown and his colleagues focuses exclusively on women, but many of the basic ideas about the social causation are likely to apply to men, albeit in slightly different ways due to their different social circumstances (see Brown, 1989). Earlier research (see Brown & Harris, 1978) clearly showed that in an inner-city sample, working-class women were more likely to suffer from depression than were middle-class women. Working-class women are also much more likely to have experienced a life event with severe long-term threat or to have experienced a major difficulty. A severe event is one which was consider-ably unpleasant or upsetting for the women concerned, and had a negative threatening aspect which was still evident after about 2 weeks from the event's occurrence, for example the death of a parent, child, or other very close relative; the loss of a job with no immediate prospect of another one; news of eviction, and so on. A major difficulty is an upsetting or unpleasant social situation that has continued for at least 2 years, for example very poor housing conditions; chronic, serious illness in a household member; or unemployment of the main "breadwinner" in the family. These two types of stressor, severe events and major difficulties, are termed *provoking agents*. The research showed that these provoking agents were much more likely to have occurred in the group of women who had become depressed than in the group that were not depressed. For those women who had become depressed in the past year, 89% had experienced a provoking agent in the 9 months before the onset of the depression. In the normal group, only 30% had experienced a provoking agent in the same time period (see Brown & Harris, 1986).

In addition to establishing the importance of provoking agents, the model was further refined to include a number of other social factors that were found to be associated with an increased risk of depression, if a provoking agent occurred. These factors were called vulnerability factors, and included the following: having several young children at home; not having employment outside the home; and lacking an intimate and confiding relationship with a husband or partner.

Further research has attempted to replicate these findings in different samples. This research has confirmed the importance of provoking agents in preceding the onset of depression. Only one vulnerability factor has been consistently identified across studies. This factor is the absence of a confiding relationship with a partner (see Champion, 1990, for a summary). The importance of social support more generally, in protecting against depression in the face of stress, has been the focus of a great deal of recent research; the interested reader is referred to the book edited by Brugha (1995). In addition, a highly effective approach to the treatment of depression called Interpersonal Psychotherapy (see later) directly targets the level and quality of a person's social support during treatment.

The social model outlined here, including some of the more recent developments, can be summarised as follows: vulnerability to depression and the onset of a depressive disorder are regarded as the result of adverse experiences in the environment rather than the result of internal faults, such as those of biology or cognition. Adverse social experiences can occur early in life; one example is the lack of adequate parental care in childhood. This early adversity is then associated with an increased risk of continuing adversity later, as demonstrated in a 20-year follow-up study of children in Camberwell (Champion, Goodall, & Rutter, 1995). Sex, class, culture, and life stage are all important factors in assessing the type of social vulnerability that is likely to be implicated in an increased risk of depression. There is more than one route by which these early adverse social experiences can have their effect (see Maughan & Champion, 1990). Two examples would be: first, the continuation of external stress; second, a negative effect on internal resources such as the inadequate development of self-esteem. To give one example of this second route, a failure to establish an adequate degree of self-esteem may make it more difficult to plan for, establish, and sustain supportive relationships in adult-life; these problems may also increase the risk of experiencing unpleasant and upsetting events in the area of relationships (see Champion, 1990; Rutter, Champion, Quinton, Maughan, & Pickles, 1995). It is at this point in discussing the refinements of a social model that it becomes clear that the model is not entirely social, but includes many aspects of the person, such as cognition, behaviour, and almost certainly biology and genetics. So, finally, this chapter will briefly consider how each of the models described can be usefully integrated to provide a more complete understanding of depression.

INTEGRATION

The aim of this chapter has been to introduce the reader to the subject of clinical depression and to impart some basic knowledge about the main models or approaches to understanding the causes of the disorder and its treatment.

By now, it should be clear that while each approach represents a different angle and emphasises different causal factors, there are a great many similarities between the approaches. Taken together, all the approaches outlined emphasise the many facets of this complex disorder. In practice, most researchers and clinicians will consider biological, genetic, cognitive, behavioural, and social factors when thinking about depression. Which aspect takes precedence will depend on the aims of the particular study or clinical intervention in question.

Some of the strengths and weaknesses of each of the approaches will be considered below: first, the cognitive approach is useful in that it forces us to think about how depression represents certain types of distortion in perception and thinking. This approach points out that there can be a marked discrepancy between the objective and the subjective view of the same event and that this discrepancy can create problems. However, the psychoanalytic approaches would argue very much the same, but from a different theoretical perspective. The psychoanalytic approach is helpful in the following ways: It provides a detailed framework for explaining how the misperceptions may have come about and forces us to think about depression in a developmental context, especially with the continuing growth of interest in Bowlby's attachment theory. In addition, the idea that much of what governs our perception and behaviour in depression is unconscious is an important contribution of this approach, though more recent cognitive models have striven to take greater account of unconscious and automatic processes (Power & Dalgleish, 1997). Both the cognitive and psychoanalytic approaches can be informed by the social approach in regard to the types of external circumstances that are associated with both vulnerability to depression and to the onset of the disorder itself. Biological approaches provide another level of explanation and description. They are especially useful in increasing our understanding of the most severe disorders.

All approaches provide methods of treatment, some of which will be more suitable than others for certain types of depression and certain individuals. Behavioural and biological approaches are likely to be especially useful for the initial treatment of the most severe depressions. Cognitive and psychoanalytic approaches generate different types of treatment which may appeal to different types of practitioners and clients. Behavioural and cognitive compared to psychoanalytic approaches to treatment are relatively short-term, which can offer advantages in terms making better use of limited resources of time and money. There is not much research which genuinely addresses all the approaches considered here, however, there is a move towards integration especially of the social and biological approaches (see Bebbington & McGuffin, 1989).

No attempt has been made here to consider the relative effectiveness of the different approaches to the treatment of depression. This is a highly complex and controversial area. The outcome of any treatment will be influenced by a host of different factors including, for example, the severity of the disorder, the characteristics of the depressed person, and so on. In addition, how outcome is assessed presents a complex problem. A number of studies have demonstrated that cognitive therapy can be at least as effective as drug treatment in the acute phase of depression and that cognitive therapy may be more effective than drugs in preventing relapse. The interested reader is referred to Williams (1992). Psychoanalytic approaches tend to report their effectiveness by clinical case studies. An example of these for both severe and mild depression can be found in Arieti and Bemporad (1978).

One important outcome study which can be broadly interpreted in the spirit of integration is a recent, large-scale study conducted to assess the comparative effectiveness of two different types of brief psychological treatment (Cognitive Therapy and Interpersonal Psychotherapy) and drug treatment for outpatients with major depressive disorder (see Elkin, 1994; Elkin et al., 1989). The results of this research showed few clear differences in the overall effectiveness of the different treatments because all were generally effective, but it has provided a significant international boost for Interpersonal Psychotherapy (IPT) which was little known or practised outside the US previously. As an approach, IPT was developed by Klerman, Weissman, Rounsaville, and Chevron (1984) (see Klerman & Weissman, 1993, for a more recent summary); it offers a short-term therapy that combines features from all of the approaches considered in this chapter, in particular from the social and the psychodynamic, but whilst acknowledging biological and psychological factors. One considerable strength of the approach is that a focus has to be decided on one of four different types of issue that are seen as central to the onset and maintenance of depression:

(1) grief—dealing with the aftermath of the loss of a close significant other
(2) interpersonal disputes—especially those that might have continued for some time, such as in a marriage or work dispute

(3) role transitions—for example, dealing with the transition of leaving home, or of having children, or of retirement
(4) interpersonal deficits—these are typically seen in individuals who are very socially isolated or who have problems in maintaining relationships.

It seems clear that this integrative approach will establish itself internationally as another powerful psychological treatment method for depression, a development that is to be welcomed given the high cost of this disorder to individuals, their families, and to society as a whole.

RECOMMENDED READING

Arieti, S. & Bemporad, J. (1978). *Severe and mild depression: The psychotherapeutic approach*. London: Tavistock.

This book provides a good general introduction and an in-depth look at psychoanalytic ideas. There are many case examples in this book.

Coyne, J. (1985). *Essential papers on depression*. New York: New York University Press.

See pp. 1–22 for a general introduction. This book includes reprints of key papers on most of the models covered in this chapter.

Gilbert, P. (1992). *Depression: The evolution of powerlessness*. Hove, UK: Lawrence Erlbaum Associates Ltd.

A good general introduction is provided in Chapter 1 (pp. 3–26). This book is strongest on the possible evolutionary basis of depression, although it covers all approaches.

Hammen, C. (1997). *Depression*. Hove, UK: Psychology Press.

A good up-to-date introduction for facts and theories.

Williams, J.M.G. (1992). *The psychological treatment of depression: A guide to the theory and practice of cognitive-behaviour therapy* (2nd ed.). London: Routledge.

A readable account of cognitive behaviour therapy for depression.

REFERENCES

Abramson, L., Metalsky, G., & Alloy, L. (1989). Hopelessness depression: A theory-based subtype of depression. *Psychological Review, 96*, 358–372.
Abramson, L., Seligman, M., & Teasdale, J. (1978). Learned helplessness: Critique and reformulation. *Journal of Abnormal Psychology, 87*, 49–74.
APA (1994). *Diagnostic and statistical manual of mental disorders* (4th ed.) Washington, DC: American Psychiatric Association.
Arieti, S., & Bemporad, J. (1978). *Severe and mild depression: The psychotherapeutic approach*. London: Tavistock.

Bebbington, P., Katz, R., McGuffin, P., Tennant, C., & Hurry, J. (1989). The risk of minor depression before age 65: Results from a community survey. *Psychological Medicine, 19*, 393–400.

Bebbington, P., & McGuffin, P. (1989). Interactive models of depression: The evidence. In K. Herbst & E. Paykel (Eds.), *Depression: An integrative approach* (pp. 65–80). Oxford, UK: Heinemann.

Beck, A., Rush, A., Shaw, B., & Emery, G. (1979). *Cognitive therapy of depression*. New York: Wiley.

Bhugra, D., & Gregoire, A. (1993). Social factors in the genesis and management of postnatal psychiatric disorders. In D. Bhugra & J. Leff (Eds.), *Principles of social psychiatry* (pp. 424–436). Oxford, UK: Blackwell Scientific Publications.

Bibring, E. (1953). The mechanism of depression. In P. Greenacre (Ed.), *Affective disorders: Psychoanalytic contribution to their study*. New York: International Universities Press.

Bowlby, J. (1988). *A secure base: Clinical applications of attachment theory*. London: Routledge.

Brown, G. (1989). Depression: A radical social perspective. In K. Herbst & E. Paykel (Eds.), *Depression: An integrative approach* (pp. 21–44). Oxford, UK: Heinemann.

Brown, G., & Harris, T. (1978). *The social origins of depression: A study of psychiatric disorder in women*. London: Tavistock.

Brown, G., & Harris, T. (1986). Establishing causal links: The Bedford College studies of depression. In H. Katschnig (Ed.), *Life events and psychiatric disorders: Controversial issues*. Cambridge, UK: Cambridge University Press.

Brugha, T.S. (Ed.). (1995). *Social support and psychiatric disorder: Research findings and guidelines for clinical practice*. Cambridge, UK: Cambridge University Press.

Champion, L. (1990). The relationship between social vulnerability and the occurrence of severely threatening life events. *Psychological Medicine, 20*, 157–161.

Champion, L.A., Goodall, G., & Rutter, M. (1995). Behavioural problems in childhood and stressors in early adult life: I. A 20 year follow-up of London school children. *Psychological Medicine, 25*, 231–246.

Champion, L.A., & Power, M.J. (1995). Social and cognitive approaches to depression: Towards a new synthesis. *British Journal of Clinical Psychology, 34*, 485–503.

Cochrane, R. (1983). *The social creation of mental illness*. London: Longman.

Coyne, J. (1985). *Essential papers on depression*. New York: New York University Press.

Cunningham-Owens, D.J. (1998). Clinical psychopharmacology. In E.C. Johnstone, C.P.L. Freeman, & A.K. Zealley (Eds.), *Companion to psychiatric studies* (6th ed., pp. 81–148). Edinburgh, UK: Churchill Livingstone.

Elkin, I. (1994). The NIMH treatment of depression collaborative research program: Where we began and where we are now. In A.E. Bergin & S.L. Garfield (Eds.), *Handbook of psychotherapy and behavior change* (4th ed.). New York: Wiley.

Elkin, I., Shea, T., Watkins, J.T., Imber, S., Sotsky, S., & Collins, J. (1989). National Institute of Mental Health treatment of depression collaborative research program. *Archives of General Psychiatry, 46*, 971–982.

Ferster, C. (1973). A functional analysis of depression. *American Psychologist, 28*, 857–870.

Freud, S. (1917). Mourning and melancholia. In A. Richards (Ed.), *The Pelican Freud Library. II* (pp. 251–268). Harmondsworth, UK: Penguin.

Gater, R., Dean, C., & Morris, J. (1989). The contribution of childbearing to the sex difference in first admission rates for affective psychosis. *Psychological Medicine, 19*, 719–724.

Gilbert, P. (1992). *Depression: The evolution of powerlessness*. Hove, UK: Lawrence Erlbaum Associates Ltd.

Goldberg, D., & Huxley, P. (1992). *Common mental disorders: A bio-social model*. London: Tavistock/Routledge.

Goodwin, G. (1998). Mood disorder. In E.C. Johnstone, C.P.L. Freeman, & A.K. Zealley (Eds.), *Companion to psychiatric studies* (6th ed.). Edinburgh, UK: Churchill Livingstone.

Gove, W., & Tudor, J. (1973). Adult sex roles and mental illness. *American Journal of Sociology, 78*, 812–835.

Hammen, C. (1997). *Depression*. Hove, UK: Psychology Press.

Harrington, R. (1993). *Depressive disorder in childhood and adolescence*. Chichester, UK: Wiley.

Kendell, R. (1976). The classification of depressions: A review of contemporary confusion. *British Journal of Psychiatry, 129*, 15–28.

Klerman, G.L., & Weissman, M.M. (Eds.). (1993). *New applications of interpersonal psychotherapy*. Washington, DC: American Psychiatric Press.

Klerman, G.L., Weissman, M.M., Rounsaville, B.J., & Chevron, E.S. (1984). *Interpersonal psychotherapy of depression*. Northvale, NJ: Jason Aronson.

Kumar, R., & Brockington, J. (Eds.). (1988). *Motherhood and mental illness: 2. Causes and consequences*. London: Wright.

Lewinsohn, P. (1974). A behavioural approach to depression. In R. Friedman & M. Katz (Eds.), *The psychology of depression: Contemporary theory and research*. New York: Winston-Wiley.

Lewinsohn, P., Hoberman, H., Teri, L., & Hautzinger, M. (1985). An integrative theory of depression. In S. Reiss & R. Bootzin (Eds.), *Theoretical issues in behaviour therapy* (pp. 331–359). New York: Academic Press.

Maughan, B., & Champion, L. (1990). Risk and protective factors in the transition to young adulthood. In P. Baltes & M. Baltes (Eds.), *Successful aging: Perspectives from the behavioural sciences* (pp. 296–331). Cambridge, UK: Cambridge University Press.

McGuffin, P., & Katz, R. (1989). The genetics of depression and manic depressive disorder. *British Journal of Psychiatry, 155*, 294–304.

Nolen-Hoeksema, S. (1990). *Sex differences in depression*. Stanford, CA: Stanford University Press.

Paykel, E. (1989). The background: Extent and nature of the disorder. In K. Herbst & E. Paykel (Eds.), *Depression: An integrative approach* (pp. 3–20). Oxford, UK: Heinemann.

Power, M.J. (1999). Sadness. In T. Dalgleish & M.J. Power (Eds.), *Handbook of cognition and emotion*. Chichester, UK: Wiley.

Power, M., & Champion, L. (1986). Cognitive approaches to depression: A theoretical critique. *British Journal of Clinical Psychology, 25*, 201–212.

Power, M.J., & Dalgleish, T. (1997). *Cognition and emotion: From order to disorder*. Hove, UK: Psychology Press.

Rutter, M., Champion, L., Quinton, D., Maughan, B., & Pickles, A. (1995). Origins of individual differences in environmental risk exposure. In P. Moen, G. Elder, & K. Luscher (Eds.), *Perspectives on the ecology of human development* (pp. 61–93). Ithaca, NY: Cornell University Press.

Seligman, M. (1975). *Helplessness*. San Francisco: W.H. Freeman.

Storr, A. (1979). *The art of psychotherapy*. London: Heinemann.

Storr, A. (1990). *The art of psychotherapy* (2nd ed.). London: Heinemann.

Weishaar, M. (1993). *Aaron T. Beck*. London: Sage.

Weissman, M., & Klerman, G. (1985). Gender and depression. *Trends in Neuroscience*, September. Amsterdam: Elsevier.

Williams, J.M.G. (1992). *The psychological treatment of depression: A guide to the theory and practice of cognitive-behaviour therapy* (2nd ed.). London: Routledge.

WHO (1989). Pharmacotherapy of depressive disorders: A consensus statement by WHO Mental Health Collaborating Centres. *Journal of Affective Disorders, 17*, 197–198.

WHO (1992). *International statistical classification of diseases and related health problems* (Vol. 1, 10th revision, pp. 311–387). Geneva: World Health Organisation.

CHAPTER THREE

Anxiety

Margie Callanan
Salomons, Centre for Applied Social & Psychological Development,
Canterbury Christ Church University College, Kent, UK

INTRODUCTION

The nature of anxiety

Anxiety is a common form of reaction that every person experiences to a greater or lesser extent during his or her lifetime. The term anxiety is one that is as much a part of the lay person's vocabulary as it is the clinician's. Defining the concept of anxiety is, therefore, not a simple task. People may describe themselves as anxious when they are anticipating an important examination, or an important job interview. Those who report an experience of fear when left alone in the dark may also describe themselves as anxious. On the other hand, anxiety may be diagnosed when general functioning is at a level below usual competence and is accompanied by physical symptoms such as tension headaches. Do all these experiences refer to the same concept? Is anxiety to be defined in terms of excess, such as excessive worrying? Or is it to be defined with reference to its perceived impact on functioning, such as life-interfering symptoms (behavioural or physiological)? Does it involve a fearful reaction?

Without a fear reaction, which is frequently an element of anxiety, we would not survive very long. It is the fear reaction that drives us to avoid danger, for example, getting out of the path of an oncoming train; or fighting a threatening figure; or fleeing from a potentially hazardous element. Research into how anxiety is described (that is, by the sufferer) suggests that fear is a basic, fundamental discrete emotion that is universally present across ages, cultures, races, and species. Anxiety, therefore, has a clear functional value in the evolutionary sense and is vital to survival. It also seems to be a feature of being successful; thus, classic laboratory studies have shown that moderate levels of anxiety can lead to optimising task performance and that too much or too little anxiety leads to worse performance (Yerkes & Dodson, 1908). The performance of athletes, entertainers, executives, and students might, therefore, suffer without the presence of some anxiety.

Anxiety, in the simplest sense, is a form of response or reaction. Its existence in the individual does not necessarily denote abnormality. Anxiety can, however, be much more than a normal, helpful, reaction in a challenging situation: It can become intolerably destructive. As with many other conditions, whether it is regarded as a disorder depends on the extent of its negative impact on thinking and behaviour and on how much it interferes with the person's daily life. The reaction of anxiety is on a continuum from normal, even desirable, to a severe disruption in ability to function as desired or expected. The concept of anxiety has been studied along this continuum, and it is the disorder of anxiety, its more destructive presentation, that concerns this present chapter.

The features of anxiety

What are the main features of anxiety? Fear and worry would seem to be important elements to its make-up: One is worried because one fears that something undesirable will happen, or one is anxious because one is frightened of something. Though fear is considered a dominant feature in the syndrome of anxiety, there is general agreement that a number of other emotions may be present, including distress or sadness, anger, shame, guilt, and interest or excitement. A different combination of these emotions will operate in different situations and across time (Izard, 1977). This makes it difficult to talk about anxiety in a precise way.

Definition, therefore, is particularly important with the concept of anxiety as it encompasses a range of reactions and can refer to a range of possible experiences. A precise definition is not universally agreed; presented here are the main elements that may be observed in clinical cases of the anxiety syndrome.

Anxiety may be defined as an unpleasant emotion that is characterised by feelings of dread, worry, nervousness, or fear. This emotion may be experienced in response to particular events, situations, people, or phenomena; it may also be experienced in *anticipation* of such stimuli. The stimulus may be external, for example a storm, or internal. An internal stimulus might be a belief that is negative, accompanied by a sense of helplessness, so that the individual does not feel in control of the situation or his/her response to it. In addition, the individual may experience physical symptoms such as sweating, overbreathing, an increased heartbeat, nausea, or dizziness. In an attempt to deal with the distress and discomfort the individual will usually make efforts to avoid the situation that is believed to excite these feelings. This avoidance behaviour is a common characteristic in the syndrome of anxiety. The main elements of the present definition, therefore, may be summarised as follows:

- an unpleasant emotion such as dread or fear
- in response to particular external or internal events
- accompanied by feeling out of control
- with the experience of uncomfortable physical symptoms
- resulting in an effort to avoid the stimulus event.

In an attempt to illustrate the syndrome as defined, let us consider the case of a 26-year-old young man, here referred to as Jack, who was described by his GP as severely anxious. Jack works as a magazine photographer, and his job performance is successful to the extent that his input is increasingly demanded at executive-level meetings. In these meetings he would sweat profusely and experience feelings of panic. Jack described other physical symptoms such as his heart "thumping loud and fast" and he was suffering frequent headaches. He reported feeling a sense of dread whenever he was due to attend a meeting and, eventually, he began to worry about these meetings even when none were due to take place. Jack felt out of control of the situation; he did not want to lose credibility by refusing to attend the meetings, and he could not control his response to the situation. He began to devise ways of avoiding the meetings but continued to worry about the possibility of having to attend one some day. This worry began to affect his actual work.

In this case, Jack's anxiety could be described as a response to an external stimulus, the executive meeting. However, it could also be described as a reaction to an internal stimulus. The internal stimulus might be Jack's belief in his ability to take part in executive-type decisions: He may have believed that he was leaving his real area of expertise, photography, and attempting an unfamiliar role. The physical symptoms experienced in the meeting may have served to further undermine his already negative self-image.

There is one further element that is often mentioned when defining clinical cases of anxiety—the extent to which it interferes with daily life. This element is not strictly necessary to warrant a diagnosis of anxiety, but it is often the reason for the individual presenting in the consulting room for help. If Jack, in the case cited, had not experienced interference in his usual work performance he may not have presented for help. Jack's fearfulness in the face of executive meetings was not as great as his fear of losing his job.

Fear, according to evolutionary theory, is a basic innate emotion, whereas anxiety is for the most part learned. Barlow (1988) recommends acknowledging the distinction between fear and anxiety. However, it would seem generally acknowledged that fearfulness is a dominant feature in anxiety.

Phobias are usually categorised under anxiety states, as the main element of a phobia is one of fear. Phobia is the name given to an irrational fear of objects (e.g. trains), situations (e.g. open spaces), animals, or phenomena (e.g. thunderstorms). A phobia may be very specific, for example, a snake phobia, or it may be general and take the form of fearing any situation that requires interaction with a number of people (a social phobia). In the usual presentation of the phobic state, the individual will manifest anxiety when he or she is brought into contact with a phobic stimulus (that is, the feared object or situation).

As mentioned previously, a common feature of the phobic state or anxiety presentation is avoidance behaviour. This is the term given to behaviour where the objective is to avoid a particular object, place or situation. Generally this avoidance behaviour takes place in the absence of any rational or obvious reason for the activity, although the origin of the avoidance is a deep fear. Thus, a person who is afraid of open spaces, an agoraphobic, will avoid any such situation that is likely to bring contact with open spaces.

Generalised anxiety is the term usually used to describe an anxious state that does not have as its focus any particular object or situation. Individuals who describe themselves as worrying excessively about most, even minor, events to the extent that normal functioning is interfered with or reduced, are considered to be suffering from generalised anxiety. In some cases, this state of generalised anxiety may include presentation of physical symptoms, such as tension pains or diarrhoea.

The "anxious personality" is a term used to refer to someone who is identified as a "worrier", worrying about most events to some degree, whether they are major or minor. In this individual anxiety is considered to be a character trait: It permeates thinking and behaviour, though not necessarily to a destructive degree. For example, the "anxious personality" would not view a major life change as a stimulating challenge, but rather something to worry and fret about. This anxiety trait has been measured by questionnaires such as the Middlesex Hospital Questionnaire and is generally used to support the notion that "emotionality" or "nervousness" may be hereditary.

It is suggested that the difference between the "anxious personality" and the individual with a severe anxiety state is one of degree: The main elements are the same, but severity and interference are greater in the latter. There is, however, no evidence to suggest that the clinical anxiety syndrome is hereditary. Although it has been observed that families of patients suffering with anxiety are more prone to fearfulness or excessive worrying (Crowe, Noyes, Pauls, & Slymen, 1983), this finding is as supportive of the learning theory as it is the genetic. Barlow (1988) suggests that the anxious personality may be the "platform for panic" (p. 174), so that the presence of this trait makes the individual more susceptible to triggers to acute panic or anxiety. Evidence from clinical cases, albeit anecdotal, presents inconsistent support for this notion. Some anxiety syndrome patients report having always been "rather a worrier", whereas others state that they were "never inclined to fret" before their current anxiety state developed.

Spielberger (1985) considers anxiety a pesonality trait that determines how external or internal stimuli are appraised. In other words, the appraisal of threat, in Spielberger's model, will be a function of one's level of *trait anxiety*. He distinguishes trait anxiety from what he terms *state anxiety*, considering the latter to be a transitory emotional state. The personality trait of anxiety may lead the individual to be anxiety prone. According to Spielberger's state–trait model, if the individual frequently experiences state anxiety then he/she has a strong trait anxiety. This model enables one to distinguish between common anxiety reactions and more intense and consistent anxiety. The model also supports, to some extent, Barlow's (1988) notion of the "anxious personality" being more vulnerable to triggers that produce acute anxiety or panic. However, causes of individual differences in trait anxiety remain unexplained.

Anxiety as a disorder

The disorder "anxiety" appeared for the first time in the seventh revision of the International Classification of Diseases (ICD-7) in 1957, and its categorisation was influenced by contemporary theoretical conceptions of anxiety disorders (Barlow, 1988). The current ICD (10th revision; WHO, 1992) groups anxiety disorders, including panic states, under the general heading of "anxiety states". Thus, anxiety is officially classified as a disorder, though the listing does not provide a good descriptive account of its possible features.

Anxiety becomes destructive and warrants the description of disorder when it is prolonged, perceived by the sufferer to be out of his or her control, and when it begins to result in behaviour or symptoms that reduce normal or desired functioning. Many people will describe a phobic reaction to something in their environment, for example an irrational fear of, and consequent attempts to avoid, spiders. However, a phobic disorder is diagnosed when such irrational fears begin to affect behaviour and decision making to an extreme extent. Thus, a spider phobic warrants the diagnosis of a disorder when the individual requires all rooms to be thoroughly checked before entering them. As may be imagined, this extreme fear could interfere with normal or usual functioning to a great extent.

Anxiety sufferers are often unaware of the cause of their condition. One of the aims of treatment is to provide an explanation of the condition, because increased understanding helps to control the sufferer's fear of the unknown.

How anxiety develops

The nature versus nurture controversy runs through theories of the origin of anxiety, as indeed it does through all theoretical attempts to explain human behaviour and processes (see Chapter 1). The nature perspective is that our responses are primarily genetically coded in our physical and biological makeup. One may be predisposed to overreact to potential threat in the environment and, thus, may be biologically vulnerable to developing anxiety.

The nature argument is that we are born as a *tabula rasa* (a blank sheet), and we learn every movement, thought, and belief from that moment on. Vulnerability to developing anxiety is primarily a social factor: Repeated negative events, observed or experienced, teach the individual to anticipate failure and, thus, lead to an anxious state. Behavioural theories of anxiety acquisition are based on the nurture paradigm: We learn to be anxious, we are not born that way.

Cognitive and psychodynamic theorists combine nature and nurture as an explanation for anxiety acquisition. They acknowledge physiological vulnerability, a predisposition to experience events in a way that influences perceptions, thoughts, and, consequently, experiences. Psychological vulnerability to anxiety is thought to be related to attributions with regard to the intense arousal or response experienced. If the arousal is unpredictable, that is, it could happen at any time, and one is unable to explain it, then one is likely to feel more out of control and become anxious. Biological vulnerability then coincides with a social or psychological vulnerability to develop anxiety.

The prevalence of anxiety

Many individuals each year seek help for what is broadly construed as anxiety or nervousness. The prevalence of generalised anxiety in the United States, on the basis of the Epidemiologic Catchment Area survey, is 4% (Barlow, 1988). This finding suggests that anxiety disorders represent the single largest mental health problem in America. Studies in Britain have also been conducted and reveal that the percentage of the population presenting with an anxiety disorder consists of a majority of women. Prevalence rates are reported to be between one-third and two-thirds higher in women than men (Roth & Fonagy, 1996). The explanations put forward for this finding relate to culture, developmental differences, coping mechanisms, and endocrinology. It is suggested that it may be more culturally acceptable for women to express fear, that men are taught to be "tough" and overcome avoidance behaviour in early development. On the other hand, the sex difference may be explained by the fact that coping styles are different for men and women. Women may cope with anxious states by using avoidance behaviour and men by using alcohol. Although these coping responses are maladaptive in both sexes, they result in different categories of diagnoses being applied to men and women. The endocrinological explanation suggests that women may be biologically more susceptible to panic: It is acknowledged that hormonal levels, which tend to be more variable in women, can affect mood state and so may affect perceptions of threat in a negative way. It may be that a combination of these factors operate to produce the data demonstrating that more women present with anxiety than men. In summary, whatever the breakdown for gender, a recent British survey found that 16% of the population suffered from some form of pathological anxiety (Hale, 1997; OPCS, 1995). This needs to be noted in conjunction with the suggestion in the literature that some anxiety states are probably under-reported in the general population (den Boer, 1997).

Anxiety presentation/secondary anxiety

Anxiety presents itself in the consulting room in a variety of guises.

- A specific phobia may be cited as the main problem.
- Inability to cope, at work or at home, may be the major difficulty experienced.
- Worries about health may be reported, along with aches and pains that have been found to have no medical basis.
- Recent major loss or trauma may be reported as the overwhelming difficulty.
- Depression may be cited as the main problem.
- Obsessive and repetitive behaviour may be the main presenting problem.

Anxiety can be secondary to another major disorder: For example, although excessive alcohol consumption can be a maladaptive response to anxious states, it is also known that drinking makes the person more susceptible to anxiety and symptoms associated with anxiety (see Chapter 4). Another example is the individual with a diagnosis of schizophrenia who may experience extreme anxiety as a result of a delusional view: For instance, the person may fear that an outside force of some kind will control his or her movements (see Chapter 9). In these cases, the primary presenting problem is not an anxiety state; anxiety is considered to be secondary to the main disorder.

Any condition of which the individual is aware, and which reduces the ability to function normally or as desired, may produce some anxiety. It may be considered almost inevitable that one would worry if one were ill in any way, and as such, anxiety would be expected to be present to some degree. However, this secondary anxiety could develop to a stage that is debilitating by itself, that is, detrimental to functioning and interfering with the management of any other disorder present. In some cases secondary anxiety will require treatment and attention. For example, a young woman undergoing treatment on a sub-fertility programme became very anxious about her general health and the possible success of the intervention. This anxiety resulted in muscle tension and physical responses that interfered with the sub-fertility treatment. It was necessary to help her reduce tension and develop strategies to cope with her fearful thinking.

THEORIES OF ANXIETY

Outlined here are some of the major approaches that attempt to account for the origin and maintenance of anxiety. The approaches outlined constitute those responsible for the commonest approaches to treatment currently utilised in the disorder of anxiety.

Biological theory of anxiety acquisition

Although most theorists acknowledge the role of neurobiology in both anxiety and emotion, some consider it to be a primary factor in the origin and maintenance of such states. Eysenck proposed a biological theory of personality that is based on different levels or intensities of cortical arousal (1967). Positive or pleasant emotions are associated with moderate levels of arousal, whereas negative or unpleasant emotions are associated with arousal that is either too high or too low. This, according to Eysenck, motivates individuals to seek moderate levels of arousal and to avoid extremes. Level of cortical arousal at resting state, that is, when one is not emotionally or physically aroused, is biologically determined and, therefore, varies across individuals. Extravert personalities, postulated to have a low level of arousal at resting state, are thought to seek out higher levels of arousal. Introvert personalities will find their optimum levels of arousal at a much lower level of stimulation, according to Eysenck's theory.

It is postulated that neurotic individuals possess the characteristic of intense nervous system activity and very slow rates of habituation (that is, poor or slow learning ability). Without the ability to habituate it will take an individual a long time to become accustomed to something and intense nervous system activity means that the individual's response level is strong. Thus, anxiety is seen as resulting largely from the interaction of individual cortical arousal level and nervous system reactivity. Anxious individuals are thought to have both high resting levels of cortical arousal and high autonomic nervous system activity.

The "fight or flight syndrome", as it has become known, is an attempt to explain anxiety in terms of nervous system reactivity. As in most biological explanations there is a strong evolutionary factor: It is stated that human beings developed a physiological reaction to external danger signals that was designed to enable the individual to fight with great strength or flee with speed. This kind of reaction was appropriate when human beings were hunters in a world populated with numerous larger, free-roaming creatures. The human system attempted to maximise survival by developing a physiological reaction that optimised successful combat with these larger and stronger creatures. Essentially, in response to a danger signal the body emits adrenaline. This activates four main physical responses: Heartbeat is increased to pump blood more effectively to muscles; breathing quickens in order to take more oxygen into the blood; energy is redistributed within the body, away from the head and trunk and out to the limbs; and, finally, in the face of increased bodily activity, it is necessary for the cooling system to be activated and so sweating occurs. The four physical reactions described are frequently reported by patients suffering anxiety: Increased heartbeat or breathing, fluttering in the stomach, or dizziness and excessive sweating (see case example in the Introduction to this chapter).

The danger signals in today's society do not normally require this intense physiological reaction for us to cope effectively. However, when our system detects a signal of danger it instinctively reacts with the "fight or flight syndrome". This nervous system activity produces physical sensations that alarm the individual further. This added fear of symptoms increases the level of danger perceived by the physical system. This is hypothesised to be the biological basis of what is termed a panic attack—a vicious circle of fear producing symptoms that increase fearfulness and escalate or maintain the physical distress. The biological theorists postulate that this physical distress becomes associated with particular phenomena and so explain the acquisition of irrational fear. Drug treatment may be used to reduce the system's reactivity, and relaxation therapy may be used to enable the individual to learn to control the physical response. Although behavioural associations are acknowledged in the biological account of the acquisition of fear, and negative-thinking patterns recognised, the biological theorists see the primary factor to be the nervous system and its reactivity.

Behavioural theory of anxiety acquisition

Behavioural theories of the acquisition and maintenance of anxiety are based on theoretical explanations of how we learn. To understand the concepts employed by behaviourists to describe the origin of anxiety, it is necessary to consider the two main learning theories, known as Classical Conditioning and Operant or Instrumental Conditioning (see Chapter 1).

Classical conditioning

This theory originated with the work of Ivan Pavlov early in the 20th century, who was studying salivation in dogs. In the course of these experiments Pavlov observed that not only did the dogs salivate in response to the presence of food but also in response to whatever they strongly associated with food. So, for example, a bell would ring just before the dog was presented with food; eventually the animal learned to associate the sound of the bell with food and so would salivate in response to hearing it (before seeing or smelling the food itself). The dog was, therefore, *conditioned* to expect food whenever it heard the bell. In this example the food is what is known as the *unconditioned stimulus*, while the bell with which it was paired is the *conditioned stimulus*. Salivation in response to food is the *unconditioned response* and in response to the bell it is known as the *conditioned response* (see Chapter 1 for further details).

To understand how classical conditioning theory attempts to explain how one learns to be anxious, let us take the example of a road traffic accident and the responses that might occur in this situation. Let us imagine that a bus has collided with a car and one of the bus occupants panics and is made very worried or anxious by the event. This bus occupant may strongly associate buses with this feeling of panic or anxiety. Thereafter, upon seeing a bus, or entering a bus, this person becomes frightened or worried. In this example the road traffic accident is the unconditioned stimulus (UCS) and the bus occupant's panic is the unconditioned response (UCR). The bus itself, having been strongly associated with the anxiety experienced by the occupant, becomes the conditioned stimulus (CS), which can now produce the conditioned response (CR) or anxiety.

The strength of the fear acquired (the CR) relies on the number of associations between the CS and UCS and also on the intensity of the experience of fear. Certain conditions have been found to increase the likelihood of anxiety or fear developing: Confinement is one (Eysenck & Rachman, 1965) and would be a factor offered to explain the single-event learning that occurred in the collision example mentioned previously. The bus occupant was confined within the bus at the time of the collision and could not avoid the danger. Repeated presentation of the CS may also lead to increases in responsiveness. Through repeated presentation the person becomes sensitised to the stimulus and so we have the process of sensitisation.

Extinction of a conditioned response is said to occur when the CS is repeatedly presented without the UCS: For example, when travelling on the bus does not lead inevitably to a collision. The CR will occur at first, but with repeated presentation of the CS (and the absence of the UCS) the magnitude of the CR diminishes. Thus, the association between the CS (in this example, the bus) and CR (the anxiety) is extinguished.

Habituation is another frequently used term within the learning theory paradigm. The habituation process is similar to that of extinction in that it refers to a breakdown in association, but in this case between the UCS and the UCR. Repeated experience of the UCS causes the strength of the UCR to reduce and eventually be extinguished. To remain with the bus collision example: The bus occupant gets so used to collisions that she/he no longer responds to them with panic or fear. The process of habituation has been used to explain behaviour observed during wartime: People became so used to air-raid sirens that they no longer feared them and sometimes did not heed them at all.

Operant or instrumental conditioning

The second process that attempts to explain how anxious responses arise is termed *operant or instrumental conditioning* (see Chapter 1). In this process the individual involved is considered to be *instrumental* in determining what happens. The individual (for example, the unfortunate bus occupant) learns that avoiding the CS (the bus) reduces the CR (anxiety): Avoidance behaviour, therefore, results in feeling secure and so this behaviour is reinforced. The reinforcement is the avoidance behaviour and the reinforced response is a feeling of security or a reduction in anxiety. Therefore, it is postulated that a two-process learning has occurred: The bus occupant has learned to associate buses with an anxious feeling and has also learned that avoiding buses results in feeling secure. Behaviour patterns, such as avoidance of the fear-provoking object, which successfully reduce fear, are likely to be repeated and increase in strength. This two-factor learning theory was proposed by Mowrer (1939) to explain the origin and maintenance of anxiety.

Evidence for the conditioning theory of fear acquisition was drawn from a number of sources, including studies of the development of anxiety states in combat soldiers and from clinical observations (for example, dental phobias). But the strongest and most systematic evidence was drawn from a multitude of experiments on laboratory animals. However, whether laboratory experiments on animals can be generalised to non-laboratory situations with humans is debatable: The demonstration that fear can be induced in animals by a conditioning paradigm, in a contrived environment, does not necessarily indicate that this is how animals or humans ordinarily acquire fears.

The evidence that combat soldiers developed fears and anxieties as a result of traumatic incidents (e.g. Flanagan, 1948) seemed consistent with conditioning theory. However, conditioning theory does not account for why only a small number of combat soldiers developed these fears: Many that had the same experiences did not acquire lasting fears. Furthermore, fears that develop gradually (for example, social fears) cannot be traced to specific occurrences and so often are not fully accounted for by conditioning theory.

The failure of people to acquire fears in theoretically fear-provoking situations (such as air raids) is one of the major criticisms of the conditioning theory of the development of anxiety. It has been found that it is difficult to produce conditional fear reactions in human participants, even under controlled laboratory conditions. The notion of habituation and the addition of sensitisation are offered by learning theorists as a resolution to these criticisms (Watts, 1979). In theory, any object should be able to become a CS, but Seligman (1971) showed that this was not the case. The notion of preparedness was postulated to explain why some stimuli were more likely to become conditioned (Seligman, 1971). Seligman explained the non-random distribution of the fear of spiders and snakes, for instance, with the notion that these insects/reptiles are *prepared stimuli*. He suggests that human beings are predisposed to develop strong, persisting fears of them. This preparedness, it is proposed, combined with the right conditioning process, will result in the development of anxiety. However, clinical data tell us that a significant amount of phobic people recount histories that cannot be accommodated by conditioning theory. It is argued that some fears may be induced by information-giving, from society and parents.

Behavioural theorists propose that another way that one can learn to be anxious is by observing significant others in our life and basing our behaviour on theirs. This form of learning is termed *modelling*: One models the behaviour and reactions of another. This vicarious learning process is offered by conditioning theorists as a resolution to criticisms of the theory with regard to why some people do not develop fears when they might be expected to. It is suggested that fears can be reduced by vicarious processes, such as modelling, in the same way that they can be learned (Rachman, 1968). For example, in therapy the technique of the therapist walking unafraid into the feared situation is often used to model the safety of such an activity to the patient. In group work, patients watch other sufferers overcome fears and model their behaviour on this success.

Conditioning theory cannot easily account for disorders where it is not possible to clearly identify the conditioned stimuli, for example in generalised anxiety. It is proposed that secondary gain may be a factor here: Reinforcement may be given for displaying fear. For example, the partner of a person with generalised anxiety may, through concern for this loved one, pay a lot more positive attention to them. This increase in attentiveness may unwittingly reinforce the anxious behaviour.

Conditioning theory as an explanation for the development of fears has resulted in a number of treatment procedures subsumed under the title of *behaviour therapy*. Behaviour therapy's main objective is to break the association between the CS and the CR; thus, the frightened bus occupant is repeatedly exposed to or presented with buses, but hopefully without the recurrence of a collision (that is, the UCS). The hoped-for result is that the bus occupant will learn that buses are not inevitably associated with collisions and the fear and anxiety (the CR) will reduce and disappear. This is the process of extinction mentioned earlier. It is an attempt to desensitise the individual to the CS. Systematic desensitisation often includes instructions to the individual on how to relax. This process has been termed *reciprocal inhibition* (Wolpe, 1958) and is a term borrowed from physiology. The reciprocal inhibition process is where one physical or emotional state (for example, relaxation) will inhibit another (anxiety). Thus, in systematic desensitisation the repeated events of evoking small amounts of fear and immediately suppressing them with relaxation will result in fear reduction (that is, therapeutic benefit). It assumed an incompatible relationship between relaxation and fear. However, it has been noted in some studies that there can be failure to extinguish a response (Rachman, 1990) and in spite of exposure to the stimulus the fear did not reduce. Conditioning theorists attempt to explain this with the notion of sensitisation.

A further criticism that arises from clinical studies is the lack of synchrony between emotional and behavioural responses: In fact, one study demonstrated remarkable desynchrony. On the clinical application of desensitisation to reduce fear it was found that a person whose behaviour had markedly improved, did not report feeling any better (Rachman, 1990). It is postulated that cognitive factors may operate also to maintain fears, and the notion of secondary gain is offered as one reason to explain such findings.

It would seem that phobic symptoms respond best to exposure treatments and that the addition of cognitive techniques appears to add little to efficacy (Roth & Fonagy, 1996). There is reported to be some limited evidence that therapist-directed exposure is more effective than self-directed, which suggested that a combination of habituation and modelling is operating to be of therapeutic benefit here.

It is proposed by behaviourists that the individual learns to be anxious via a number of possible processes, such as the strong association of reactions or feelings with an event or place, or reinforcement of particular behaviours, or by observation of the reactions of significant others in one's life.

Cognitive theory of anxiety acquisition

Cognitive theorists postulate that the primary factor in the origin and main-tenance of anxiety is the thinking process: Cognitions, that is one's thoughts, determine one's reactions (Beck, 1985a,b,c). According to cognitive theory, it is the way an individual appraises a situation and thinks about it that determines the emotional and physical response to that situation; it is acknowledged that two individuals can undergo exactly the same process of events and yet, because they view the situation differently, each will have experienced a very different impact.

According to cognitive theorists, one is anxious because of perceived threat. It seems clear, at a simple level, that if we perceive a particular phenomenon in a very negative way, we are more likely to be adversely affected by it; we are more likely to worry and more likely to feel apprehension.

A number of cognitive processes have been described attempting to explain the development and maintenance of an anxiety state. Some of these processes incorporate physiological factors and behavioural factors; these factors are con-sidered in terms of their effect on thinking, but it is the cognitions themselves that are considered to have the primary impact on emotional reactions.

It is postulated that if the individual has a negative view of his/her physiolo-gical response, anxiety will increase as will negative thinking. Negative attribu-tions to the physiological response, for example interpreting faster breathing rhythms as being *unable* to breathe, will result in intense anxiety. This misinter-pretation model is based on Clark, Salkovskis, and Chalkey's (1985) cognitive model of panic states. The objective of therapy, based on this model, is to reproduce the feared physical sensations in the consulting room so that a non-catastrophic interpretation of the symptoms may be encouraged. For example, the patient is instructed in hyperventilation and is encouraged to observe the effects of overbreathing. These effects are then compared to the experience of a panic attack, and the patient is guided to the conclusion that hyperventilation contributes to the symptoms experienced. The patient is then instructed in a breathing technique to control hyperventilation. The objective is that the patient learns that these sensations are not due to an impending medical crisis and, in addition to learning a strategy to control the symptom, changes the negative attributions previously held.

Beck's (1985a,b,c) model of the cognitive processing proposed to be in-volved in the production of the anxiety syndrome may be broken down into three steps: primary appraisal, secondary appraisal, and reappraisal. These terms were first used by R.S. Lazarus (1966) and are employed by Beck to describe his cognitive theory of the anxiety state. The primary appraisal is the first impression on which the individual assesses the potential threat. This may be reinforced or modified by a pre-existing cognitive set. The cognitive set, basically, is how one is predisposed to think; for example, if one is thinking negatively about one's environment, then one is likely to have a predisposition to make negative assessments. Beck argues that it is during the primary appraisal that one assesses whether the threat directly affects one's vital interests. The result is that if vital interests are affected, then the individual has what Beck calls a critical response. This critical response may be produced by a range of situations, from a potential future disaster to an immediate threat to life.

While the primary appraisal is taking place the individual is making a secondary appraisal and is assessing possible resources for dealing with the potential threat. Secondary appraisal is where the individual evaluates internal resources for protecting or deflecting the possible damage that might result from the threat. The example Beck uses to illustrate primary and secondary appraisal is that of a youngster confronted with a bully in the playground: The youngster not only assesses the size and harmfulness of the bully but also assesses the resources at hand for protection or flight. Beck postulated that the level of anxiety experienced is dependent on these two appraisals: In the case of a phobic state, for example, primary and secondary appraisal of going out alone may result in negative assessments with regard to potential harm and the individual's own ability to cope. However, it is often observed in the clinical setting that an agoraphobic will go out with a trusted significant other. The secondary appraisal in this case results in a positive assessment of resources to cope because of the presence of a caretaker.

Beck states that the cognitive appraisal of the individual is not applied in any conscious way; rather, the appraisals and reappraisals occur automatically. The third stage, reappraisal, is where the individual estimates the severity of danger and as a result may have what is termed a hostile response: Whether the individual reacts with flight (due to anxiety) or fight (due to anger) depends on the level of self-confidence. A hostile response may also occur if the individual perceives that she/he is trapped, in which case the fight reaction results from anxiety rather than anger.

Self-confidence is considered to be a key factor in the appraisal of threat and may be affected by external factors, such as the assistance of a caretaker: Agoraphobics' confidence in their ability to cope is increased if someone they trust accompanies them into the feared situation. Positive thinking is considered to increase one's sense of self-efficacy, or self-confidence, and negative thinking can reduce one's belief in one's ability to cope. Our thinking is, therefore, postulated to affect how we react in threatening situations. Our reactions, in turn, can affect our performance in the situation and this performance will feed back to either confirm or reduce self-efficacy.

This feedback loop, or vicious circle, may be illustrated by considering an individual in the act of public speaking. The individual may be concerned to make a good impression and so good performance is of the utmost importance: The cognitive set may now predispose the individual to be critical of his or her own performance. If the person estimates that there is a good chance of getting it wrong, and is feeling inadequate with regard to coping with this possibility, then anxiety will occur. If, during the speech, this person makes a slip, this flaw in performance increases anxiety, which in turn increases the potential to make further mistakes. Eventually there may even be an audience reaction to these mistakes; this also feeds into the vicious circle to increase anxiety.

Anxiety is maintained within the vicious circle until an appraisal of the situation takes place that restructures the perception of the threat. If the public speaker decides that his or her flaws in performance are not important and may not even be noticed, then his or her cognitive focus has shifted from negative to positive and anxiety is likely to reduce. A reduction in anxiety can result in more positive appraisal and less likelihood of flaws in performance. Cognitive therapy in the case of anxiety focuses on negative thinking (especially negative appraisals) and attempts to shift this to a more positive appraisal: This is known as *cognitive restructuring*. Cognitive restructuring is a therapeutic approach that may also be used with depressed patients, though it would not generally apply to specific contexts as in the case of an anxious patient.

People generally accept that, although it may be difficult, it is possible to change behaviour. Most people, at some point in their lives, attempt to give up a bad habit of one kind or another. When it comes to how we think, however, there is often a belief that thinking is involuntary and, therefore, cannot be changed. "That's how I think. I can't help it!" is often heard both inside and outside the therapist's consulting room. In fact, it is argued that we learn to think in much the same way as we learn to behave. Our perceptions and cognitions are shaped by experience. As may be seen from the vicious circle described previously, it is possible for our thinking to shape our experiences and so changing how we think can be important. It may be said that, although we cannot change the world, we can perhaps affect how it impacts on us by changing how we think about it. For example, if we were to think always of the possibility of threat without taking into account the probability of it, we would be likely to be continuously anxious (as almost anything is possible). Most irrational thinking focuses on possibilities and uses this to justify the cognitive activity and the consequent behavioural activity. For example, if one feared that the roof would fall in and considered the possibility alone, then that fear would not be easily argued away (ceilings do fall in—it is possible). However, most individuals consider the probability of the roof caving in and quite rightly assess the danger as minimal given the very low probability of occurrence. Appraisals of potential threat, therefore, need to take into account probability as well as possibility.

Physiological factors are also taken into account in the cognitive theory of anxiety states. Beck recognises anxiety as complex responses with evolutionary, biological, emotional and cognitive components. It is acknowledged that the most basic emotions are innate, survival-oriented responses to an environment that has changed greatly over the course of evolution.

The locus of the problem in anxiety disorders is where reality is continually interpreted as dangerous. Information about oneself, the world and the future is continually processed in a distorted way as dangerous. Consequently, states of anxiety are associated with automatic thoughts and images relevant to danger. These thought processes trigger physiological and emotional components of the anxiety response. It is under conditions where emotions are inappropriate or exaggerated that Beck emphasises the importance of cognitive factors. Therapy is directed at altering these automatic thoughts and the underlying misperceptions responsible for distorted processing of information.

Some cognitive theorists (for example, Spielberger, 1985) view anxiety as a trait: The individual has a disposition to experience anxiety frequently or to be anxiety prone. This view of the anxiety syndrome is primarily concerned with cognitions but relates the nature of thinking to innate and learned processes that may predispose the individual to be more fearful. A vulnerability factor, that is the predisposition to attribute negative outcomes to anticipated events and to own physical response, is recognised as the core of the anxiety syndrome. When one feels threatened, one feels more vulnerable and this affects the appraisals that are then processed.

Cognitive theory has the explanatory power to account for irrational anxiety, because the cause of anxiety is seen to reside in faulty processing of information rather than a clear, rational perception of threat. It is not unusual for individuals to report that their fears are irrational, yet this knowledge, or insight, does not stop continuous thoughts of threat and impending doom. The problem, as Beck sees it, is that there is a tendency to overestimate danger and underestimate the ability to cope. Individuals in therapy often come to realise that it is their thinking that frightens them, not the so-called feared stimulus. For example, when a patient is instructed to examine the elements of danger to them in open spaces, or in a supermarket, they are often unable to identify them: Yet his/her thinking has assumed a danger element.

A recent cognitive paradigm for anxiety is proposed by Riskind (1997) who postulates the *looming vulnerability* model. Looming vulnerability is conceptualised as a cognitive component of the danger that elicits anxiety, sensitises the individuals to threat, biases cognitive processing, and makes the anxiety more persistent. It relates to movement of the threatening stimuli and suggests that this increases anticipatory anxiety in a significant way. Riskind states that this model helps to subsume psychological, ethological, and physiological literatures in the explanation of anxiety (1997). A recent report on the evidence of the efficacy of cognitive therapy in anxiety states concluded that, when delivered by experienced therapists, this approach benefits panic symptoms in particular (Roth & Fonagy, 1996).

Psychodynamic theory of anxiety acquisition

Psychodynamic theory is concerned in part with the unconscious. Events that have occurred early in life, and which have had an impact on the individual's emotions, are stored in the unconscious and are postulated to affect the adult's functioning (see Chapter 1). The disorder of anxiety occurs when one has thoughts or feelings that one cannot cope with, when external demands or internal impulses represent a major threat. Psychodynamic theorists postulate that anxious feelings arise from internal conflicts or impulses of which the individual is not consciously aware. In other words, the origin of the anxiety is in the unconscious, and the feeling is triggered in the present by a variety of associations. Freud stated that missing someone who is loved and longed for is the key to an understanding of anxiety. For example, early loss or separation, though not consciously remembered or thought of, may produce anxiety in the adult individual.

In psychodynamic theory, anxiety is related to the persistence of remembered danger situations that seemed real at an earlier stage of development. For example, the developmentally immature fears of separation may be activated by the emergence of a symbolically linked situation currently present in one's environment. A young adult who lost his mother in childhood may have difficulty forming deep relationships with girlfriends. The psychodynamic theorist would hypothesise that this man was afraid to get close to another woman because he was afraid of the loss that might result.

In Freud's later reconceptualisation of anxiety in "Inhibitions, symptoms and anxiety" (1926), one of the proposed functions of anxiety is to warn of a potential danger situation, which thereby triggers the recruitment of internal psychological and/or external protective mechanisms. The employment of effective psychological defence mechanisms is considered adaptive because it serves the purpose of protecting the individual and allowing a higher and more mature level of functioning. Anxiety may also be adaptive in recruiting help from others when there is real danger.

Sometimes defensive reactions are inadequate and lead to the formation of symptoms. The solution to the problem becomes the problem. These may include phobic or compulsive symptoms that are symbolically related to the unconscious wishes or fears that have generated the anxiety. So, for example, Freud might view anxiety about being alone in a raging storm as the possibility of unconscious separation fears. One is alone in the storm, cut off from others, rendered helpless. This may be eliciting a childhood anxiety about separation from a loved one when all those emotions would have been intensely felt.

Freud saw anxiety as the psychic reaction to danger. A situation can be defined as dangerous if it threatens a person with helplessness in the face of hazard. Anxiety is self-defeating or pathological when it is noticeable, intense, disruptive, and paralysing, or when it triggers self-defeating defensive processes (also called symptoms).

All evidence for the psychodynamic theory of the acquisition of anxiety arises from clinical material, that is, therapeutic contact with anxious individuals. Supporting evidence for the explanatory power of the theory is taken from reports of outcome of psychodynamic therapies that use the theory to drive the intervention employed.

Malan (1979) proposed a two-triangle model of psychotherapy in dealing with, for example, anxious individuals: the Triangle of Conflict and the Triangle of Person. These are represented standing on an apex (see Fig. 3.1). The Triangle of Conflict has at its three points defence, anxiety, and hidden feeling. The Triangle of Person has other (O), transference (T), and parent (P) at its three points. "Other" represents current or recent significant individuals, and transference is a psychoanalytic term that refers to the feelings expressed towards the therapist within the therapy. It is hypothesised in psychodynamic therapy that feelings acted out with the therapist represent a transference of feelings from other important relationships in the client's life, particularly from the past (see Chapter 1). The aim of psychotherapy is to reach beneath the defence and anxiety to the hidden feeling and then to trace this feeling back from the present (O or T) to its origins in the past, usually in relation to the parents (P). The therapist does this by making interpretations, that is, suggesting what feelings might be hidden behind what the client is actually presenting with. The therapist enables the client to relearn how to tolerate and understand these hidden feelings within the psychotherapeutic relationship. Such relearning can lead to a reduction in the anxiety and the use of more adaptive mature defences; hence a reduction in symptoms. Therapy, therefore, provides a new positive experience of how anxiety can be dealt with via this process of working through.

The psychodynamic theory of anxiety acquisition offers a way of examining and understanding unusual fears and, perhaps just as importantly, provides a framework for understanding the therapist–client relationship. As with all other

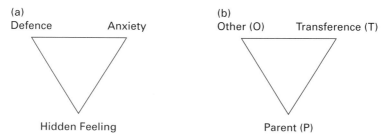

FIG. 3.1   Malan's two-triangle model of therapy (1979), (a) the Triangle of Conflict, and (b) the Triangle of Person.

theories in their purist form, the psychodynamic theory does not appear to fully account for all the manifestations of anxieties and fears presented in our society. There is a dearth of studies on the efficacy of psychodynamic interventions with anxiety states (Roth & Fonagy, 1996), so it is not possible to be conclusive about its benefit in the therapeutic sense.

AN INTEGRATED MODEL OF ANXIETY ACQUISITION?

John Bowlby's (1973) proposed model for the explanation of the development of anxiety states includes the notion that there is no single key. Instead he suggests that fear and anxiety are aroused in situations of many kinds. Basically, Bowlby's theory is an evolutionary one: Fears are normal and phylogenetically determined. Ontogeny (the development of the individual) recapitulates phylogeny (the development of the human race): In other words, our development as individuals reflects the process of development the human race has been through.

Bowlby proposes that individuals have an innate propensity to make emotional bonds: Once attachment is made it determines our emotional state. If the attachment is a secure one and we do not lose it at a vulnerable stage, then we are more likely to be healthy emotionally. Anxiety is seen to be related to fears of separation and insecure attachment. Bowlby considers levels of, and susceptibility to, anxiety to be dependent on the quality of the infant–caregiver relationship in early childhood. This incorporates elements of the psychodynamic theory and also refers to a learning process with some regard to innate disposition.

More recently, Bowlby (1988) states that change can go on throughout the life cycle. Therefore, there is potential to revise failures in the early relationship or to create anxiety in those who have had adequate early care. Because fear is seen to arise in a "compound" situation, for example, being alone *and* in the dark *and* hearing strange noises, then an integrative or interactive model to explain its development might be more appropriate.

Eysenck (1976) advocated the interactive role of learning and conditioning in the formation and expression of biologically based or innate emotions such as anxiety. There is recognition of the interaction between biological and cognitive systems, as well as the role of learning in the full expression of personality. It also seems reasonable to accept the psychodynamic theorists' view that early experience affects emotional development and the expression of these emotions.

An integrative approach in the therapeutic situation may also be more acceptable with some anxious patients. When patients present in the consulting room in a state of distress because they are frightened of the physical symptoms that they are experiencing, it can be reassuring for them to have a way of understanding their body's reactions. This reassurance is often provided by explaining the "fight or flight syndrome". Because many of the same physiological reactions occur when running for a bus (increased heartbeat, increased breathing, maybe even sweating), it is often useful to use this analogy to reduce their fear of the symptoms. This constitutes a two-pronged attack on the patients' dysfunctional state; it attends to the physical symptoms, making the patient feel "listened to", and at the same time, it is an attempt to restructure their thinking. By shifting the negative explanation of the symptoms, the therapist attempts to deal with patients' cognitions as well as their bodily reactions.

When patients are in acute distress, it is not always appropriate to take a purist approach and attend only to their thinking processes. Nor would it prove helpful to stop with the description of the "fight or flight syndrome". Using the theory of reciprocal inhibition and teaching patients relaxation techniques gives them a strategy to begin to combat their uncomfortable sensations.

In the previous case, three different theories of anxiety acquisition drive the therapist's intervention: biological, cognitive, and behavioural. This is a common approach in short-term work with patients suffering panic attacks or acute anxiety. Other groups of patients may have different needs, however. For example, a patient with generalised anxiety may need to explore the underlying reasons for this state: Cognitive and psychodynamic approaches provide a way of understanding and intervening with such a case. Exploring past and current relationships in the patient's life, and assessing his or her thinking processes, provides much information on what might be operating to create the anxiety.

Each approach to anxiety acquisition has unique tools to offer the therapist. For example, biological accounts of the anxious state offer patients a way of understanding what is happening to their own bodies. Behavioural techniques offer a way to begin making change and attempting to reduce the level of interference that may be caused by the anxiety. Cognitive assessment and intervention, on the other hand, provide a way of understanding and dealing with anxieties that are irrational and seem to have no single-event source. When working closely and repeatedly with someone, it is important to have a way of understanding the therapeutic relationship: This is offered by the psychodynamic approach. Although many approaches offer strategies for dealing with anxiety problems, the psychoanalytic therapy offers a way of exploring their source and increasing self-knowledge.

Given the range of possible presentations of anxiety, and bearing in mind Bowlby's notion that fear occurs in many forms, it would seem that the more tools available to aid understanding and intervention the better. There are many classifications of anxiety disorders (ICD-10; WHO, 1992) and they may have different optimal treatments (Hale, 1997). The purist approach in research activity may be important in order to identify which tools are most effective with certain emotional states. However, as mentioned earlier, while anxiety presentation itself is variable, it must be borne in mind that the complexity of the human being in the consulting room is infinite. For this reason an integrative approach to treatment is often necessary.

RECOMMENDED READING

Barlow, D.H. (1988). *Anxiety and its disorders: The nature and treatment of anxiety and panic.* New York: Guilford Press.

Beck, A.T., & Emery, G., with Greenberg, R.L. (1985). *Anxiety disorders and phobias: A cognitive perspective.* New York: Basic Books.

Rachman, S.J. (1990). *Fear and courage* (2nd ed.). New York: W.H. Freeman & Co.

Wells, A. (1997). *Cognitive therapy of anxiety disorders: A practical manual and conceptual guide.* Chichester, UK: John Wiley & Sons.

REFERENCES

Barlow, D.H. (1988). *Anxiety and its disorders: The nature and treatment of anxiety and panic.* New York: Guilford Press.

Beck, A.T. (1985a). The cognitive model of threat reactions. In A.T. Beck & G. Emery, with R. Greenberg (Eds.), *Anxiety disorders and phobias: A cognitive perspective* (pp. 37–53). New York: Basic Books.

Beck, A.T. (1985b). Cognitive structures and anxiogenic rules. In A.T. Beck & G. Emery, with R. Greenberg (Eds.), *Anxiety disorders and phobias: A cognitive perspective* (pp. 54–66). New York: Basic Books.

Beck, A.T. (1985c). Vulnerability: The core of anxiety disorders. In A.T. Beck & G. Emery, with R. Greenberg (Eds.), *Anxiety disorders and phobias: A cognitive perspective* (pp. 67–81). New York: Basic Books.

Bowlby, J. (1973). *Separation: Anxiety and anger, Vol. 2.* London: Hogarth.

Bowlby, J. (1988). *A secure base: Clinical applications of attachment theory.* London: Routledge.

Clark, D.M., Salkovskis, P.M., & Chalkey, A.J. (1985). Respiratory control as a treatment for panic attacks. *Journal of Behaviour Therapy and Experimental Psychiatry, 16*, 23–30.

Crowe, R.R., Noyes, R., Pauls, D.L., & Slymen, D.J. (1983). A family study of panic disorder. *Archives of General Psychiatry, 40*, 1065–1069.

Den Boer, J.A. (1997). Social phobia: Epidemiology, recognition and treatment. *British Medical Journal, 315*, 796–800.

Eysenck, H.J. (1967). *The biological basis of personality.* Springfield, IL: Thomas.

Eysenck, H.J. (1976). The learning theory model of neurosis: A new approach. *Behaviour, Research and Therapy, 14*, 251–267.

Eysenck, H.J., & Rachman, S.J. (1965). *The causes and cures of neurosis.* London: Routledge & Kegan Paul.

Flanagan, J. (1948). *The aviation psychology program in the Army Air Forces* (USAAF Aviation Psychology Research Report, No. 1). Washington, DC: US Government Printing Office.

Freud, S. (1926). Inhibitions, symptoms and anxiety. In J. Strachey (Ed.), *The Standard Edition of the Complete Works of Sigmund Freud, Vol. 20* (pp. 77–172). London: Hogarth Press/Institute of Psycho-analysis.

Hale, A.S. (1997). ABC of mental health: Anxiety. *British Medical Journal, 314*, 1886–1889.

Izard, C.E. (Ed.). (1977). *Human emotions.* New York: Plenum Press.

Lazarus, R.S. (1966). *Psychological stress and the coping process.* New York: McGraw-Hill.

Malan, D.H. (1979). *Individual psychotherapy and the science of psychodynamics.* London: Butterworths.

Mowrer, O.H. (1939). Stimulus response theory of anxiety. *Psychological Review, 46,* 553–565.

OPCS (1995). *Surveys of psychiatric morbidity in Great Britain.* In H. Meltzer, B. Gill, & K. Hinds (Tech. Report No. 3). London: HMSO.

Rachman, S.J. (1968). *Phobias: Their nature and control.* Springfield, IL: Thomas.

Rachman, S.J. (1990). *Fear and courage* (2nd ed.). New York: W.H. Freeman & Co.

Riskind, J.H. (1997). Looming vulnerability to threat: A cognitive paradigm for anxiety. *Behaviour, Research and Therapy, 35,* 685–702.

Roth, A., & Fonagy, P. (1996). *What works for whom.* New York: Guilford Press.

Seligman, M.E.P. (1971). Phobias and preparedness. *Behaviour Therapy, 2,* 307–320.

Spielberger, C.D. (1985). Anxiety, cognition and affect: A state–trait perspective. In A.H. Tuma & J.D. Maser (Eds.), *Anxiety and anxiety disorders. Part I: Basic biological and psychological research approaches to anxiety* (pp. 171–182). Hillsdale, NJ: Lawrence Erlbaum Associates Inc.

Watts, F.N. (1979). Habituation model of systematic desensitisation. *Psychological Bulletin, 86,* 627–637.

Wolpe, J. (1958). *Psychotherapy by reciprocal inhibition.* Stanford, CA: Standford University Press.

WHO (1957). *International classification of diseases: Manual of the international statistics classification of disease, injuries and causes of death* (7th ed.). Geneva: World Health Organisation.

WHO (1992). *International classification of diseases: Manual of the international statistics classification of disease, injuries and causes of death* (10th ed.). Geneva: World Health Organisation.

Yerkes, R.M., & Dodson, J.D. (1908). The relation of strength of stimulus to rapidity of habit formation. *Journal of Comparative Neurology and Psychology, 18,* 459–482.

CHAPTER FOUR

Drug and alcohol dependence

Jane Powell
Department of Psychology, Goldsmiths College, University of London, UK

INTRODUCTION

It is probably fair to say that all of us experiment with recreational drugs at some time or other in our lives. For the most part, however, these drugs are socially acceptable and do not become problematic: Drinking alcohol in social situations to relax, taking caffeine in the form of tea or coffee to increase alertness, or smoking the occasional cigarette (inhaling nicotine) to calm ourselves down, are all examples of "normal" drug use. These substances all exert psychoactive effects, that is, they alter our mental functioning via an effect on brain activity. Indeed, this is often the very reason for which we take them. They may, however, be taken in excessive amounts, and then can lead to a range of medical, social, and psychological problems.

As an example, heavy alcohol consumption is associated with damage to the liver (cirrhosis) and to the brain (alcoholic dementia, or Korsakoff's syndrome). Over a period of frequent drinking, tolerance develops: The body is geared to maintaining equilibrium in its physiological processes, and therefore gradually adapts its functioning to accommodate the disturbance created by ingestion of the drug. This means that in order to achieve the original effects, the drinker must consume progressively larger quantities. Often associated with this is physical dependence, which arises because the adaptations made by the tolerant body means that it no longer functions normally without the alcohol; thus, for instance, when an alcoholic goes without drink for longer than usual, he or she experiences unpleasant withdrawal symptoms such as shaking, sweating, and even hallucinations. Tolerance and physical dependence characterise prolonged use of some but not all addictive drugs, and are often seen as significant obstacles to becoming abstinent.

Social functioning will be progressively disrupted as the drinker/drug user spends more and more time inebriated or suffering from the after-effects of drug use. At the extreme, addicts may be unable to hold down stable employment, and may become abusive or dismissive towards family and friends, eventually resulting in isolation and alienation. Lack of work creates financial difficulties, and, particularly if illicit and expensive drugs such as heroin or cocaine are used, the addict may become involved in criminal activity or prostitution. The psychological consequences can be equally grim. With increasingly severe social and financial problems to contend with, and possibly physical ill-health as well, the addict is likely to become anxious and depressed. If, as is likely by this time, there are few people left to whom he or she can turn for emotional support, then alcohol or other drugs may be seen as a way of achieving temporary relief—and so a vicious circle is established.

There is a vast range of psychoactive drugs which can be used to excess, some illicit but many legal. The effects they produce vary, and the consequences of heavy sustained use differ, depending partly on the particular drug and partly on personal characteristics of the drug user. Some people, for example, become intoxicated with much smaller amounts of alcohol than others, and this is influenced by their sex, their body mass, their recent daily intake of alcohol, and so on. Likewise, the likelihood that someone will turn to crime to finance their drug use will be affected by factors such as opportunities for legal employment and their personal moral code. Drugs can nevertheless be classified according to the psychoactive effects which they produce through their action on the central nervous system (the CNS, which includes the brain), and one such classification system is described in the following section.

GENERAL CLASSES OF PSYCHOACTIVE DRUGS

The Royal College of Psychiatrists (1987) has listed five main categories of psychoactive drugs which are frequently misused: opiates, depressants, stimulants, hallucinogens, and minor tranquillisers. Examples of drugs falling into each category, with details of their main effects are as follows.

The opiates

These include natural extracts from the opium poppy (e.g. morphine, codeine), drugs derived from these via some chemical modification (e.g. heroin), and a range of synthetic compounds which have similar chemical structures (e.g. methadone, dihydrocodeine). Opiates are medically prescribed for pain relief, but also tend to produce pleasant mood states, and in some cases a transient euphoric "high" or "rush", which occurs shortly after drug ingestion. They are capable of inducing tolerance and physical dependence, and the withdrawal syndrome includes severe 'flu-like symptoms such as sweating, shaking, weakness, runny eyes and nose, aching, and nausea. As yet no permanent medical consequences have been directly associated with opiate use, though, as discussed later, lack of care in the way the drugs are used may lead indirectly to numerous health hazards.

General depressants

The most common members of this class are alcohol and barbiturates, and they act by reducing (depressing) brain activity and thus decreasing mental exertion. Early effects include decreased anxiety, and reduced control over behaviour, experienced as a relaxation of normal inhibitions and often manifest as excitability. Later, however, the sense of relaxation progresses into general sedation and eventually unconsciousness. Tolerance and physical dependence can develop, with unpleasant withdrawal symptoms, which include shaking and hallucinations.

Minor tranquillisers

These are the benzodiazepines, of which two of the most well-known are diazepam (a well-known brand-name is Valium) and nitrazepam (Mogadon). They have very similar effects to the general depressants, and are commonly prescribed for the relief of anxiety and insomnia. Over recent years, increasing attention has been drawn to their addictive potential, and although they were originally thought not to induce physical dependence, it is now clear that many long-term users do experience extreme physical discomfort when they attempt to cut down or stop.

Stimulants

These include, for example, cocaine, amphetamines ("speed"), and caffeine. They stimulate brain activity, leading initially to increased alertness, elevation of mood, and an enhanced sense of mental and physical energy. Heavy stimulant use can produce feelings of paranoia and occasionally frank psychosis. The existence of tolerance and physical dependence is more controversial than with the preceding classes of drug, though there is some evidence for a withdrawal syndrome characterised by general weakness and low mood (which may be severe).

Hallucinogens

Drugs falling into this category include synthetics such as LSD (lysergic acid diethylamide) and a variety of plant products such as mescalin and psilocybin ("magic mushrooms"). They accentuate sensory experience, often inducing bizarre perceptual distortions and hallucinations, and altering normal thought processes in a variety of ways. Their spectrum of effects can range from enjoyable fantasy to terrifying nightmare and dangerous delusions. Some individuals experience "flashbacks" when drug-free, weeks or even months later, though these gradually disappear. There does not appear to be any tolerance or physical dependence.

Other drugs

A comparatively small number of drugs do not fit into the above classification, and these include some of the synthetic "designer" drugs (e.g. ecstasy). Three of the most widely used exceptions are nicotine, cannabis, and volatile inhalants. Nicotine is the psychoactive substance present in tobacco, and has complex effects, acting both as a stimulant and a sedative. It often induces some degree of physical dependence, though in comparison with the opiates and alcohol the physical withdrawal symptoms are mild. Cannabis is extracted from the Indian hemp plant, and has mixed depressant and hallucinogenic properties. Although it is clear that tolerance to many of its effects develops, there is some controversy over whether it also induces physical dependence. Volatile inhalants, such as glues, industrial solvents, and lighter fuels, can produce a wide variety and mixture of effects, including sedative and hallucinogenic experiences.

MEDICAL PROBLEMS ASSOCIATED WITH DRUG USE

The most dramatic danger associated with use of many of the drugs listed previously is the risk of fatal overdose: Above a certain threshold, drug effects may be so powerful that they disable some aspects of normal body function and eventually cause death. For example, opiates can suppress the respiratory system to the point where inadequate oxygen reaches the brain. In some cases, taking the drug over a period of time can have a cumulative effect which endangers life, as in the case of smoking tobacco, which is associated with an increased incidence of lung cancer and heart disease, and heavy drinking, which may lead to liver disease.

In addition to hazards posed directly by the drugs themselves, there is also a long list of indirect problems arising as secondary consequences or from the way in which they are used. Many infectious diseases, for instance, can be passed on through unhygienic methods of drug administration, notably when the drug is injected and needles are shared between two or more users. Contaminated blood can be transferred in this way, leading to the spread of conditions such as hepatitis or HIV. Secondary consequences of drug use include increased risk of illness arising from reduced attention to self-care, or from inadequate nutrition. Another set of problems is associated with the illegality of certain drugs: In these cases the black market price of the drug may be high, increasing the likelihood that the user will finance his/her habit through risky criminal activity or prostitution.

DEVELOPMENT OF THE CONCEPT OF
DRUG DEPENDENCE

Although media coverage often leads us to think of drug addiction as a modern-day phenomenon, excessive drug use has occurred at most periods in history and in most cultures. In Victorian England, for instance, not only was alcoholism rife in the inner-city slums, but opiates were used heavily in the form of laudanum, sold commercially for the relief of minor aches and pains. Prior to the 18th century, heavy drug use was usually considered a vice, and it was only towards the end of the 19th century that medical explanations conceptualising "inebriety" as a disease began to gain a significant foothold. These early medical models focused primarily on the phenomenon of physical dependence, identifying the onset of withdrawal symptoms as the main impediment to abstinence. This meant that substances such as alcohol and opiates, which have particularly florid withdrawal syndromes, became prototypical of addictive drugs, whereas others such as nicotine, which either do not induce physical dependence or where the withdrawal symptoms are very subtle, were for a long time not considered to be addictive at all. To quote Rolleston (1926), a highly influential authority on drugs at the time, "To regard tobacco as a drug of addiction is all very well in a humorous sense, but it is hardly accurate."

Increasingly, however, it has become recognised that people can develop psychological as well as physical dependence on drugs, experiencing a strong and apparently irresistible urge or "craving" for the substance in question even when they are not in the grip of withdrawal symptoms. Indeed, in 1964 the World Health Organisation (WHO, 1964) gave greater weight to the psychological than to the physical symptoms, defining drug dependence as follows:

> A state, psychic and sometimes also physical resulting from the interaction between a living organism and a drug, characterized by behavioural and other responses that always include a compulsion to take the drug on a continuous or periodic basis in order to experience its psychic effects, and sometimes to avoid the discomfort of its absence. Tolerance may or may not be present.

There have been numerous hypotheses regarding the underlying causes of psychological dependence, with varying implications for treatment. On the one hand it has often been suggested that certain personality traits may be associated with proneness to addiction; as yet there is little convincing evidence that this is so. Other theories focus on particular drug effects that the individual experiences, and conceptualise psychological dependence as an inability to cope with the void that cessation of drug use would leave. Whereas psychoanalytic models may postulate that the drug serves crucial symbolic functions, cognitive-behavioural formulations emphasise very practical needs such as dealing with stress, or acceptance within a particular sub-culture. This theoretical framework will be discussed at greater length later.

As it has been recognised that addiction to drugs is largely a psychological phenomenon, parallels have been drawn with other types of compulsive behaviour such as gambling or over-eating, and it is now common to hear the term "addiction" applied to these behavioural abnormalities; similarly, the word "workaholism" has been coined to describe what is perceived as pathological over-working. This terminology assumes that these superficially diverse behaviours are maladaptive responses to a range of underlying needs, excessive drug use representing just one example of such a general process.

APPROACHES TO UNDERSTANDING AND TREATING ADDICTION

As is clear from the foregoing discussion, addiction is a complex and multi-faceted disorder, and interventions are correspondingly diverse. Although a proportion of addicts either quit unaided, or seek help to do so because, for one reason or another, they have come to see their dependence as undesirable in itself, there is a substantial proportion who would prefer to carry on using drugs and do not consider drug use *per se* to be a problem. This divergence of view is reflected also in the societal debate over the legalisation of currently illicit drugs and the ambivalent attitude that is seen in the essentially arbitrary distinction made between those drugs that are legal, such as alcohol and nicotine, and those that are not.

The appropriate "treatment" for addiction, therefore, depends on where the impetus for change is coming from. At the societal level, there is an emphasis on persuading—and if necessary, coercing—addicts into becoming abstinent, with heavy sanctions for those caught breaking the law; at the same time, a realistic recognition of the limitations of this approach means that there are parallel programmes designed to minimise the problems of drug use both to the individual and to the community via education about the health hazards and "least risky" practices, provision of clean syringes, and in some circumstances, prescription of pharmacologically pure opiates. If and when an individual drug user has come forward to seek help with either giving up or altering his or her pattern of drug use, then interventions will vary depending on the stage in the addictive cycle and on the treatment resources and perspectives available within the local service.

A transtheoretical model of the stages involved in attempting to overcome addiction has been proposed by Prochaska and DiClemente (1983). They describe the sequence of stages through which addicts progress in seeking to achieve abstinence as comprising: (a) precontemplation, (b) contemplation, (c) action, (d) maintenance, and, all too often, (e) relapse. Each stage represents a different motivational state and entails different problem-solving strategies and behaviour. At precontemplation, the addict has not yet identified any compelling need or desire to change, whereas at the stage of contemplation his priorities are shifting away from continued drug use towards the possibility of quitting. When contemplation progresses to action, he is actively involved in an attempt to become drug-free, and, once this is achieved, he confronts the various obstacles to maintaining the abstinent state. If he relapses, then he may revert to any one of the previous stages. The issues and problems which he, and/or involved professionals, need to work on at each stage are clearly different if successful progression is to be achieved.

This model provides a useful framework within which to consider specific treatment approaches developed within different theoretical domains. Rather than being seen as mutually contradictory or in competition with each other, each technique can be evaluated with reference to the particular stage at which it is likely to be applicable, with the overall aim of identifying a repertoire of interventions that may enable addicts to make successful and adaptive changes.

The pharmacological approach

It may at first sound counterintuitive that the problem of addiction to drugs should be treated by drugs. However, there are a number of pharmacological treatments that have already been found useful, or whose potential usefulness is currently being explored.

First, as discussed earlier, many addictive substances induce a state of physical dependence, such that if the addict misses a dose he experiences a physically uncomfortable set of withdrawal symptoms. This presents an early obstacle to quitting, and various types of drug may be prescribed in an attempt to help the addict through this early "action" stage. The drugs used vary according to the particular addictive substance, but the principles are similar for most substances. Taking opiate dependence as an example, many addicts find it impossible to stop all at once and so request help with a graduated reduction, where the dose is tapered off over a period of time. This period may be anything from a few days to several months, depending on the addict's preference and the policy of the prescribing physician. With small reductions, the intensity of the withdrawal discomfort is not so great; however, compared with a sudden cessation of drug use the symptoms will last for longer. An opiate addict can be transferred to any form of opiate for withdrawal purposes, since all opiates have similar effects. However, some types, such as methadone, have longer-lasting effects than others, such as heroin or morphine, and doctors often prefer to prescribe the former type because it does not need to be taken so frequently in order to allay withdrawal symptoms. Methadone also tends not to produce the euphoric effects that heroin does, and this is often given as another reason for transferring the addict to methadone.

The main alternative to the graduated reduction method is to stop all opiate use at once, and to prescribe non-opiate drugs for a short period to provide symptomatic relief. Clonidine, for instance, can help to alleviate some opiate withdrawal symptoms such as sweating and shaking, and thus make the withdrawal syndrome easier to endure. This method has the advantage of minimising the duration of discomfort whilst reducing its overall severity; however, the drugs used may produce side-effects, thus limiting their usefulness. A fuller discussion of these withdrawal regimes is available in Ghodse (1995).

Although help with physical withdrawal undoubtedly makes it easier for many addicts to achieve abstinence in the short term, it is far from a complete cure for addiction. Hunt, Barnett, and Branch (1971) reviewed the literature on relapse to drug use, and found that whether the substance in question was opiates, alcohol, or nicotine, about 70% of addicts used again within 6 months of successful detoxification. Similarly, Gossop, Green, Phillips, and Bradley (1987), with opiate addicts who completed detoxification in an in-patient setting, revealed that the majority used at least once within 6 months of leaving and about 50% became re-addicted within this period. A second application of pharmacological treatment therefore attempts to protect the addict *after* detoxification, that is, in the "maintenance" stage.

A comparatively recent treatment of this type, which is currently attracting a lot of attention, is the use of a drug called naltrexone. All drugs exert their effects by attaching themselves to receptors within the body—rather like putting a plug in a socket in order to run an electrical appliance. It follows, therefore, that if the receptors are already occupied then the incoming drug cannot plug itself in, and is eventually excreted from the body without having had any effect. Naltrexone is known as an opiate antagonist, because it attaches itself to the same receptors as opiates. It does not appear to produce any addictive effects in its own right, and if taken by a detoxified opiate addict will "block" the action of any opiates taken subsequently. This may therefore protect the addict against succumbing to a momentary impulse to use opiates, since he knows that he will not achieve the desired effect. For the addict who continues to take naltrexone on a regular basis, it potentially encourages him to develop a lifestyle within which drugs have no place. Each dose of naltrexone blocks the opiate receptors for a limited period of time, however, so that if the addict is really determined to use he simply has to wait until the naltrexone has passed out of his system. Interestingly recent research suggests that alcoholics may also benefit from naltrexone treatment in a similar way; this is consistent with the view that alcohol stimulates endogenous (i.e. the body's own) opioid activity and that blocking this effect therefore reduces the subjective reward gained from drinking. Alcoholics are also sometimes prescribed a drug called disulfiram (or Antabuse) which interacts with any alcohol which is consumed to cause nausea and vomiting. Clinical experience to date (e.g. Rabinowitz, Cohen, Tarrasch, & Kotler, 1997; Volpicelli, Volpicelli, & O'Brien, 1995) indicates that addicts or alcoholics who take these drugs after becoming abstinent are indeed less likely to relapse; however, a significant proportion fail to comply with the medication regime. For these individuals it may be the case either that they stop taking the medication because they have already decided to recommence drug/alcohol use, or that cessation of the protection afforded by the medication makes them more vulnerable to using for other reasons. In a review of this literature in relation to alcoholism, Moncrieff and Drummond (1997) note that many of the studies conducted so far have been methodologically problematic, limiting the conclusions that can be drawn, and stress the need for more rigorous evaluations of pharmacological evaluations in the future.

Psychological models

The social learning theory perspective

Social Learning theory (SLT; Bandura, 1977a,b) has its origins in the behavioural principles of instrumental learning (Skinner, 1938). In essence, this analyses animal and human behaviour in relation to its consequences: A behaviour that leads to a rewarding outcome tends to be repeated, whereas one that is punished tends to be avoided in future. The more frequently and/or intensely the behaviour is rewarded, the more habitual it becomes; the more frequent or intense the punishment, the greater the likelihood it will be avoided.

The application of this framework to understanding drug dependence is straightforward if we define dependence operationally as an excessive tendency to engage in drug-taking behaviour. This implies that the rewards to the addict are so salient, and sufficiently reliable, that he or she has become motivated to take the drug progressively more often in order to achieve these effects, eventually reaching a point where the desire overwhelms all else. Likewise, the decision to try to break a habit can be seen as reflecting the strength of its punishing outcomes. Since most habits produce mixed effects, some pleasant and others aversive, the addict may find him/herself in an approach-avoidance conflict, where motivation fluctuates between wanting to use and wanting to stop. Most of us can identify with such ambivalence, which accompanies many important transitions in our lifestyles.

As discussed in a previous section, different classes of drug exert quite disparate pharmacological effects, so that the rewards that have contributed to development of the addiction will vary from drug to drug. The particular effects which are most powerfully rewarding will differ between individuals according to their personal needs and desires, which in turn will depend on some combination of their past experience (learning history), basic personality traits, and current life circumstances. To illustrate this, let us consider two people (Mark and Claire) both addicted to heroin. Heroin is an opiate and, as we saw earlier, has the dual effects of producing a transient euphoric "high" and of alleviating emotional distress through its more protracted sedative action. Mark has used heroin recreationally about once a month for 2 years, and has always enjoyed the relaxation it produces. However, 6 months ago his girlfriend left him for another man, and he has become very depressed and anxious about the future. Such an intense reaction is typical of Mark: His parents divorced when he was a child, and since then he has been highly sensitive to perceived rejection. He has few other friends to help him through this difficult period, and has begun to use heroin on a daily basis because it gives him a short-term escape from his distress. If he seeks help to overcome his addiction, it will be crucial to address his particular vulnerability to depression since it is otherwise likely that when it recurs in the future it will put him at renewed risk of turning to drugs.

Claire, by contrast, considers herself to be a generally relaxed person with no current sources of worry, but enjoys the "high" she experiences after injecting heroin. Although she, too, began to use recreationally, her social circle is now composed predominantly of other drug users, and she has lost touch with non-using friends. Her intermittent use has therefore escalated to the point where she, like Mark, is taking heroin every day; she has become physically dependent, and she feels she would be lost without the excitement and social life attached to her drug use. The issues she faces in becoming drug-free are clearly very different from those faced by Mark, as discussed in more detail later.

Another basic principle of instrumental learning theory is that a specific behaviour will be more rewarding in some contexts than others, and that individuals are able to learn to distinguish favourable from unfavourable contexts. In theoretical terms, features that distinguish these contexts are known as discriminative stimuli (DSs) (see also Chapter 1). Referring back to the two addicts described earlier, Mark will have learned that heroin use is more rewarding when he is feeling low in mood than when he is happy, and depression will have become a DS that triggers the response of drug use. Claire, on the other hand, may have learned that heroin is particularly exciting when used in company but not so thrilling when she is on her own: In this case, drug-using acquaintances will have become DSs for her use.

Social learning theory (SLT) is an elaboration of instrumental learning theory, which emphasises the important contribution of cognitive processes to goal-directed behaviour in humans. Whereas learning theory has its origins in the analysis of animal behaviour, SLT enables these same principles to be applied to the understanding of human activity by taking into account our much more complex perceptual and reasoning skills. For instance, we do not need to experience the outcomes of every action directly in order to modify our behaviour, but can learn through observing other people or listening to what they say. Similarly, the significance of a particular occurrence will be perceived differently from one individual to another, depending on personality, learning history, alertness, etc.; the panoply of cognitive processes involved in perception will thus influence the impact that an event has on overt behaviour.

The application of SLT to the understanding and treatment of addictive behaviours has been formalised by Marlatt and Gordon (1985) in a model they have labelled "Relapse Prevention" (RP). The RP model concentrates particularly on the factors that will influence the success or failure of an addict who attempts to become abstinent, but there is a great deal of overlap with processes that may be involved in the initial development of an addiction. The model is too complex to discuss completely here, and the interested reader is referred to the references by Marlatt and his colleagues, given at the end of this chapter (e.g. Cummings, Marlatt, & Gordon, 1980; Marlatt & Gordon, 1985; Marlatt, 1996). However, the main principles are as follows.

For any addict, there will be a range of DSs for drug use. If, after becoming drug-free, he encounters one of these stimuli, then he will be at high risk of a lapse to drug use. The presence of one or more DSs thus constitutes a high-risk situation. So, if Mark is feeling depressed or Claire meets one of her drug-using contacts, the likelihood that they will take drugs is increased. Marlatt argues that a cognitive process is involved here, the DSs arousing *positive outcome expect-ancies* and thus triggering a motivation to use drugs. However, the ability of an addict to survive this threat to his abstinence will be influenced by various other factors including the strength of his motivation not to use, his knowledge of alternative strategies for coping with the situation, and his *self-efficacy*, that is, his belief in his personal control or ability to master the situation. A shortfall in any one of these factors will increase vulnerability to relapse, as illustrated in Fig. 4.1 below.

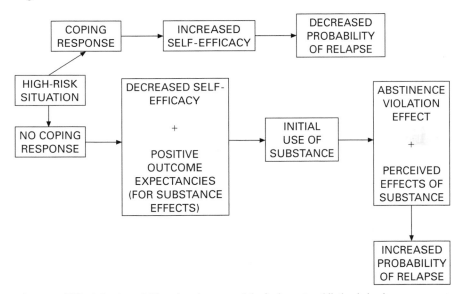

FIG. 4.1   A social learning theory model of relapse to addictive behaviour.

For example, Mark may know in principle that an alternative strategy for combating low mood is to listen to a favourite piece of music. If, however, he has temporarily lost sight of his reasons for wanting to stay drug-free (a common problem in treatment), he may be insufficiently motivated to try this strategy and may therefore go straight for the easier option of drug use. Likewise, if his self-efficacy is very low and he feels that he does not have the strength within himself to apply the effort that is needed to let the music work, then he is likely to dismiss it as a possibility. It is essential, then, that intervention focuses not only on equipping the addict with adequate strategies but also on the personal resources that allow him to use them effectively. Conversely, a high degree of self-efficacy combined with strong motivation to remain abstinent may be insufficient if the addict does not have the knowledge or skill to resolve the situation in some other way. Thus, for instance, Claire may be determined not to use again, and may feel confident in her ability to resist, but may nevertheless lapse when she meets a friend who urges her to use with him because she has not thought through or practised how to resist this kind of social pressure. The fewer alternatives that an individual has accessible for dealing with a situation, the more salient his positive outcome expectancies for drug use will become.

The outcome of the high-risk situation, and the way in which the individual interprets it, has important consequences for his future progress. If he has successfully resisted drug use, and attributes this to his personal ability, then his level of general self-efficacy will be raised and he will feel more confident in his ability to handle future threats successfully. This increased self-efficacy will, as discussed already, make it more likely that he will attempt alternative coping strategies in other high-risk situations, and thus improve his chances of long-term abstinence. Assume, for instance, that Mark sees his ex-partner with another man. Instead of resorting to heroin use to block out his distress, he goes away for a long weekend to visit his sister, and to his surprise has an enjoyable time and is able to put the incident to the back of his mind. He returns feeling good about himself and optimistic that he will be able to help himself through future stresses in an equally constructive way. Although such a process may happen spontaneously, the fact that Mark has a deeply ingrained tendency to construe things negatively means that he will probably need substantial help and support in learning to approach his life in such a positive manner. This would consequently be a central focus of his treatment. By contrast, if he did in fact lapse, either because he was inadequately prepared with coping strategies or because he lacked the self-efficacy to try them out, then he may be at risk of a full-blown relapse to addictive use. Again, however, cognitive factors are important.

Marlatt has identified one particularly destructive cognitive process, the Abstinence Violation Effect (AVE). Here, the individual sees that his drug use is incompatible with his previous determination to remain abstinent, creating a state of "cognitive dissonance"; he then resolves this dissonance by assuming that some intrinsic personal quality makes abstinence impossible for him ("personal attribution"). He may tell himself, for instance, "Addiction is a disease I have, which I can't shake off—so there's no point in trying any more." Such an interpretation will clearly undermine his resistance to future temptations. A more constructive way of assessing a lapse would be to identify circumstantial factors that made it difficult to resist, permitting contingency plans for the future to be developed. Viewed in this way, lapses can be used as learning experiences.

A substantial amount of evidence has accrued in support of the general principles of the RP model. By way of example, Cummings, Gordon, and Marlatt (1980) found that alcoholics, smokers, opiate addicts, gamblers, and overeaters were particularly likely to lapse when they experienced negative emotional states: 35% of all lapses were identified as having been preceded by negative mood, with a further 16% following some form of interpersonal conflict, and another 20% being attributed to social pressure. These findings are consistent with the view that addictive behaviour is often engaged in because of its effectiveness in escaping stress, and suggest therefore that stress situations may be particularly risky to recent "quitters". Other authors have noted, however, that there are numerous methodological problems associated with accurate depiction of antecedents to lapses, and research in this area is currently flourishing; indeed, a whole issue of the specialist journal, *Addiction* (1996, Vol. 91), was recently devoted to this topic. Other evidence consistent with the RP model has been reported by Miller, Westerberg, Harris, and Tonigan (1996), who followed the progress of alcoholics being treated as outpatients and found that one of the strongest predictors of relapse was lack of coping skills.

What are the implications of the RP model for treatment? From the foregoing discussion, it is evident that there is no single treatment or educational package that can be applied identically with every client. Rather, the therapist must be aware of the many different factors that can influence attitudes to and expectations about use of a wide variety of drugs, and be willing to approach each individual's dependence with a mind free of assumptions about underlying factors. Within the broad theoretical framework, there are at least four elements to developing an individual treatment, as follows:

(1) Detailed assessment of the addict's personal risk factors and existing coping resources. Intervention will start with a reasonably extensive assessment, but information will continue to emerge throughout the treatment.
(2) Helping the addict to identify alternative strategies for avoiding or coping with risk situations. These strategies may comprise both cognitive techniques (e.g. talking oneself through difficult issues, or challenging inappropriate assumptions) and behavioural techniques (e.g. taking up new leisure pursuits, or learning how to relax physically).
(3) Enhancing the addict's self-efficacy and skill in using alternative strategies, for instance by assisting him to practise them and thereby identify and tackle potential difficulties.
(4) Preparation for how to deal with a lapse. This might entail discussion of the AVE, together with the development of a structured plan of what to do in such an eventuality (e.g. contact a particular person, go somewhere private for a period of reflection).

All of these four elements can take many different forms, depending on characteristics of the therapist, the patient, and the resources available. Most general cognitive-behavioural methods, as described elsewhere in this volume in connection with other disorders, are applicable to the treatment of underlying psychological disturbances or vulnerabilities, and Marlatt and Gordon's (1985) book offers suggestions for approaching more specific problems such as the AVE. One specialised technique widely incorporated within the RP approach is that of "motivational interviewing" (Miller, 1983), which focuses on enhancement of addicts' resolution and commitment to the process of change. The highly interactive nature of this type of intervention, where the therapist and patient work together to identify problem areas and evaluate different coping strategies, should generate a supportive atmosphere for the patient's efforts at change: This is clearly a vital component of the treatment process. Since the aim is for abstinence and psychological well-being in the long term, beyond the limited duration of formal therapy, it is important that the patient should also be helped to establish durable social supports outside the treatment setting, whether in the form of developing new non-drug-using relationships or of attending peer support groups such as Alcoholics/Narcotics Anonymous (see later).

The Relapse Prevention treatment approach, implemented in various formats, has been evaluated in a number of recent studies with encouraging results. For example, Allsop, Saunders, Phillips, and Carr (1997) randomly allocated 60 alcoholics who were already receiving detoxification and basic drugs education as either in- or outpatients to receive either no additional treatment, a Relapse Prevention package, or extra discussion sessions. At 6-month follow-up, RP subjects showed significantly higher abstinence rates (eight subjects compared with only one in each of the other two groups), and had spent more time drug free before any initial lapses to alcohol use. By 12 months, however, these initial treatment effects had been eroded, with fewer subjects remaining abstinent, indicating that in future trials more attention should be given to factors affecting maintenance of initial gains.

The classical conditioning model

Classical conditioning is the form of learning associated with Pavlov's work in the early part of this century. His best-known demonstrations were with dogs, showing that when the sound of a bell reliably preceded the arrival of their food, they eventually began to salivate when they heard the bell (see Chapter 1). In the normal course of events, the smell and taste of food tends to elicit this reaction automatically (as an unconditioned reflex or UCR), whereas the sound of bells does not. Pavlov therefore deduced from his experiments that animals can learn about associations between two stimuli, so that one becomes a signal that the other is about to occur and triggers an anticipatory physical reaction. These learned reactions are largely involuntary, and are termed conditioned reflexes (CRs); the stimuli that trigger them are referred to as conditioned stimuli (CSs).

The relevance of this type of learning to addiction was first formally proposed by an American physician, Abraham Wikler (1948, 1980), who observed that several opiate addicts whom he had detoxified experienced renewed physical discomfort when they returned to the areas in which they had formerly bought and used drugs. Their symptoms resembled those of withdrawal, including, for instance, watering eyes and a runny nose. Wikler's explanation is shown schematically in Fig. 4.2.

Briefly, his model is as follows. The withdrawal syndrome is a UCR which occurs when the drugs are metabolised by the body and lose their effect. Most addicts experience withdrawal symptoms repeatedly in the course of their addiction, since there are often delays in finding the drug and the symptoms begin before the addict succeeds in procuring his next dose. Since the addict will react to the onset of symptoms by looking for and using drugs, a whole range of environmental cues may potentially become associated with the experience of withdrawal, including the places where the drugs are bought and used, and stimuli such as drug using paraphernalia (e.g. needles and syringes) which are regularly present in those settings. Through classical conditioning, these cues can become CSs capable of eliciting withdrawal-like symptoms as CRs.

If this is true, then detoxification from opiates is not enough to ensure abstinence, because when the detoxified addict encounters one of these cues his body will automatically react with the conditioned withdrawal response. This may put him at risk of relapse, as his past experience indicates that the quickest way of alleviating the symptoms is to take drugs. Wikler has therefore argued that the CRs may elicit drug craving; whether or not a lapse actually ensues will be

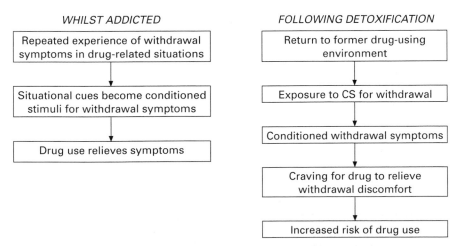

FIG. 4.2 Wikler's model of the role of classical conditioning in relapse.

influenced by other factors such as determination to stay drug-free, possession of alternative coping strategies, drug availability, and so on.

A number of studies have yielded support for this analysis. First of all, experiments with animals and with humans have demonstrated that it is possible to produce classical conditioning of withdrawal symptoms in the laboratory. O'Brien, O'Brien, Mintz, and Brady (1975) studied current (i.e. non-detoxified) opiate addicts, and manipulated the onset of their withdrawal symptoms by giving them naloxone, an opiate antagonist drug which immediately displaces opiates from their receptors, thus causing the addict to experience withdrawal symptoms. Simultaneously with administration of the naloxone, an unusual odour was presented. This was repeated several times, in order to produce an association between the odour and the onset of withdrawal. In a subsequent test trial, the odour was presented in the absence of naloxone. Over half of the subjects still reacted with withdrawal symptoms, indicating that for these subjects the odour had indeed become a CS for a conditioned withdrawal response.

It has furthermore been shown in many studies that addicts react very differently from non-addicts when they are exposed to drug-related cues. For instance, Teasdale (1973) showed opiate addicts pictures of drug stimuli and neutral stimuli, and found that their ratings of withdrawal-like symptoms were much higher during exposure to the drug-related material. Other experiments, with both opiate addicts and alcoholics, have shown that physiological responses (e.g. heart rate, temperature) are greater to drug-related than to neutral stimuli, with non-addict control subjects tending to show little or no reaction (e.g. O'Brien, Ehrman, & Ternes, 1986). It should, however, be noted that the physiological responses such as these are not unequivocal evidence of conditioned withdrawal, since similar changes occur in emotional states such as anxiety or excitement. An equally plausible alternative explanation, therefore, is that exposure to these stimuli is anxiety-provoking to addicts but not to non-addicts. Ambiguity also surrounds the interpretation of increases in subjective craving which are seen during cue exposure, since both cognitive and conditioning models predict such reactions. A detailed overview of cue-reactivity experiments can be found in Drummond, Tiffany, Glautier, & Remington (1995), in which contemporary researchers describe current issues and findings.

Several variations on Wikler's original theory have been proposed. Siegel (1983) has argued that the withdrawal-like symptoms elicited by drug-related cues are in fact conditioned *opponent processes* (OPs). He has cited evidence that when drugs cause changes in normal physiological processes, the body reacts to restore equilibrium by producing effects opposite in direction to the drug effects. These OPs are adaptive, because they provide protection against potentially dangerous effects. For example, if a drug slows respiration rate, then at an extreme level breathing may stop altogether. The body's OP would be to increase breathing rate, counteracting the drug effect and protecting life. Siegel's view is that the OPs that occur after drug ingestion can become conditioned to environmental cues, so that a detoxified addict may experience conditioned OPs when he encounters drug-related cues. Because OPs are the reverse of direct drug effects, they appear very similar to withdrawal symptoms.

In addition to the conditioned withdrawal and conditioned OP theories, there is also evidence that at least some addicts, in some situations, show conditioning of acute, directly produced, drug effects. It has been argued that the experience of such positive conditioned sensations could have a "priming" effect, that, is effectively whetting the addict's appetite for desired drug effects and thus increasing their motivation to use. O'Brien's team has consistently found a minority of their subjects reporting and opiate-like "high" during exposure to drug-related material (O'Brien et al., 1986), and there is also clinical evidence in the form of "needle-freak" behaviour: Some intravenous drug users report that if they are unable to find a supply of their drug, they can achieve some degree of pleasure or alleviation of withdrawal from injecting water instead. Experimental support has come from a study by Meyer and Mirin (1979) in which detoxified addicts were given access to heroin after they had been pre-treated with either naltrexone (an opiate antagonist) or placebo, using a double-blind design so that neither subjects nor experimenter knew which of the two substances they had received. Although the dose of naltrexone was adequate to block completely the effects of the subsequently injected heroin, there was a tendency for these subjects to show weak but objectively measured opiate-like effects such as pupillary constriction and a reduction in respiratory rate. Powell (1995) found that when heroin addicts were assessed whilst preparing to inject their regular dose, they showed improvements in their physical state even before injection; this contrasts with the more typical findings of withdrawal-like reactions in detoxified addicts, and may suggest that situational factors such as drug availability or drug attitude are crucial mediators in determining what type of reaction is elicited.

Regardless of the form of conditioned responses, if they give rise to a subjective desire or craving to use, and/or actually increase the likelihood of a lapse to drug use, they should clearly become a target of intervention. There is now substantial evidence that high levels of self-reported craving are among the strongest predictors of subsequent relapse (e.g. Killen & Fortmann, 1997); Drummond and Glautier (1994) have also found certain aspects of physiological reactivity to alcohol-related cues to be predictive. A number of studies have supported the theoretical premise that cue-elicited craving and possibly other physiological reactions can be eliminated through systematic cue exposure, a treatment based on conditioning principles (see reviews by Dawe & Powell, 1995; Rohsenow, Monti, & Abrams, 1995). The addict is exposed to drug-related material whilst refraining from actual drug use, on the theoretical basis that this weakens and eventually extinguishes the conditioned response. In other words, the cue ceases to be a signal that drug effects are about to occur, and the anticipatory response (the CR) therefore dies away. The rationale is identical to that underlying exposure treatment for phobias (see Chapter 3). Bradley and

Moorey (1988) exposed two opiate addicts and a solvent abuser to drug-related cues, and observed that their subjective craving gradually waned over the course of the exposure (*within-session habituation*; see Fig. 4.3a). A number of single-case reports have demonstrated that when addicts are exposed to the same stimuli for several consecutive sessions, the magnitude of subjective craving experienced declines from one session to the next (*between-session habituation*; see Fig. 4.3b).

Initial research concerning the clinical usefulness of this approach was encouraging. Thus, for example, Blakey and Baker (1980) worked with six individual alcoholics, systematically exposing them to situations associated with drinking and encouraging them to resist actually having an alcoholic drink. Average levels of self-reported craving dropped from one session to the next, and five of the six patients managed to remain abstinent for at least two months. Their subsequent progress is uncertain, as further follow-up was not carried out. O'Brien's team have likewise reported between-session habituation of craving in opiate and cocaine addicts (Childress, McLellan, & O'Brien, 1986), as have other researchers (e.g. Bradley & Moorey, 1988; Powell, Bradley, & Gray, 1992). However, in the small number of randomised controlled clinical trials that have so far been conducted the long-term benefits of this approach are more equivocal. Dawe et al. (1993) found that 6 months after treatment opiate addicts

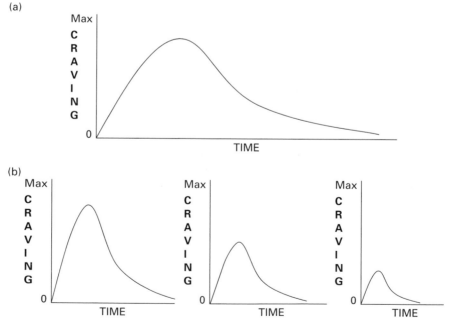

FIG. 4.3   (a) Within-session habituation of craving ratings; (b) Between-session habituation of craving ratings.

who had received cue exposure were no more likely to be drug-free than those who had not; nor did the groups differ in extent of drug use once an initial lapse had occurred. More encouragingly, Drummond and Glautier (1994) found in alcoholics that although cue exposure did not reduce overall abstinence rates, those who received cue exposure took longer to relapse to heavy drinking than did a comparison group who received relaxation training. This has led to the suggestion that cue-exposure treatment may enable alcoholics to exert restraint over their drinking, opening up the possibility of moderate (or controlled) drinking rather than abstinence as a goal. This whole area, however, remains controversial. It is possible that the slight advantage of cue exposure in this study compared to that found by Dawe et al. with opiate addicts reflected methodological differences. For example, whereas Drummond and Glautier exposed their subjects to real alcohol, which they held and smelled, Dawe et al. used a range of drug-related cues which, for ethical and clinical reasons, did not include real opiates: This may have reduced the potency of their treatment. Alternatively, the many social problems routinely associated with illicit drug use, as opposed to alcohol use, may mean that the relative importance of conditioned responses differs between substances.

The current evidence for the relevance of conditioning to understanding addiction is therefore mixed. Although there is a large body of support for the development and elicitation of conditioned responses to drug-related cues, the effects of cue-exposure treatment seem at best to be subtle and to be affected by as yet undetermined parameters of the methodology, patient characteristics, or type/form of substance use. A number of clinical trials of cue exposure in different substance-using groups, with varying methodologies, are currently in progress and their outcomes will be critical in determining whether there are any consistent and clinically significant benefits to be gained from such intervention.

The disease model

This discussion would not be complete without at least brief consideration of an opposing conceptualisation of addiction, that it is a disease (i.e. a disorder, presumed or known to have an organic cause, and largely beyond the individual's control). The most prominent advocate of this view is the Alcoholics Anonymous (AA) organisation. The disease model began to develop in the early 1990s, and reflected a transition from the prevalent perception of addiction as a vice. AA's original argument was that some people have a physical allergy to the intake of alcohol which causes them to react to a single drink with an intense craving for more, so that they have abnormal difficulty in limiting their consumption. The "allergy" component of this argument has, scientifically unsupported, receded, but the more general concept of addiction as a "disease of the will" has gained in strength and been broadened to apply to other forms of addiction. There is now a host of organisations associated with AA, including

Narcotics Anonymous (NA) for other drug users, Gamblers Anonymous (GA), and various groups such as Al-Anon which provide contact for families of addicts. The remainder of this discussion will focus on AA as an example of the stance taken by all these groups.

In the absence of any known physical cure for the underlying disease process, AA has adopted a spiritual framework, calling on addicts to subjugate their own will to that of a "higher power" which imposes a set of rules for structuring beliefs and behaviour. The "higher power" is not necessarily identified as God, although some individuals with pre-existing religious convictions may well do so. When an addict engages with AA, he progresses through a set of 12 steps, each of which involves recognition and acceptance of a new spiritual/moral code. The addict effectively commits himself to a new way of life, one aspect of which is abstinence, and is given massive support for this conversion by the other AA members. There are various levels of support, via regular meetings held in the community, individual contact, and residential treatment where addicts progress through a very structured programme and move through levels of seniority in a rigid hierarchy. Deviation from the rules of the programme is systematically and severely penalised, and the addict may be required to move down a tier in the hierarchy, or even be expelled. When addicts have completed the programme, there is often a system of half-way houses to facilitate their transition to a drug-free life in the community.

Alongside its spriritual emphasis, AA also encourages its members to use a range of strategies to help themselves in conforming to the new code of abstinence. These overlap noticeably with the practical interventions of the RP model, and include various cognitive manoeuvres such as calling to mind the benefits of abstinence, or the aversive consequences of drug use, and behavioural tactics such as the avoidance of certain risky situations (e.g. pubs).

There has been an expansion of research in recent years substantiating the central postulate of the disease model that there may be a biological basis to addiction-proneness, in at least a sub-group of individuals. For example, some genetic studies have reported high heritability for addiction to various substances (see e.g. True et al., 1997), and differences in drinking characteristics have been observed between alcoholics with no prior family history of drinking and those with alcoholic parents, the latter often showing more severe dependence (Cloninger, 1987).

It is only in the last few years that empirical evaluation of the effectiveness of 12-step interventions have been conducted, and this has usually been in the context of studies comparing outcomes for addicts exposed to either relapse prevention or 12-step approaches. The two largest and most recent studies, following up alcoholics who have either made their own choices between the two treatments (Ouimette, Finney, & Moos, 1997) or who have been randomly allocated between them (Project MATCH Research Group, 1997), have both found good clinical outcomes for both treatments and little if any evidence for superiority of one over the other. The similarities in outcomes may reflect overlap between the behavioural guidance offered within each framework, or, alternatively, be attributable to non-specific factors such as provision of professional support or client commitment and readiness to change. It is difficult to exclude the latter possibility, since no randomised trial with a meaningful follow-up period can ethically allocate one group of addicts to a "no treatment" condition; however, consistent with this interpretation, a third group of subjects in the Project MATCH study who received only four sessions of "motivational enhancement therapy" did equally well at follow-up.

INTEGRATION

The most obvious conflict between the approaches outlined previously lies in the fundamental disagreement between the disease and the SLT models concerning the degree of control an individual has over his addiction. AA argues that addiction is a disease over which, by definition, the individual has little control; the SLT model sees it as largely reflecting inadequate resources for coping with life without drugs, and stresses that the addict can actively take control by acquiring the resources, psychological or material, which will enable him to remain abstinent. The two theories are diametrically opposed, then, in the view which they encourage an addict to take of himself—victim or master. In terms of practical guidance, however, there is much overlap.

Both approaches recommend a range of practical coping strategies for avoiding or dealing with the temptation to use, and clinically there is often a good working liaison between them. For example, a psychologist applying SLT principles might well recommend a client to attend AA for the contact with successful abstainers, who will both provide a new non-using social network and serve as encouraging role models. Likewise, AA often values the specialised help psychologists can offer the individual in learning strategies which will aid him in adhering to their abstinence-oriented philosophy. It is often argued that the approach most likely to benefit an individual addict will be strongly influenced by his or her personal preferences and belief system; thus, some individuals find themselves alienated by the quasi-religious framework promoted by AA, whereas others may be so psychologically vulnerable and lacking in social support or self-confidence that the SLT emphasis on personal mastery seems unrealistic and they may find it easier to identify with the affiliation offered by the AA disease model. However, contradicting this plausible assumption, the Project MATCH study described earlier, which compared outcomes following RP, 12-step, and brief motivational enhancement treatments in a huge sample of 1726 alcoholics, in fact found no evidence that any one of the treatments was especially appropriate for a particular sub-group of alcoholics defined according either to drinking characteristics, family history, psychiatric symptoms, beliefs, or other demographic and psychological variables.

The pharmacological approach is complementary to the other frameworks, which deal primarily with the difficulties of long-term abstinence. Too often, pharmacological treatments are identified with a very narrow "medical" model which sees addiction as a disease rooted exclusively in physical dependence. This represents an injustice to the majority of doctors working in the area who, through hard clinical experience, are well aware not only that withdrawal is merely the first step towards sustained abstinence, but also that the clinical effectiveness of any withdrawal regime depends on the psychological prepared- ness of the addict and the resources he has to draw on to tolerate these first difficult days. Indeed, the development of post-detoxification pharmacological treatments (naltrexone, disulfiram) is clear testimony to medical recognition of the more persistent impact of psychological needs and desires. Thus, GPs often work in collaboration with other professionals to develop a structured plan for helping the addict through both the immediate difficulties of detoxification and the longer-term problems of remaining drug-free. So, for instance, the SLT model of addiction recognises the relevance of well thought-out reduction regimes in enabling people to tolerate the discomfort of detoxification. The emphasis, however, is on identification of psychological factors which may help or hinder the course of any withdrawal regime, with therapeutic input directed at developing necessary resources. On the basis of such an assessment, therapists working within this framework might well liaise with the prescribing physician to negotiate a withdrawal programme most likely to suit the individual patient (e.g. a short, sharp reduction versus a gentle, protracted one). Similarly, the idea of prescribing a pharmacological substance as a block to impulsive drug use originates as much in the psychological as in the medical analysis. The psy- chologist would, however, ideally couple the drug treatment with sessions for identifying any high-risk situations experienced during this period and helping the client to develop appropriate coping strategies.

Although the conditioning model of addiction has been derived from a differ- ent branch of learning theory, it too is easily accommodated within an overarching SLT model. Thus, it is possible that classical conditioning may account for a significant proportion of the craving experienced by detoxified addicts; but whether or not they respond to their craving by actually using drugs is one of the central concerns of SLT. Whereas one intervention is to extinguish conditioned responses via cue exposure, an alternative approach is to help the addict develop a repertoire of strategies to counteract the impulse to use. Furthermore, it is plain that conditioning cannot account for all of the temptations to use drugs, with social pressure, for instance, being another important influence (see Tiffany, 1995, and Niaura et al., 1988, for discussions of the relationships between cognitive factors, cue reactivity, and behaviour). Even the firmest believer in cue exposure would currently see this as but one component of intervention.

The "Stages of Change" framework of Prochaska and DiClemente (1983), described earlier, provides a constructive way of considering how the different models and treatment techniques reviewed here might be employed in individualised combinations to support and facilitate progress towards abstinence. Thus, psychological techniques such as Motivational Interviewing and Relapse Prevention may assist the addict in the shifts from contemplation to action and from action to maintenance, and in preparing for and responding to the possibility of relapse, whereas cue exposure would be particularly relevant to the stage of maintenance. The "12-steps" approach advocated by Alcoholics Anonymous provides an alternative conceptualisation that focuses on the instigation of action and on maintenance of abstinence; whereas pharmacological treatments provide specific and complementary mechanisms for facilitating both action and/or maintenance through symptomatic relief and blocking of drug effects.

The last five to ten years have seen an upsurge in the numbers of systematic, large-scale, and rigorous studies evaluating a whole range of treatments in substance dependence. Although these have been encouraging in many respects, they have inevitably generated as many questions and new hypotheses as they have answered, and there is no doubt that developments will continue unabated over the next decade. The increasing availability and use of new technologies, such as neuro-imaging and behavioural genetics, is adding an exciting new dimension to research in the area, in principle enabling a more fine-grained analysis of the mechanisms involved in drug effects and treatments and of individual differences in responses at a physiological level. The future is consequently rich with possibilities for finding out more about both biological and psychological bases of dependence, and for defining interventions that will integrate these sources of information with an understanding of the social contexts within which drug dependence occurs.

RECOMMENDED READING

Drummond, D.C., Tiffany, S.T., Glautier, S., & Remington B. (Eds.). (1995). *Addictive behaviour: Cue exposure theory and practice*. Chichester, UK: John Wiley & Sons Ltd.

This volume brings together theoretical and clinical perspectives on the classical conditioning model and its treatment implications, reviewing recent literature in relation to a range of substances.

Ghodse, H. (1995). *Drugs and addictive behaviour* (2nd ed.). Oxford, UK: Blackwell Scientific Publications.

A useful overview of assessment and treatment of drug addiction from a variety of perspectives, and a good source of information regarding pharmacological issues specific to particular classes of drug.

Marlatt, G.A., & Gordon, J.R. (1985). *Relapse prevention: Maintenance strategies in the treatment of addictive behaviors*. New York: Guilford Press.

A well-written and detailed account of the SLT approach to addiction.

Orford, J. (1985). *Excessive appetites: A psychological view of addictions.* Chichester, UK: John Wiley & Sons Ltd.

A fascinating account of developments in the concept of dependence, this book considers differences and similarities between approaches to a range of addictive behaviours, including gambling, eating, and sexuality alongside substance use.

Royal College of Psychiatrists. (1987). *Drug scenes: A report on drugs and drug dependence.* London: Gaskell.

A concise book summarising the basic issues in drug dependence, also considering the socio-political dimension.

REFERENCES

Allsop, S., Saunders, B., Phillips, M., & Carr, A. (1997). A trial of relapse prevention with severely dependent male problem drinkers. *Addiction, 92,* 61–74.

Bandura, A. (1977a). Self-efficacy: Toward a unifying theory of behavioural change. *Psychological Review, 84,* 191–215.

Bandura, A. (1977b). *Social learning theory.* Englewood Cliffs, NJ: Prentice-Hall.

Blakey, R., & Baker, R. (1980). An exposure approach to alcohol abuse. *Behaviour Research and Therapy, 18,* 319–325.

Bradley, B.P., & Moorey, S. (1988). Extinction of craving during exposure to drug-related cues: Three single case reports. *Behavioural Psychotherapy, 16,* 45–56.

Childress, A.R., McLellan, A.T., & O'Brien, C.P. (1986). Abstinent opiate abusers exhibit conditioned craving, conditioned withdrawal, and reductions in both through extinction. *British Journal of Addiction, 81,* 655–660.

Cloninger, C.R. (1987). Neurogenetic adaptive mechanisms in alcoholism. *Science, 236,* 410–416.

Cummings, C., Gordon, J.R., & Marlatt, G.A. (1980). Relapse: Prevention and prediction. In W.R. Miller (Ed.), *The addictive behaviours* (pp. 291–321). New York: Pergamon Press.

Dawe, S., Powell, J., Richards, D., Gossop, M., Marks, I., et al. (1993). Does post-withdrawal cue exposure improve outcome in opiate addiction? A controlled trial. *Addiction, 88,* 1233–1245.

Dawe, S., & Powell, J. (1995). Cue exposure treatment in opiate and cocaine dependence. In D.C. Drummond, S.T. Tiffany, S. Glautier, & B. Remington (Eds.), *Addictive behaviour: Cue exposure theory and practice* (pp. 197–210). Chichester, UK: Wiley.

Drummond, D.C., & Glautier, S.P. (1994). A controlled trial of cue exposure treatment in alcohol dependence. *Journal of Consulting and Clinical Psychology, 62,* 809–817.

Drummond, D.C., Tiffany, S.T., Glautier, S., & Remington, B. (Eds.). (1995). *Addictive behaviour: Cue exposure theory and practice.* Chichester, UK: Wiley.

Ghodse, A.H. (1995). *Drugs and addictive behaviour: A guide to treatment* (2nd ed.). Blackwell Science Inc.

Gossop, M., Green, L., Phillips. G., & Bradley, B. (1987). What happens to opiate addicts immediately after treatment: A prospective follow-up study. *British Medical Journal, 294,* 377–1380.

Hunt, W.A., Barnett, L.W., & Branch, L.G. (1971). Relapse rates in addiction programs. *Journal of Clinical Psychology, 27,* 455–459.

Killen, J.D., & Fortmann, S.P. (1997). Craving is associated with smoking relapse: Findings from three prospective studies. *Experimental and Clinical Psychopharmacology, 5,* 137–142.

Marlatt, G.A. (1996). Taxonomy of high-risk situations for alcohol relapse: Evolution and development of a cognitive-behavioural model. *Addiction, 91,* S37–S49.

Marlatt, G.A., & Gordon, J.R. (1985). *Relapse prevention: Maintenance strategies in the treatment of addictive behaviors*. New York: Guilford Press.

Meyer, R.E., & Mirin, S.M. (1979). *The heroin stimulus: Implications for a study of addiction*. New York: Plenum Press.

Miller, W.R. (1983). Motivational interviewing with problem drinkers. *Behavioural Psychotherapy*, *11*, 147–182.

Miller, W.R., Westerberg, V.S., Harris, R.J., & Tonigan, J.S. (1996). What predicts relapse? Prospective testing of antecedent models. *Addiction*, *91*, S155–S172.

Moncrieff, J., & Drummond, D.C. (1997). New drug treatments for alcohol problems: A critical appraisal. *Addiction*, *92*, 939–947.

Niaura, R.S., Rohsenow, D.J., Binkoff, J.A., Monti, P.M., Pedraza, M., & Abrams, D.B. (1988). Relevance of cue reactivity to understanding alcohol and smoking relapse. *Journal of Abnormal Psychology*, *97*, 133–152.

O'Brien, C.P., Ehrman, R.E., & Ternes, J.W. (1986). Classical conditioning in human opioid dependence. In S.R. Goldberg, & I.P. Stolerman (Eds.), *Behavioural analysis of drug dependence* (pp. 329–356). San Diego, CA: Academic Press.

O'Brien, C.P., O'Brien, T.J., Mintz, J., & Brady, J.P. (1975). Conditioning of narcotic abstinence symptoms in human subjects. *Drug and Alcohol Dependence*, *1*, 115–123.

Ouimette, P.C., Finney, J.W., & Moos, R.H. (1997). Twelve-step and cognitive-behavioural treatment for substance abuse: A comparison of treatment effectiveness. *Journal of Consulting and Clinical Psychology*, *65*, 230–240.

Powell, J.H. (1995). Classical responses to drug-related stimuli: Is context crucial? *Addiction*, *90*, 1089–1095.

Powell, J.H., Bradley, B., & Gray, J.A. (1992). Subjective craving for opiates: Evaluation of a cue exposure protocol for use with detoxified opiate addicts. *British Journal of Clinical Psychology*, *32*, 39–53.

Prochaska, J.O., & DiClemente, C.C. (1983). Stage processes of self-change of smoking: Toward an integrative model of change. *Journal of Consulting and Clinical Psychology*, *51*, 390–395.

Project MATCH Research Group. (1997). Matching alcoholism treatments to client heterogeneity: Project MATCH post-treatment drinking outcomes. *Journal of Studies on Alcohol*, *58*, 7–29.

Rabinowitz, J., Cohen, H., Tarrasch, R., & Kotler, M. (1997). Compliance to naltrexone treatment after ultra-rapid opiate detoxification: An open label naturalistic study. *Drug and Alcohol Dependence*, *47*, 77–86.

Rohsenow, D.J., Monti, P.M., & Abrams, D.B. (1995). Cue exposure treatment in alcohol dependence. In D.C. Drummond, S.T. Tiffany, S. Glautier, & B. Remington (Eds.), *Addictive behaviour: Cue exposure theory and practice* (pp. 169–196). Chichester, UK: Wiley.

Rolleston, H. (1926). Medical aspects of tobacco. *The Lancet*, *i*, 961–965.

Royal College of Psychiatrists (1987). *Drug scenes: A report on drugs and drug dependence by the Royal College of Psychiatrists*. London: Gaskell.

Siegel, S. (1983). Classical conditioning, drug tolerance and drug dependence. In Y. Israel, F.B. Glaser, H. Kalant, R.E. Popham, W. Schmidt, & R.G. Smart (Eds.), *Research advances in alcohol and drug problems* (Vol. 7, pp. 207–246). New York: Plenum Press.

Skinner, B.F. (1938). *The behaviour of organisms*. New York: Appleton Century-Crofts.

Teasdale, J.D. (1973). Conditioned abstinence in narcotic addicts. *International Journal of the Addictions*, *8*, 273–292.

Tiffany, S.T. (1995). The role of cognitive factors in reactivity to drug cues. In D.C. Drummond, S.T. Tiffany, S. Glautier, & B. Remington (Eds.), *Addictive behaviour: Cue exposure theory and practice* (pp. 137–165). Chichester, UK: Wiley.

True, W.R., Heath, A.C., Scherrer, J.F., Waterman, B., Goldberg, J., Lin, N., Eisen, S.A., Lyons, M.J., & Tsuang, M.T. (1997). Genetic and environmental contributions to smoking. *Addiction*, *92*, 1277–1287.

Volpicelli, J.R., Volpicelli, L.A., & O'Brien, C.P. (1995). Medical management of alcohol dependence—clinical use and limitations of naltrexone treatment. *Alcohol and Alcoholism, 30,* 789–798.

WHO (1964). *Thirteenth report, WHO expert committee on addiction-producing drugs.* (Technical Report Series No. 273). Geneva: World Health Organisation.

Wikler, A. (1948). Recent progress in research on the neurophysiologic basis of morphine addiction. *American Journal of Psychiatry, 105,* 329–338.

Wikler, A. (1980). *Opioid dependence: Mechanisms and treatment.* New York: Plenum Press.

CHAPTER FIVE

Eating disorders

Jean Mitchell
Anglian Harbours NHS Trust, Suffolk, UK

Helen McCarthy
Gwent Community NHS Trust, Newport, UK

ANOREXIA NERVOSA

Historical overview

Although English language references to anorexia nervosa can be found in 17th-century medical writings, the disorder was first described in detail in 1873, by Sir William Gull in England, and Dr Lasegue in France. Their two independent publications described a condition (named "anorexia nervosa" by Gull) whereby young females were apparently anorexic in the absence of any observable organic illness. These individuals typically became hyperactive, were preoccupied with their bodies being thin, and would refuse food, even though severe emaciation and amenorrhoea (cessation of menstruation) were often consequences of their actions. Both Gull and Laseque stressed the fact that they considered anorexia to be a psychological rather than a physical disease.

Historically, debate has focused on the issue of whether or not anorexia nervosa represents a distinct clinical entity, or whether it is a variant of other psychiatric illness, such as depression, schizophrenia, obsessive-compulsive disorder, and hysterical disorder. A further debate has centred on whether or not anorexia nervosa represents a non-specific symptom or a group of disorders linked only by the fact that significant weight loss occurs as a result of emotional problems. However, the contemporary viewpoint is that there is a syndrome of primary anorexia nervosa, which has characteristic signs and symptoms that distinguish it from other causes of weight loss (Garfinkel & Garner, 1982).

What is anorexia nervosa?

The criteria for anorexia nervosa proposed by the 4th edition of the North American Diagnostic and Statistical Manual (DSM-IV; American Psychiatric Association, 1994) are presented in Table 5.1.

Russell (1995) has noted how anorexia nervosa, like other psychiatric disorders, can be seen to change and evolve over time. For example, the psychological expression of anorexia nervosa (its psycho-pathology) is liable to change in response to social pressures. Joan Brumberg (1988) has described the contemporary social pressures that promote dietary restraint, and other researchers have documented how the perception of the "ideal" woman's weight has declined over recent decades, such that beauty contestants' weights fall well below the national norm, and have steadily declined over a period of two decades (Garner & Garfinkel, 1980). Furthermore, this recent shift towards a thinner ideal for western women is associated with an increase in the incidence of anorexia nervosa (e.g. Lucas, Beard, O'Fallon, & Kurland, 1991). Further evidence that socio-cultural factors influence both the psychological content of eating disorders and their mode of expression comes from research that suggests that the sudden appearance of bulimia nervosa in the late 1970s is a new variant of eating disorder, rather than being a previously undetected problem (Kendler et al., 1991; Lucas & Soundy, 1993).

What does this mean in terms of trying to define and classify anorexia nervosa? Russell (1995) has contrasted the medico-clinical approach to defining

TABLE 5.1
DSM-IV criteria for anorexia nervosa

A. Refusal to maintain body weight at or above a minimally normal weight for age and height (e.g. weight loss leading to maintenance of body weight less than 85% of that expected; or failure to make expected weight gain during period of growth, leading to body weight less than 85% of that expected).

B. Intense fear of gaining weight or becoming fat, even though underweight.

C. Disturbance in the way in which one's body weight or shape is experienced, undue influence of body shape and weight on self-evaluation, or denial of the seriousness of current low body weight.

D. In post-menarchal females, amenorrhea, i.e. the absence of at least three consecutive menstrual cycles. (A woman is considered to have amenorrhea if her periods occur only following hormone, e.g. oestrogen, administration.)

Specify type:

Restricting type: During the episode of anorexia nervosa, the person does not regularly engage in binge eating or purging behaviour (i.e. self-induced vomiting or the misuse of laxatives or diuretics).

Binge eating/purging type: During the episode of anorexia nervosa, the person regularly engages in binge eating or purging behaviour (i.e. self-induced vomiting or the misuse of laxatives or diuretics).

psychiatric disorder, in which clinical features deemed necessary for a diagnosis become enshrined within diagnostic criteria (e.g. DSM-IV) with the socio-cultural approach, which views the patterning of an illness as a response to prevailing social and cultural systems (e.g. Brumberg, 1988). Russell suggests that we may need a broader formulation of the psycho-pathology of anorexia than the current precise formulation exemplified by contemporary psychiatric diagnostic systems, such as DSM-IV, to allow for the influence of socio-cultural factors in the expression of this disorder.

A striking feature of anorexia nervosa concerns the observation that people with this condition typically exhibit a distortion of their body image, to the extent that even when they are very thin, they often claim to feel fat and bloated (Bruch, 1962). There is evidence that this is representative of a more general difficulty with thinking and perceptual processes, because they also tend to misperceive their affective (emotional) and visceral (bodily) sensations (Bruch, 1978).

The characteristic amenorrhoea seems primarily to be a consequence of the weight loss because in 70% of cases periods cease shortly after dieting commences (Fries, 1977; Hurd, Palumbo, & Gharib, 1977). Many of the other phenomena ascribed to the anorexic syndrome also appear to be direct consequences of starvation, because they can be found in all starving people, irrespective of the cause of the starvation (Casper & Davis, 1977). We know this as a result of a series of studies, known as "the Minnesota studies", in which psychologically normal men were placed on semi-starvation diets for 6 months in order to investigate some of the likely consequences of being detained as a prisoner of war (Keys, Brozek, Henschel, Mickelson, & Taylor, 1950). These studies revealed that, in common with their anorexic counterparts, the men experienced an intense preoccupation with food, they tended to approach eating with various rituals and great secrecy, and they also showed other strange food habits, such as combining odd mixtures of food. Bulimia, the rapid consumption of a large amount of food in a short period of time (see later), occurred in four of these subjects (Schiele & Brozek, 1948) and a few of the men were observed to steal small items that they were able to afford, which again has parallels with the behaviour of some anorexics with bulimic features, or some individuals who suffer from bulimia nervosa (Russell, 1979). This suggests that once an individual has embarked on an anorexic regime, irrespective of the underlying reasons that first led to the development of anorexia nervosa, the consequent starvation will itself produce characteristic features that will intensify and strengthen the anorectic behaviour. Specifically, the person will become locked in a vicious circle where fears about being in control lead to a restriction of food intake, which eventually in itself will result in a preoccupation with food and eating that escalates the fear about control issues, thereby leading to an exacerbation of dietary restriction.

Prolonged caloric restriction also leads to the emergence of symptoms such as irritability, poor concentration, anxiety, depression, apathy, lability of mood, and fatigue (Garfinkel & Garner, 1982). Sleep disturbance, in the form of reduced time spent sleeping and early morning wakening, are common in anorexia nervosa (Crisp, Stonehill, & Fenton, 1971). Disturbances in sleep and mood have also been related more generally to under-nutrition (Crisp, 1980).

However, it is very characteristic of individuals with anorexia nervosa to deny the adverse consequences of the disorder, such as the weight loss, feelings of hunger, and mood swings. This is done with a conviction and tenacity that can appear totally baffling to the observer; despite clear evidence to the contrary, the person with anorexia will often steadfastly deny that there is anything wrong.

There are several physical signs of starvation, the most striking of which is the weight loss. The extent of weight loss is variable but can be greater than 50% of the matched population mean weight. Other physical signs of the disorder include dry, cracking skin, thinning hair on the scalp, brittle nails, lanugo hair (fine, downy hair growth over the body, especially over the back and face), and coldness in the extremities of the body. There are marked hormonal disturbances, including low levels of testosterone, follicle-stimulating hormone, and luteinising hormone (for a comprehensive review of this area, see Garfinkel & Garner, 1982, pp. 58–99).

BULIMIA NERVOSA

Historical overview

It has been known for many years that some individuals with anorexia nervosa show bulimic features, that is, have periods in which they binge eat, vomit voluntarily, or abuse laxatives and purgatives. Bulimia nervosa was only named and identified as a distinct disorder from anorexia nervosa by Russell in 1979. In this study, he identified patients with bulimic symptoms, some of whom could not be classified as anorexic in terms of weight loss, and furthermore had no previous history of anorexia nervosa. These individuals typically alternated periods of food restriction with periods when they binged, that is, rapidly consumed a large quantity of food over a short period of time. Following a binge they would usually make themselves vomit or abuse laxatives or other purgatives, ostensibly to avoid the consequences (in terms of weight gain) of ingesting such an enormous number of calories, and also to alleviate the physical discomfort that is experienced as a result of bingeing. Russell also demonstrated that there was a clear overlap between patients with bulimia nervosa and the bulimic subgroup of anorexia nervosa patients.

Russell's viewpoint has been endorsed by other researchers (Casper, Eckert, Halmi, Goldberg, & Davis, 1980; Garfinkel, Moldofsky, & Garner, 1980) and it is now known that people with anorexia and people with bulimia can be differentiated on a number of demographic features. For example, when compared to individuals with anorexia nervosa, people with bulimia nervosa tend to be older (Casper et al., 1980) and are less likely to come from middle- or upper-class backgrounds (Lacey, 1983). There is also evidence that individuals with bulimia nervosa are more likely to have been overweight in the past (Fairburn & Cooper, 1983; Russell, 1979) and to engage in self-destructive or antisocial impulsive behaviours, such as shoplifting, abusing drugs, or deliberate self-harm (Abraham & Beaumont, 1982; Casper et al., 1980; Pyle, Mitchell, & Eckert, 1981; Russell, 1979). Although it is difficult to draw any definite conclusions, evidence suggests that bulimia nervosa is a more intractable condition to treat than anorexia nervosa, and that those who suffer from bulimia have a poorer prognosis (Russell, 1979).

What is bulimia nervosa?

The DSM-IV criteria for bulimia nervosa are presented in Table 5.2. Unlike their anorexic peers, individuals with bulimia nervosa are not necessarily thin and may be normal weight, or even overweight, and are more likely to have been significantly overweight in the past (Fairburn & Cooper, 1983; Russell, 1979). High carbohydrate, easily ingested food usually constitutes "binge" food, with bulimic individuals reporting consuming energy contents between three and twenty-seven times the recommended daily energy allowance on a "bad day" (Abraham & Beaumont, 1982).

Following a binge most sufferers induce vomiting, take large quantities of laxatives, or both. There are various physical complications associated with

TABLE 5.2
DSM-IV criteria for bulimia nervosa

A. Recurrent episodes of binge eating. An episode of binge-eating is characterised by both (1) eating, in a discrete period of time (e.g. in any 2-hour period), an amount of food that is definitely larger than most people would eat in a similar period of time (taking into account time since last meal and social context in which eating occurred); and (2) a sense of lack of control over eating during the episodes (e.g. feeling that one can't stop eating or control what or how much one is eating).

B. Recurrent use of inappropriate compensatory behaviour to avoid weight gain, e.g. self-induced vomiting.

C. A minimum average of two episodes of binge eating and two inappropriate compensatory behaviours a week for at least 3 months.

D. Self-evaluation is unduly influenced by body shape and weight.

E. The disturbance does not occur exclusively during episodes of anorexia nervosa.

Specify type:
Purging type: These individuals regularly purge after binge eating via self-induced vomiting or the abuse of laxatives.
Non-purging type: These individuals do not engage in self-induced vomiting or laxative abuse. Some may use compensatory methods of dieting and exercising.

vomiting, including loss of electrolytes, an increased risk of developing urinary infections and renal failure, and increased susceptibility to epileptic seizures (Russell, 1979).

Depressive symptoms are a common feature in patients with bulimia nervosa (Halmi, 1995; Pyle et al., 1981) and there is also evidence that they experience considerable lability of mood (Fairburn, 1980; Johnson & Larson, 1982). It is not unusual for sufferers to contemplate suicide after bingeing, or to actually make suicide attempts (Abraham & Beaumont, 1982). As noted previously, bulimic features (both in individuals with anorexia nervosa and bulimia nervosa) have been observed to be associated with poor impulse control and with a variety of impulsive, self-destructive, and antisocial behaviours, such as drug abuse, self-mutilation, and stealing. In contrast to individuals with anorexia nervosa, denial is not usually a feature of bulimia nervosa and sufferers are generally well aware that they have a serious problem and require help.

PICA

Pica (from the Latin word meaning "magpie") has been documented as far back as the 16th century (Parry-Jones, 1991). It is the desire to eat, or the eating of, substances usually considered inedible. The ingested substances may be plaster, dirt, carpet fibres, etc. Pica is a normal developmental feature of infants, which usually declines by the age of 2 years (Bicknell, 1975). It has also been commonly observed among pregnant women who may have cravings for substances such as chalk or coal.

The biological explanation is that it is a behavioural sign of iron deficiency or general malnourishment. This may explain many cases, but psychological research indicates that other factors may be relevant. Millican, Lourie, and Layman (1956) looked at pica in older children and identified three main contributing factors:

(1) organic brain damage in the child
(2) disturbance in the mother–child relationship
(3) socio-economic factors such as poor housing.

They later pointed out the importance of separation from one parent as an additional causal factor.

OBESITY

What is obesity?

"Obesity" is a difficult construct to define and assess for a number of reasons. Sobal (1995) has reviewed how in industrialised societies, fatness varies in association with different social roles, such as gender (women are generally fatter), age (fatness tends to increase until people become elderly, especially for women), ethnicity (e.g. African American women are fatter in the United States), socio-economic status (lower socio-economic status women are fatter), marriage (married men are fatter), and parenthood (the more children a woman has, the fatter she is likely to be, relatively speaking).

A further complicating factor in the accurate assessment of obesity concerns the difficulty inherent in actually measuring this construct. Most studies simply measure height and weight, a problematic method that only provides a crude indication of the body's fat content (Royal College of Physicians, 1983) and fails to take into account individual differences in overall physical size, shape, build, or metabolism. For example, people who are fit and athletic and therefore have a muscular physique may weigh above the average for their age and height although they are not fat. At this point it is worth noting that irrespective of the assessment method that is employed, the limits of "normality" (i.e. where the boundary between "normal" and "obese" should be placed) need to be defined. At present we define overweight and obesity in adults by reference to life insurance company standards that present the association between weight range and mortality rate (DHSS/MRC, 1976). Using this method, "overweight" is typically defined as individuals who weigh 110–119% of standard weight, which is the weight range associated with the lowest mortality rate for each height category in an insured population. Obesity is generally defined as a body weight in excess of 120% of the standard weight (i.e. if the optimum weight, in terms of longevity, for a particular age and height band was 10 stone, an individual would have to weigh 12 stone or more to be classified as "obese"), although estimates for the precise point at which increasing weight is deemed to threaten health range from 5% to 30% above ideal weight (Brownell, 1995). Brownell also highlights the fact that the most cited contemporary measure for estimating obesity, the Body Mass Index (weight in kilograms per height in metres squared) is more strongly associated with percentage of body fat and health complications, and is therefore a more valid measure of obesity than simple weight norms. Using this method, figures adopted by the National Centre for Health Statistics define overweight as a BMI of 27.3 for women and of 27.8 for men, with a BMI of 32.3 and 31.1 or above corresponding to severe overweight in women and men respectively.

When one considers the health risks associated with obesity, there is considerable evidence that substantial degrees of obesity increase morbidity and mortality. For example, obesity plays a role in the development of coronary heart disease (Garrow, 1981), high blood pressure (Bray, 1979; DHSS/MRC, 1976), gallbladder disease (Rimm, Werner, van Yserloo, & Bernstein, 1975), and certain types of cancer (Lew & Garfinkel, 1979).

As well as an increased risk to physical well-being, it is well known that being overweight or obese has adverse consequences for the psychological health of the individual, especially for females. People who are overweight tend to be stigmatised against, certainly in Western cultures. Staffieri (1967) found that children as young as 4 or 5 years of age begin to produce unfavourable stereotyped responses towards endomorphic (obese) silhouettes. Richardson (1961) found that children aged 10 and 11 shown drawings of children with various physical disabilities (e.g. sitting in a wheelchair) together with drawings of a "normal" and an obese child, almost invariably saw the obese child as the least desirable.

Unfortunately, obese people are not only subjected to prejudicial attitudes but at times find themselves on the receiving end of overt discrimination. For example, Canning and Mayer (1966) suggested being obese adversely influenced whether high school students were accepted into the college of their choice. Stunkard and Sobal (1995) cite evidence that obese people face severe discrimination in the job market, and found that young obese women were far less likely to marry than were their non-obese peers, and when obese women do marry, they are far more likely to fall in social class than do non-obese women. There is also evidence that obese people are subjected to discrimination and prejudice from health-care professionals, and typically report being treated with disrespect by the medical profession, who have been shown to view their obese patients as "weak-willed, ugly and awkward" (see Stunkard & Sobal, 1995).

WHO DEVELOPS EATING DISORDERS?

Anorexia nervosa typically affects young, well-educated middle-class females. For example, a study of schoolgirls conducted in the United Kingdom in 1976 found that it was present in its severe form in 1 in 100 girls in the 16–18 age range in the independent sector of education, with a figure of 1 in 300 in the state education system (Crisp, Palmer, & Kalucy, 1976). However, because this study concerned itself solely with very severe cases of anorexia nervosa, and only with secondary school-age girls, these figures may represent an underestimation of the problem. It is important to emphasise here that eating disorders occur on a continuum—many young women, although not fulfilling the diagnostic criteria for anorexia or bulimia, nevertheless experience considerable difficulty in this area, and can be thought of as "sub-clinical" cases. Some researchers have reported that the disorder appears to be becoming more equally distributed through all social classes (Garfinkel & Garner, 1982), although others report more equivocal findings (Jones, Fox, Babigan, & Hutton, 1980). Most studies report an age range of between 12 and 25 years for developing anorexia (Garfinkel & Garner, 1982). In contrast, individuals showing bulimic features tend to be older. Russell (1979) for example, presented a mean age of onset for bulimia of 21.2 years (range 13–37).

Research suggests that bulimia nervosa has a higher prevalence rate than anorexia nervosa and that binge eating occurs frequently amongst women (Hawkins & Clement, 1980; Wardle, 1980). One study that looked at American college students found that 19% of the females reported experiencing all the major symptoms of bulimia (Halmi, Falk, & Schwartz, 1981). In the United Kingdom a community study of bulimia nervosa was conducted in which 20.9% of women reported bingeing, 2.9% reported using vomiting as a means of weight control, and there was a prevalence rate of 1.9% fulfilling diagnostic criteria for bulimia nervosa (Fairburn & Cooper, 1983). There is also evidence that women who develop bulimia nervosa are less likely to come from middle- or upper-class backgrounds than women who develop anorexia nervosa (e.g. Lacey, 1983).

One of the most striking demographic features of anorexia nervosa concerns the fact that the vast majority of sufferers, approximately 90–95% of reported cases, are female (Bemis, 1978; Jones et al., 1980). This observation supports the contention that cultural factors are extremely significant in the aetiology (development) of anorexia. However, there is some evidence that male anorexics are more likely to be found in the chronic group and to have a poorer prognosis than females in general (Crisp, Kalucy, Lacey, & Harding, 1977). The same researchers have also stated their belief that males are more likely to develop the bulimic form of the disorder, a hypothesis given some support by Halmi et al.'s (1981) finding that 5% of a sample of male college students reported experiencing all the major symptoms of bulimia. However, in clinical practice male patients with bulimia nervosa have been found to represent less than 5% of total reported cases (Russell, 1979). It is also worth noting that male anorexics do not show the typical social class skewing that females do (Crisp & Toms, 1972; Marshall, 1978).

Until recently, reliable information concerning the proportion of British children and adults who are overweight was somewhat lacking. However, results are now available from two major surveys that examined the prevalence of overweight in children (Stark, Atkins, Wolff, & Douglas, 1981) and in adults (Office of Population Censuses and Surveys, 1981). In the Stark et al. (1981) study, a nationally representative cohort of over 5000 children, born in a particular week in 1946, had their weights and heights measured at age 6, 7, 11, 14, 20, and 26 years. This demonstrated that the prevalence of obese children (i.e. weighing more than 120% of the standard figure) was relatively low (for example, 1.4% of boys and 2.1% of girls at age 6). However, there was a trend for weight to increase with age such that by their mid-20s, 31% of men and 27% of women were substantially overweight (more than 110% of standard weight), whereas 12.3% of men and 11.3% of women were obese. The second study (Office of Population Censuses and Surveys, 1981) assessed a number of factors, including the heights and weights of all adults between 16 and 64 years of age in a sample of 5000 households drawn from a random sample of 100 Local Authority districts. The findings revealed that across all age groups, an average of 39% of men and 32% of women were overweight, with 6% of men and 8% of women being classified as obese.

In America, estimates for the prevalence of overweight are 24.2% in men (15.4 million men) and 27.1% for women (18.6 million women), with estimates for severe overweight being 8% for men (5.1 million men) and 10.6% for women (7.4 million women) (reviewed by Williamson, 1995).

WHAT IS THE OUTCOME IN EATING DISORDERS?

Reported mortality figures for anorexia nervosa range from 0 to 24% (Farquharson & Hyland, 1966; Williams, 1958), with an average of about 9%. However, studies that follow up anorexic patients for several years have found a higher death rate than this. Theander (1983) observed a total mortality rate of 17% and a more recent study by Ratnasuriya, Eisler, Szmukler, and Russell (1991) reported a 20-year follow-up study of 41 patients with anorexia nervosa that demonstrated a mortality rate of 15% from causes related to the eating disorder. At least 15% of this sample had developed bulimia nervosa. Only 30% had what was considered to be a good general outcome, with 32.5% rated as having an intermediate outcome, and 20% (not including those who had died) having a poor (chronically ill) outcome. Herzog et al. (1992) suggest a mortality rate for anorexia nervosa of approximately 0.5–1% per year of observation, with mortality being highest amongst those who have the most severe degree of weight loss (115-fold greater if weight is less than 35kg, Patton, 1988) but lower in those who have received specialised treatment (Crisp, Callender, Halek, & Hsu, 1992). Suicide is consistently reported as being the commonest cause of death. The reader is referred to Treasure and Szmukler (1995) for a review of the medical complications of chronic anorexia nervosa.

Theander (1970) reported that for 58 of his patients, 47% were anoretic for a duration of less than 3 years, 31% for 3–5 years, and 22% for greater than 5 years. Although recovery in terms of weight gain and stabilisation has been observed to occur in more than 50% of patients, concerns with weight and a fear of fatness remain common, as do dietary restriction and feelings of anxiety when eating with others (Hsu, Crisp, & Harding, 1979; Morgan & Russell, 1975).

The early studies tended to suggest that bulimia is associated with a poor outcome. Russell (1979, p. 448), for example, said that "bulimia nervosa is more resistant to treatment, physical complications are more frequent and dangerous, and the risk of suicide is considerable". More recent studies have qualified this belief. For example, Hsu (1995) summarised the findings of five short-term retrospective studies that indicated that most patients do well at 1 year after treatment, with at least 75% having no bulimic symptoms. However, due to various methodological problems (discussed by Hsu), these data may be misleading. Hsu also reviewed six studies where patients were followed up for two or more years that revealed a low mortality rate (0.7%), although this may not be a reliable estimate because there was a high rate of untraced patients in four of the studies. One of the studies (Swift et al., 1987, cited in Hsu, 1995) reported a nine-fold increase in mortality, although the fact that their sample, composed of inpatients (who may have been more severely ill), could have influenced this result: In addition, it was not clear whether or not they received specific treatments targeted at their bulimic symptoms, which have been shown to improve outcome. When taken together, these studies suggest that most bulimic patients do improve with time, although 20% will develop a chronic, entrenched form of the disorder, and 30% will continue to exhibit some residual difficulties. Olmsted et al. (1984) reported a relapse rate of 31% during a 2-year follow-up study, with factors such as younger age, higher vomiting frequency, and elevated scores on specific sub-scales of certain eating disorder questionnaires being the strongest predictors of relapse.

It is almost a certainty that most readers of this chapter will know people who wish to lose weight and therefore diet, because it has been reported that at any one time a staggering 65% of British women and 30% of British men are trying to lose weight ("Slimming Foods", 1980). However, the chances are that few of them will succeed in reducing their weight on a permanent basis, as illustrated by the observation that excessive weight and obesity are continuing problems in Britain, despite the widespread efforts that are made to diet. Although it is relatively easy for people to achieve short-term weight loss, longer-term follow-up studies have shown that the majority of people regain weight over time (O'Neil, Currey, Sexaner, Riddle, & Molony-Sinnot, 1980; Stunkard & Penick, 1979). Indeed, there is a growing body of opinion that holds that far from improving matters, the restriction of food intake may lead to the development of binge eating and actually make people fatter (Cannon & Einzig, 1983; Orbach, 1979; Wardle & Beinart, 1981). Dwyer (1995, p. 496) cites the factors that are associated with long-term success in maintaining weight loss, namely: "physical activity and exercise, gradual changes in diet, therapy that deals with obesity as a disorder that will respond to an altered social milieu and individualisation of treatment to fit patients' lifestyle realities. Weight loss should be maintained for at least one year before renewed efforts to lose even more weight are attempted."

PSYCHOLOGICAL MODELS OF EATING DISORDERS

Behavioural models

Behavioural approaches are concerned with assessing, and where appropriate changing, a person's behaviour or performance directly, with little or no reference to dispositional or mentalistic processes (see Chapter 1). Thus, behavioural models do not infer the existence of any underlying causes of psychological problems, but hold that it is maladaptive behaviour patterns, acquired through traumatic or inappropriate learning, that constitute the "problem" that needs to be changed. Behavioural change is achieved by manipulating the environmental factors that maintain the problem behaviour by, for example, modifying the pleasurable or painful consequences of behaviour. Thus, in eating disorders, analysis will focus on how positive and negative reinforcers maintain the learned problem behaviour, namely avoidance of food in the case of anorexia, bingeing and vomiting in the case of bulimia, and overeating/eating high caloric foods in the case of obesity.

Techniques derived from behavioural theories have been demonstrated to have a role to play in alleviating some of the maladaptive behaviours associated with eating disorders. Operant conditioning procedures have been shown to be effective in promoting weight gain in anorexia nervosa, with negative reinforcers such as bed rest and isolation, and positive reinforcers such as increased social and physical activities contingent on food intake or weight gain, being employed (for example, Garfinkel, Kline, & Stancer, 1973; Halmi, Powers, & Cunningham, 1975). Rosen and Leitenberg (1982) reported that exposure to food and vomiting response prevention led to the complete cessation of vomiting and bingeing in a single subject, and that this improvement was maintained at 10-month follow-up. The behavioural treatment of obesity typically aims to teach people how to recognise the factors which maintain their eating habits and then how to devise methods to overcome these difficulties and establish new patterns of behaviour (Stuart, 1967). Thus, the home or work environment can be modified to minimise stimuli that can lead to inappropriate eating. For example, high calorie foods such as cakes and confectionery can be eliminated from the home. The eating pattern itself can be modified by, for example, encouraging the person to eat only at specific times in a particular room in the house. Regular exercise has been shown to be the single strongest correlate of long-term maintenance of weight loss, with the current emphasis being placed on regular, low-level activity with adherence as the focus (Grilo, Brownall, & Stunkard, 1993). Self-monitoring is another crucial behavioural technique employed in behavioural programmes for obesity.

The behavioural treatment of obesity has been shown to produce significant weight loss in those suffering from mild to moderate obesity, with the loss being maintained well at 1 year follow-up (cited by Wilson, 1995), although at 5-year follow-up virtually all patients will have returned to their pre-treatment baseline. There is evidence that perhaps behavioural techniques are best directed at obese children rather than adults. For example, Epstein, Valoski, Wing, and McCurley (1994) reported that a family-based programme focusing on lifestyle changes and weight control in both obese children *and* their parents was associated with 34% of the children having decreased weight, with 30% no longer being obese at 10-year follow-up.

However, behavioural models can be criticised for failing to address the underlying difficulties that eating disorders are symptomatic of, for example, depression, issues about sexuality and relationships, and fears about not being in control of one's life. Attempting to treat serious eating problems such as anorexia nervosa solely by using behavioural techniques could be potentially dangerous, because it will strengthen the fears that the sufferer has of not being in control of her life and could well result in an exacerbation of disordered eating patterns, as well as the subjective experience of feeling depressed, helpless, and having low self-esteem. Although the judicious and sensitive application of behavioural techniques may be of some use in dealing with the symptomatic aspects, such as food refusal and weight loss for anorexia nervosa, other intervention strategies need to be employed to tackle the underlying problems. Furthermore, in recognition of the fact that eating disorders are complex and multidetermined, it is rare to find behavioural techniques employed in their "pure" form; rather, one typically finds that cognitive-behavioural techniques are used.

Cognitive models

Cognitive models stress the vital role of cognition in mediating behaviour and focus on the relationship between maladaptive thinking patterns and psychological problems (see Chapter 1). Cognitive models of anorexia nervosa have focused on three major areas: Disordered sensations of satiety and hunger, errors in thinking (conceptual distortions), and perceptual distortions, namely body image disturbance.

It is generally acknowledged that anorexics have difficulty in monitoring and reporting on their emotional and physical states, and that descriptions of their inner states may show inaccuracies. Furthermore, their perceptions may be unduly influenced by external factors. For example, when food was directly introduced into their stomachs, individuals suffering from anorexia were found to be less accurate than normal controls in perceiving the quantity that they were given (Coddington & Bruch, 1970). They also display delayed gastric emptying when compared with controls (Dubois, Gross, Ebert, & Castell, 1979), and have been shown to fail to develop an aversion to sweet tastes, unlike normal controls (Garfinkel, Moldofsky, Garner, Stancer, & Coscina, 1978). Although these findings suggest an internal deficit in the mechanisms for regulating food/ carbohydrate intake, Garfinkel (1974) reported that anorexic patients' feelings of fullness following a meal persist longer if they believe they have eaten a high calorie meal, suggesting that cognitive factors influence their satiety experience. Thus, it is possible that cognitive factors mediating intake may be sufficiently prominent that they prevail over the internal, physiologically mediated regulatory mechanisms.

Bruch (1977) has drawn attention to the disturbances in thinking that occur in anorexia nervosa and has emphasised the importance of relabelling misconceptions and errors in the anorexic's thinking during psychotherapy. Drawing on the work of Beck (1976) on depression and anxiety disorders, Garner and Bemis (1982) have developed a cognitive model of anorexia nervosa focusing on conceptual processes leading to faulty thinking. Their categories of aberrant conceptual processes, based on those proposed by Beck (1976), include selective abstraction (e.g. "I am special if I am thin"), over-generalisation (e.g. "I was not happy at my normal weight, so I know that gaining weight won't make me feel better"), magnification (e.g. "gaining five pounds would push me over the brink"), dichotomous or all-or-none reasoning (e.g. "if I gain one pound, I'll gain a hundred pounds"), personalisation and self-reference (e.g. "I am embarrassed when other people see me eat"), and superstitious thinking (e.g. "I can't enjoy anything because it will be taken away"). Garner and Bemis have detailed the basic assumptions, or principles, that underlie and organise the irrational ideas of the anorexic patient, for example, that weight, shape, or thinness can serve as the sole or predominant basis for inferring personal value or self-worth, that complete self-control is necessary or even desirable, and that absolute certainty is necessary in making decisions.

Williamson, Davis, Duchman, McKenzie, and Watkins (1990) proposed a cognitive-behavioural model of anorexia nervosa, hypothesising that distorted thoughts (cognitions) concerning body weight and shape generate high levels of anxiety, and that the urge to reduce anxiety motivates the extreme weight reduction methods (behaviour) employed by individuals with anorexia nervosa. Wilson (1989) has suggested a comprehensive "cognitive-social learning model of bulimia nervosa", which proposes that cognitions are a key factor in bulimia, specifically, the knowledge that one has violated dietary "rules". For the reader interested in exploring the role of dietary restraint in the aetiology of binge eating in more depth, the following papers are recommended: Herman and Polivy (1984); and Wardle and Beinart (1981).

Thus, when adopting a cognitive-behavioural model, a major task of therapy would be to help the patient to develop more realistic, functional ways of organising her internal world of thoughts and beliefs, as well as employing behavioural techniques to decrease maladaptive behaviours and to facilitate more positive behaviours. The reader is referred to de Silva (1995) for an overview of cognitive-behavioural models in eating disorders, and to Freeman (1995) for a summary of treatment.

Feminist models

Feminist models address themselves to the question of why the vast majority of individuals suffering from eating disorders are female and relate the development and maintenance of eating disorders to psychological and social factors relating to the position of women in society. Boskind-Lodahl (1976) has interpreted the anorexic's symptoms as a reflection of contemporary women's striving to please others and validate their self-worth from external sources, often by controlling their appearance. She believes that these women have never questioned their assumptions that wifehood, motherhood, and intimacy with men are the fundamental components of femininity. She also draws attention to the ascetic dimension of fasting, and the false sense of "power", "goodness", and "control" that this provides, and suggests that, in seeking to control bulimic behaviour, fasting represents a struggle against a part of the self.

In contrast, an alternative viewpoint is that the thin ideal emerged in relation to contemporary women's *increased* power, as a response to women "taking up too much space" (see Striegel-Moore, 1995, for a general review). This perspective sees the "thin ideal" as serving the function of controlling and containing women's social ambitions by redirecting their energies to realising a beauty ideal that is not readily attainable, and requires enormous effort to achieve. The fact that so few women can achieve this ideal can lead to feelings of shame and self-doubt which further undermine one's sense of self-empowerment.

Other writers, such as Marilyn Lawrence (1979, 1984, 1987), have placed great emphasis on the asceticism of fasting and suggested that the desire of the anorectic to engage in a battle with her body and to subdue and take control of it is the result of an underlying sense of lack of control in other areas of life. Lawrence (1979, p. 49) points out that anorexia typically develops at or around adolescence and is associated with young women "feeling caught up in a struggle for autonomy with which they felt unable to cope". She hypothesises that adolescence, which demands increased autonomy and independence from the individual, is especially problematic for young women. Girls are brought up to be "good" (i.e. passive and compliant) which makes it more difficult for females to negotiate the transition to independence. There has also been an historical association between sickliness and "femininity" (Ehrenreich & English, 1978). In contrast, a certain degree of resistance and rebellion is regarded as healthy in boys, which makes for a smoother passage to independence. It also leads to the development of true self-esteem based on the individual having a sense of genuine self-worth. In contrast, because passivity, compliance, and acquiescence to the needs of others are attributes that are encouraged in girls, the development of their self-esteem tends to be based on pleasing other people and meeting the needs of others. Thus, it is more difficult for girls to develop a sense of fundamental self-value and to take their own needs seriously.

This approach therefore suggests that, for the anorexic, anorexia nervosa represents the solution (albeit a maladaptive one) to a problem that she finds impossible to deal with in any other way at the time, with the symptoms of anorexia functioning as a protective outer shell that hides and protects the real, needy person inside. Lawrence also emphasises the theme of symbolic nurturing through feeding which appears recurrently throughout women's lives. The relationship that women have with food is frequently extremely ambivalent. For example, the role of being the provider of food for one's family is one that is often associated with feelings of guilt. If you give your children what they like to eat, the chances are that it is not good for them, whereas, if you provide healthy food, they will probably complain that they are being deprived and demand chips and confectionery! Ambivalence also pervades the area of women as eaters, because food is a source of pleasure that is "not allowed" for those who have the primary responsibility for providing it.

Other feminist writers have also focused on the role of women as providers and nurturers and how this occurs at the expense of their own physical and emotional needs, to the extent that many women do not even recognise their needs (e.g. Eichenbaum & Orbach, 1984; Orbach, 1979). For example, it is not uncommon for women to feed their families before they themselves eat, irrespective of how hungry they are themselves, and, as any woman who has cared for a very young baby will attest, one's need for essentials such as food, sleep, companionship, and time and space for oneself becomes totally subsumed under the demands and needs of the infant. Relationships with adults are not immune to this effect, and many women allow the needs and wishes of their partners to take precedence over their own, apparently without question.

This perspective views eating disorders as defensive, protecting the person concerned from having to acknowledge or address the conflict between her own unmet needs and those of other people. Thus, using this approach (and grossly simplifying matters) anorexia nervosa can be seen as a total denial of neediness; the behaviour, values, and professed beliefs of the individual with anorexia proclaim that she is without needs or desires, whether they be for food, warmth, relationships, sex, etc. The person who develops bulimia as a means of dealing with the issue of conflicting needs presents a much more ambivalent picture. Although the bulimic woman can take in food, which is symbolic of nurturance in general, she cannot retain it, and furthermore, often takes in "bad" food. Other areas of her life will also have this quality of ambivalence. For example, she may crave to have close relationships but feel overwhelmed when this becomes a possibility, and therefore withdraw. Some bulimic women can sustain relationships, but only with partners who are unsatisfying and incapable of meeting their real needs, just like "binge" food. Compulsive eating represents an attempt to meet emotional needs inappropriately, by using food. For example, as detailed by Orbach (1979), eating can provide an inappropriate means of dealing with feelings such as anxiety, boredom, and anger. For an anthology of feminist writing on eating disorders, see Fallon, Katzman, and Wooley (1994).

Psychodynamic models

Psychodynamic approaches stress the importance of internal, unconscious thoughts and hidden feelings in generating psycho-pathology. These approaches attempt to assess and, where appropriate, change a person's psychological make-up by dealing as directly as possible with thoughts, feelings, and desires. These models look at the internal world and the role of early relationships with others in forming that world. For the internal world of the adolescent, for example, psychodynamic models propose that when an individual is faced with painful, conflicting feelings (for example, the desire to become more independent conflicting with anxiety about becoming more separate from parents) or real external threat, defence mechanisms are summoned to protect the individual's sense of herself or her ego. Defence mechanisms are unconscious strategies (see Chapter 1) that offer some degree of protection from feeling bad. Using this model, one can conceptualise the aberrant behaviours associated with eating disorders as defensive, and therefore as protecting the person from painful feelings. For example, to simplify matters grossly, the total denial of needs that one sees in anorexia nervosa (e.g. the need for food, warmth, friendship, etc.) can be seen to protect the person from the realisation of how needy and vulnerable she feels. Bulimia and vomiting often enable the sufferer to dispose of bad feelings that she finds overwhelming or frightening (e.g. if she feels angry with someone close to her, bingeing and then being sick will make these feelings disappear as if by magic). Compulsive eating can represent an attempt to meet needs inappropriately by using food. Thus these behaviours can be viewed as protective, which helps to account for the fact that many people with eating disorders are extremely reluctant to give them up, and, even where they wish to do so, find this very difficult.

In providing a model for the formulation of the internal world, contemporary psychodynamic formulations of eating disorders have focused on object relations, that is, the internal or cognitive representations of very early relationships between mother and baby, and how this relates to later difficulties. Such theories would argue that as object relations are established early on in development and are unconscious they can remain unchanged, adversely affecting adult functioning. In terms of eating disorders, it has been suggested that the inner world of object relations typically generates fears for the consequences of getting close to others (Dare & Crowther, 1995a).

Bruch (1978) has suggested that infants who later develop anorexia nervosa are extremely well cared for, but that this is done according to the mother's decisions and feelings, not according to the child's demands. Thus, a mother may respond to her crying infant by always feeding her, rather than trying to discern whether her distress is attributable to needs other than hunger, such as needing to be changed, cuddled, and comforted, or provided with more or less warmth. The child thus fails to learn to differentiate between hunger and other sources of discomfort, and grows up unable to discriminate between different bodily sensations and without having a sense of control over them. The subsequent lack of autonomy and difficulties with decision making that manifest themselves are praised by parents and teachers as "special goodness", when in effect the young person is never testing her own ideas and capacities. Bruch suggested that anorexia nervosa develops when such individuals feel at a disadvantage, and represents a struggle for self-mastery and a self-respecting identity that is maladaptively pursued through control over one's body. It also represents an attempt to escape from the over-demanding role that the family, which may have extremely high achievement expectations, sets. An overview of psychodynamic models/eating disorders can be found in Dare and Crowther (1995b).

A key issue in the psychodynamic treatment of eating disorders, therefore, concerns the attempt to identify and help resolve the unconscious conflicts the eating disorder attempts to solve. For example, short-term focal psychotherapy for bulimia nervosa (interpersonal psychotherapy, IPT) seeks to identify and modify interpersonal problems such as unresolved grief and difficulties with relationships. One study found that although IPT did not appear as effective as cognitive-behavioural therapy at the end of treatment, it "caught up" over time and was just as effective at 1- and 6-year follow-up (Fairburn, Jones, Peveler, Hope, & O'Connor, 1993). Dare and Crowther (1995a) provide a description of a series of research trials conducted at the Maudsley Hospital that examine the efficacy of different therapies, including psychotherapy, for anorexia nervosa. This ongoing work will hopefully help to provide information about the outcome in patients with severe anorexia nervosa who undergo psychotherapy, and to clarify the factors that can help identify which patients are most likely to benefit from this form of treatment.

Social-cultural models

The fact that anorexia nervosa occurs with a particular age, sex, and social class distribution, as well as its apparent increased incidence, suggests that socio-cultural factors may play an important role in the development of the disorder. Socio-cultural models therefore examine how socio-cultural factors precipitate the disorder in those who are vulnerable or predisposed to developing it.

Several authors have stressed the important role that culture plays in the preferred or "ideal" appearance of women. For example, one can find examples throughout history of potentially unhealthy customs that derived from the expectation that women should conform to an idealised appearance, such as footbinding in China (Lyons & Petrucelli, 1978) and the wearing of corsets in 19th-century Europe (Vincent, 1979). As Garfinkel and Garner (1982) point out, particular illnesses have also been romanticised at times, and the characteristic look associated with them has become desirable. For example, the "look" associated with tuberculosis was glamorised in the 19th century and the tubercular appearance was thought to be a sign of a romantic personality (Sontag, 1978). Garner and Garfinkel suggest that thinness and anorexia nervosa have likewise been glamorised in the 20th century.

Some authors (Garner & Garfinkel, 1980; Garner, Garfinkel, & Olmstead, 1983) suggest that the current, and relatively recent, cultural emphasis on thinness in women represents an important social and cultural trend in the development of anorexia nervosa. They draw attention to how the conflict between the trend towards a smaller ideal shape, together with increases in actual body weights of females, can account for the persuasiveness of dieting among women (Dwyer, Feldman, Seltzer, & Mayer, 1969; Huenemann, Shapiro, Hampton, Mitchell, & Behnke, 1966; Jakobovits, Halstead, Kelley, Roe, & Young, 1977). Furthermore, there is indirect evidence that increased cultural pressure to diet and be slim facilitates the development of anorexia nervosa in individuals who must focus increased attention on a slim body (professional models and ballet students), particularly if they are in a competitive environment (Garner & Garfinkel, 1980). Other authors have focused on the changing role of women in society and social change generally, and how this relates to both the current "epidemic" of anorexia and bulimia, and the patterning of symptoms such as vomiting and hyperactivity. Brumberg (1988), for example, has pointed out that bulimia could only emerge as a prevalent syndrome in modern, industrial-capitalist societies; lack of privacy and basic plumbing and sanitary amenities would have made it extremely difficult for young women to adopt bulimic behaviour patterns in the 1800s, and a plentiful supply of pre-processed food is also necessary to live a bulimic lifestyle. Bingeing would be difficult, if not impossible, if one had to prepare "binge" foods, such as bread and cakes, from scratch.

Family models

Family theories of eating disorders assume that the family of the patient has a role in causing or maintaining the disorder. There are many schools of family therapy (see Chapter 8), but the basic model behind them is the same; the eating disorder in the patient is a symptom of underlying family disturbance.

Minuchin (1978) noted several cases in his own practice where adolescent patients showed considerable improvement in their eating problems when treated as inpatients in hospital, but relapsed soon after returning home. He proposed that relationships and processes in the family (the family "dynamics") in some way caused the patient to become ill again. A corollary of this proposal was that the patient's illness served an important function in the family and was necessary for the family's continued ability to function as a unit.

Attempts have been made to define the characteristics of families who have an anorexic member. For example, linked with the high incidence of the disorder in middle-class families, it has been suggested that the parents have very high performance expectations of their children and that this causes the children great stress. Another suggestion is that, in such families, open rebellion is not permitted for the adolescent children and so their teenage reaction against parental values will have to be covertly rather than openly expressed.

Some studies have examined the issue of sexual abuse in relation to eating disorders and typically report an incidence of about 30% (reviewed by Connors & Morse, 1993), that, although higher than the general population (15–30%), presents a relatively small difference.

Minuchin's clinical observations led him to develop a theory based on the functioning of the whole family. His "structural" theory describes the family structure which reflects healthy family relationships (see Chapter 8). In anorexic families he found a different structure. He described them as "enmeshed", that is, over involved with each other so that individuals in the family are too close to one another and the excessive togetherness leads to a lack of privacy. Members become unduly concerned about each other's welfare and they intrude on each other's thoughts and feelings. An additional feature of the families is the very high value they place on harmony. Open conflict is avoided and so underlying conflicts do not get addressed and dealt with.

Other family approaches present alternative descriptions. For example, Selvini-Palazzoli's (1974) description is of families with disturbed patterns of communication. Although contradiction is common in the family, there is little acknowledgement of conflict. The unspoken disagreements lead to covert coalitions and the child becomes a secret ally to both mother and father. The parents compete, for example, for a sense of moral superiority in who has made greater sacrifices for the sake of the family.

Both these theories emphasise how children reared in such families may have particular difficulty in becoming autonomous during adolescence. Although the theories present a model for understanding why someone in the family becomes ill, family theories generally do not explain why the illness that develops should be an eating disorder, nor why one child rather than another should become ill.

Carrying out research on families is extremely problematic; definitions of what constitutes normal family functioning and definitions of dimensions of family functioning are extremely difficult to derive. The family background and experiences of the researchers will colour their interpretation of any available definition. These points mean that more "objective" measures are attempted, but then the problem arises that if you measure simple, observable features of the family, how can you then infer anything about complex interrelationships and interactions within the family?

Research on families has provided some support for the theories. Bruch (1978) found that parents often suffered depression, and marital problems came out into the open when the anorexic child recovered. Kalucy, Crisp, and Harding (1977) found an unusual interest in food, weight, and shape in families of anorexic patients. Problems of dependency and insecurity were also common. Obesity was unusually common in the mothers, especially when the daughter suffered bulimic symptoms. A high incidence of alcoholism has been reported in the families, especially among the fathers. Martin (1983) found that anorexic families conformed to Minuchin's description of being enmeshed, but also found variation between families in the study. This variability has been repeatedly restated by other authors. In a review of questionnaire studies, Eisler (1995) noted that most "anorectic" families reported lower levels of closeness than they would ideally like, and that there was a tendency for these families to exhibit poor communication, especially affective (i.e. emotional) expression.

Research using family therapy as a treatment for anorexia nervosa indicates that it is more effective than individual, supportive psychotherapy for those with an early onset (less than 19 years of age) and shorter history (less than 3 years duration) of the disorder, a finding that holds at 5-year follow-up (Dare & Eisler, 1995). These authors also report that two-thirds of those treated with family therapy show a good or intermediate outcome at 1 year post-treatment, but that this method of treatment does not appear to benefit those suffering from bulimia nervosa. For some families where one or more parent demonstrates high expressed emotion (e.g. makes more critical comments than one would generally expect), family counselling has been shown to be more efficacious than conjoint family therapy in the treatment of anorexia nervosa.

INTEGRATION

Garfinkel and Garner (1982) emphasised that eating disorders are multidetermined: That is, there is no single cause but a number of factors that operate together. Those factors are the ones we have identified in this chapter, and they are relevant both to what triggers the disorder in the first place, and what then maintains it.

Cultural factors provide the setting in which norms and ideals exist and change over time. Those ideals that relate to body shape may be present with different intensities in different cultures and many authors have linked the intense pressure on young women to be thin in contemporary Western societies with the increase in incidence of anorexia nervosa and bulimia nervosa in the past 30 years. The feminist approaches link closely with this in looking at how women's position in society promotes the development of unhealthy eating patterns. These considerations, however, do not explain why different people react to the prevailing pressures in different ways.

If a girl or young woman in such a culture also grows up in a family where tension is not expressed and conformity is valued, the pressure to behave and appear in certain ways is further raised. Eating problems in one family member can lead to battles in the family (overt or covert) over who is in control of the eating. The issue of control is particularly live during adolescence, when the young person faces the developmental task of separating from her parents and developing her own autonomy. This task is typically acted out by rebelling against parental values and adopting those of the peer group. The adolescent can then reach her own compromise between the two sets of values to arrive at her own way of seeing things. In families that cannot tolerate the rebellion or the autonomy of the young person, the process may become blocked, and if the block is severe, battles over autonomy may become pathological (e.g. if they are always over food) and lead to the development of eating problems.

Apart from external factors, there are features of the individual which influence whether or not she will develop eating problems. Her very early relationships influence how she experiences things in later life. If food is provided whenever she is upset, the child will come to link eating with the alleviation of not only hunger but also loneliness or other discomfort. Food will then hold an inflated place in her life. Alternatively, if the child experiences withdrawal of love and affection by her mother whenever she does not perform mother's wishes, she may come to work hard at pleasing her mother in order to keep her love. Conforming to what the mother wants includes, in most families, issues around accepting food prepared by the mother. In both of these examples, feeding and emotional satisfaction or deprivation are linked. This link then influences how the individual thinks and behaves over food.

Given this complicated backdrop of pressures and influences, external events may bring things to a head. Stress, either acute or long term, which lowers the self-worth and sense of self-control of a young girl, may lead to something of a crisis. If her response to these feelings is to diet in order to enhance her self-image, or to eat increasing amounts for comfort or other satisfaction, food and dieting then become bound up with the problems. The dieting may be experienced as successful, or compelling to continue if partly successful, and may increasingly take over. Similarly, overeating may be experienced as satisfying in some way. The person may find that it offers many secondary gains, added to which chronic and severe dieting, or chronic overeating, will lead to physiological changes in her body. The complex cycle of underlying problems and eating-related symptoms is then established.

Many factors in the individual, family, and culture may play a role in eating disorders. Exact causal mechanisms are not known, but the disorders are syndromes that are the result of an interaction of a number of forces. These forces predispose the individual to develop an eating disorder, precipitate its emergence, and maintain it once it has started. For any individual, the circumstances contributing will interact in a complex way.

Research has not been done on why other vulnerable individuals, such as sisters of patients, do not develop the disorder. It is clear that many people have the individual, family, and cultural characteristics we have described, and these lead to the development of a full-blown eating disorder within the context of stressors that initiate dieting, weight loss, and the pursuit of thinness. Eating disorders are not discrete identifiable illnesses, but people show degrees of eating-related pathology, the extremes of which are called anorexia nervosa, bulimia nervosa, or obesity.

RECOMMENDED READING

Crisp, A.H. (1980). *Anorexia nervosa: Let me be.* London: Academic Press.

This presents the view that anorexia nervosa represents a psycho-biological regression, and includes many references to research, while remaining readable.

Garfinkel, P.E., & Garner, D.M. (1982). *Anorexia nervosa: A multidimensional perspective.* New York: Brunner Mazel.

A useful reference book which covers the main factors which contribute to eating problems; it is the closest to a textbook of anorexia nervosa.

Garner, D.M., & Garfinkel, P.E. (1997). *Handbook of treatment for eating disorders* (2nd ed.). New York: Guilford Press.

Macleod, S. (1981). *The art of starvation*. London: Virago.

An extremely thoughtful first-hand account of the experience of suffering from anorexia nervosa that was MIND book of the year.

Schmidt, U., & Treasure, J. (1993). *Getting better bit(e) by bit(e): A survival kit for sufferers of bulimia nervosa and binge eating disorders*. Hove, UK: Psychology Press.

Treasure, J. (1997). *Anorexia nervosa: A survivor's guide for families, friends, friends and sufferers*. Hove, UK: Psychology Press.

REFERENCES

Abraham, S.F., & Beaumont, P.J.V. (1982). How patients describe bulimia or binge eating. *Psychological Medicine*, *12*, 625–635.

American Psychiatric Association (1994). *Diagnostic and statistical manual of mental disorders* (4th ed.). Washington, DC: American Psychiatric Association.

Beck, A.T. (1976). *Cognitive Therapy and the emotional disorders*. New York: International Universities Press.

Bemis, K.M. (1978). Current approaches to the etiology and treatment of anorexia nervosa. *Psychological Bulletin*, *85*, 593–617.

Bicknell, D.J. (1975). *Pica*. London: Butterworths.

Boskind-Lodahl, M. (1976). "Cinderella's stepsister": A feminist perspective on Anorexia and Bulimia. *SIGNS: Journal of Women in Culture and Society*, *2*, 342–356.

Bray, G.A. (Ed.). (1979). *Obesity in America*. Proceedings of the 2nd Fogarty International Centre Conference on Obesity (No. 79). Washington, DC: US DHEW.

Brownell, K.D. (1995). Definition and classification of obesity. In K.D. Brownell & C.G. Fairburn (Eds.), *Eating disorders and obesity: A comprehensive handbook* (pp. 386–390). New York: Guilford Press.

Bruch, H. (1962). Perceptual and conceptual disturbances in anorexia nervosa. *Psychosomatic Medicine*, *24*, 187–194.

Bruch, H. (1977). Psychological antecedents of anorexia nervosa. In R. Vigersky (Ed.), *Anorexia nervosa* (pp. 1–10). New York: Raven Press.

Bruch, H. (1978). *The golden cage: The enigma of anorexia nervosa*. Cambridge, MA: Harvard University Press.

Brumberg, J.J. (1988). *Fasting girls: The emergence of anorexia nervosa as a modern disease*. Cambridge, MA: Harvard University Press.

Canning, H., & Mayer, J. (1966). Obesity: Its possible effect on college acceptance. *New England Journal of Medicine*, *275*, 1172–1174.

Cannon, G., & Einzig, H. (1983). *Dieting makes you fat*. London: Century.

Casper, R.C., & Davis, J.M. (1977). On the course of anorexia nervosa. *American Journal of Psychiatry*, *134*, 974–978.

Casper, R.C., Eckert, E.D., Halmi, K.A., Goldberg, S.C., & Davis, J.M. (1980). Bulimia: Its incidence and clinical importance in patients with anorexia nervosa. *Archives of General Psychiatry*, *37*, 1030–1035.

Coddington, R.D., & Bruch, H. (1970). Gastric perceptivity in normal, obese and schizophrenic subjects. *Psychosomatics*, *11*, 571–579.

Connors, M., & Morse, W. (1993). Sexual abuse and eating disorders: A review. *International Journal of Eating Disorders*, *13*, 1–11.

Crisp, A.H. (1980). Sleep, activity, nutrition and mood. *British Journal of Psychiatry*, *137*, 1–7.

Crisp, A.H., Callender, J.S., Halek, C., & Hsu, L.K.G. (1992). Long-term mortality in anorexia nervosa: A 20-year follow-up of the St George's and Aberdeen Cohorts. *British Medical Journal*, *161*, 104–107.

Crisp, A.H., Kalucy, R.S., Lacey, J.H., & Harding, B. (1977). The long-term prognosis in anorexia nervosa: Some factors predictive of outcome. In R. Vigersky (Ed.), *Anorexia nervosa*. New York: Raven Press.

Crisp, A.H., Palmer, R.L., & Kalucy, R.S. (1976). How common is anorexia nervosa? A prevalence study. *British Journal of Psychiatry*, *218*, 549–554.

Crisp, A.H., Stonehill, E., & Fenton, G.W. (1971). The relationship between sleep, nutrition and mood: A study of patients with anorexia nervosa. *Postgraduate Medical Journal*, *47*, 207–213.

Crisp, A.H., & Toms, D.A. (1972). Primary anorexia nervosa or weight phobia in the male: Report on 13 cases. *British Medical Journal*, *1*, 334–338.

Dare, C., & Crowther, C. (1995a). Living dangerously: Psychoanalytic psychotherapy of anorexia nervosa. In G. Szmukler, C. Dare, & J. Treasure (Eds.), *Handbook of eating disorders*. Chichester, UK: John Wiley & Sons.

Dare, C., & Crowther, C. (1995b). Psychodynamic models of eating disorders. In G. Szmukler, C. Dare, & J. Treasure (Eds.), *Handbook of eating disorders*. Chichester, UK: John Wiley & Sons.

Dare, C., & Eisler, I. (1995). Family therapy. In G. Szmukler, C. Dare, & J. Treasure (Eds.), *Handbook of eating disorders*. Chichester, UK: John Wiley & Sons.

De Silva, P. (1995). Cognitive-behavioural models of eating disorders. In G. Szmukler, C. Dare, & J. Treasure (Eds.), *Handbook of eating disorders*. Chichester, UK: John Wiley & Sons.

DHSS/MRC. (1976). *Report on research on obesity* (Compiler W.P.T. James). London: HMSO.

Dubois, A., Gross, H.A., Ebert, M.H., & Castell, D.O. (1979). Altered gastric emptying and secretion in primary anorexia nervosa. *Gastroenterology*, *77*, 319–323.

Dwyer, J. (1995). Popular diets. In K.D. Brownell & C.G. Fairburn (Eds.), *Eating disorders and obesity: A comprehensive handbook* (pp. 491–497). New York: Guilford Press.

Dwyer, J.T., Feldman, J.J., Seltzer, C.C., & Mayer, J. (1969). Body image in adolescents: Attitudes toward weight and perception of appearance. *Journal of Nutritional Education*, *1*, 14–19.

Ehrenreigh, B., & English, D. (1978). *For her own good: 150 years of the experts'advice to women*. New York: Pluto Press.

Eichenbaum, L., & Orbach, S. (1984). *What do women want?* London: Fontana.

Eisler, I. (1995). Family models of eating disorders. In G. Szmukler, C. Dare, & J. Treasure (Eds.), *Handbook of eating disorders* (pp. 155–176). Chichester, UK: John Wiley & Sons.

Epstein, L.H., Valoski, A., Wing, R.R., & McCurley, J. (1994). Ten-year outcomes of behavioural family-based treatment of childhood obesity. *Health Psychology*, *13*, 573–583.

Fairburn, C.G. (1980). Self-induced vomiting. *Journal of Psychosomatic Research*, *24*, 193–197.

Fairburn, C.G., & Cooper, P.J. (1983). The epidemiology of bulimia nervosa. *International Journal of Eating Disorders*, *2*, 61–67.

Fairburn, C.G., Jones, R., Peveler, R.C., Hope, R.A., & O'Connor, M. (1993). Psychotherapy and bulimia nervosa: The longer-term effects of interpersonal psychotherapy, behaviour therapy and cognitive behaviour therapy. *Archives of General Psychiatry*, *50*, 419–428.

Fallon, P., Katzman, M.A., & Wooley, S.C. (1994). *Feminist perspectives on eating disorders*. New York: Guilford.

Farquharson, R.F., & Hyland, H.H. (1966). Anorexia nervosa: The course of 15 patients treated from 20 to 30 years previous. *Canadian Medical Association Journal*, *94*, 411–419.

Freeman, C. (1995). Cognitive therapy. In G. Szmukler, C. Dare, & J. Treasure (Eds.), *Handbook of eating disorders* (pp. 309–332). Chichester, UK: John Wiley & Sons.

Fries, H. (1977). Studies on secondary amenorrhoea, anorectic behaviour, and body image perception: Importance for the early recognition of anorexia nervosa. In R. Vigersky (Ed.), *Anorexia nervosa*. New York: Raven Press.

Garfinkel, P.E. (1974). Perception of hunger and satiety in anorexia nervosa. *Psychological Medicine, 4*, 309–315.

Garfinkel, P.E., & Garner, D.M. (1982). *Anorexia nervosa: A multidimensional perspective*. New York: Brunner Mazel.

Garfinkel, P.E., Kline, S.A., & Stancer, H.C. (1973). Treatment of anorexia nervosa using operant conditioning techniques. *Journal of Nervous and Mental Disease, 157*, 428–433.

Garfinkel, P.E., Moldofsky, H., & Garner, D.M. (1980). The heterogeneity of anorexia nervosa: Bulimia as a distinct subgroup. *Archives of General Psychiatry, 37*, 1036–1040.

Garfinkel, P.E., Moldofsky, H., Garner, D.M., Stancer, H.C., & Coscina, D.V. (1978). Body awareness in anorexia nervosa: Disturbance in body image and satiety. *Psychosomatic Medicine, 40*, 487–498.

Garner, D.M., & Bemis, K. (1982). A cognitive-behavioural approach to anorexia nervosa. *Cognitive therapy and research, 6*, 1–27.

Garner, D.M., & Garfinkel, P.E. (1980). Socio-cultural factors in the development of anorexia nervosa. *Psychological Medicine, 10*, 647–656.

Garner, D.M., Garfinkel, P.E., & Olmstead, M.P. (1983). An overview of sociocultural factors in the development of anorexia nervosa. In P.L. Darby et al. (Eds.), *Anorexia: Recent developments in research*. New York: Alan R. Liss.

Garrow, J.S. (1981). Obesity and energy balance. In A.M. Dawson, N. Compston, & G.M. Besser (Eds.), *Recent advances in medicine* (No. 18, pp. 75–92). London: Churchill Livingstone.

Grilo, C.M., Brownall, K.D., & Stunkard, A.J. (1993). The metabolic and psychological importance of exercise in weight control. In A.J. Stunkard & T.A. Wadden (Eds.), *Obesity: theory and therapy* (2nd ed., pp. 253–273). New York: Raven Press.

Gull, W.W. (1874). Anorexia nervosa (apepsia hysterica, anorexia hysterica). *Trans. Clin. Soc. London, 7*, 22–28.

Halmi, K.A. (1995). Current concepts and definitions. In G. Szmukler, C. Dare, & J. Treasure (Eds.), *Handbook of eating disorders*. Chichester, UK: John Wiley & Sons.

Halmi, K.A., Falk, J.R., & Schwartz, E. (1981). Binge eating and vomiting: A summary of a college population. *Psychological Medicine, 11*, 697–706.

Halmi, K.A., Powers, P., & Cunningham, S. (1975). Treatment of anorexia nervosa with behaviour modification. *Archives of General Psychiatry, 32*, 92–96.

Hawkins, R.C., & Clement, P.F. (1980). Development and construct validation of a self-report measure of binge eating. *Addictive Behaviour, 5*, 219–226.

Herman, C.P., & Polivy, J. (1984). A boundary model for the regulation of eating. In A.J. Stunkard, & E. Stellar (Eds.), *Eating and its disorders* (pp. 141–156). New York: Raven.

Herzog, W., Deter, H.C., Schelberg, D., Seilkopf, S., Sarembe, E., Kroger, F., Minne, H., Mayer, H., & Petzold, (1992). Somatic findings at 12 year follow up of 103 anorexia nervosa patients: Results of the Heidelberg-Mannheim follow up. In W. Herzog et al. (Eds.). Berlin, German: Springer-Verlag.

Hsu, L.K.G. (1995). Outcome of bulimia nervosa. In K.D. Brownell & C.G. Fairburn (Eds.), *Eating disorders and obesity: A comprehensive handbook* (pp. 238–244). New York: Guilford Press.

Hsu, L.K.G., Crisp, A.H., & Harding, B. (1979). Outcome of anorexia nervosa. *Lancet, 1*, 61–65.

Huenemann, R.L., Shapiro, L.R., Hampton, M.C., Mitchell, B.W., & Behnke, R.A. (1966). A longitudinal study of gross body composition and body conformation and their association with food and activity in a teenage population: Views of teenage subjects on body conformation, food, and activity. *American Journal of Clinical Nutrition, 18*, 325–338.

Hurd, H.P., Palumbo, P.J., & Gharib, H. (1977). Hypothalamatic-endocrine dysfunction in anorexia nervosa. *Mayo Clinic Proceedings*, *52*, 711–716.

Jakobovits, C., Halstead, P., Kelley, L., Roe, D.A., & Young, C.M. (1977). Eating habits and nutrient intakes of college women over a thirty year period. *Journal of the American Dietetic Association*, *71*, 405–411.

Johnson, C., & Larson, R. (1982). Bulimia: An analysis of mood and behaviour. *Psychosomatic Medicine*, *44*, 341–351.

Jones, D.J., Fox, M.M., Babigan, H.M., & Hutton, H.E. (1980). Epidemiology of anorexia nervosa in Monroe County, New York: 1960–1976. *Psychosomatic Medicine*, *42*, 551–558.

Kalucy, R.S., Crisp, A.H., & Harding, B. (1977). A study of 56 families with anorexia nervosa. *British Journal of Medical Psychology*, *50*, 381–395.

Kendler, K.S., Maclean, C., Neale, M., Kessler, R., Heath, A., & Eaves, L. (1991). The genetic epidemiology of bulimia nervosa. *American Journal of Psychiatry*, *148*, 1627–1627.

Keys, A., Brozek, J., Henschel, A., Mickelsen, O., & Taylor, H.L. (1950). *The biology of human starvation* (2 vols). Minneapolis, MN: University of Minnesota Press.

Lacey, J.H. (1983). The bulimia syndrome at normal body weight: Reflections on pathogenesis and clinical features. *International Journal of Eating Disorders*, *2*, 59–62.

Lasegue, C. (1873). De l'anorexie hysterique. *Archives Générales de Médicine*, *21*, 385–403.

Lawrence, M. (1979). Anorexia nervosa: The control paradox. *Women's Studies International Quarterly*, *2*, 93–101.

Lawrence, M. (1984). *The anorexic experience*. London: The Women's Press.

Lawrence, M. (Ed.). (1987). *Fed up and hungry: Women, oppression and food*. London: The Women's Press.

Lew, E.A., & Garfinkel, L. (1979). Variations in mortality by weight among 750,000 men and women. *Journal of Chronic Diseases*, *32*, 563.

Lucas, A.R., Beard, C.M., O'Fallon, W.M., & Kurland, L.T. (1991). 50 year trends in the incidence of anorexia nervosa in Rochester, Minn: A population-based study. *American Journal of Psychiatry*, *148*, 917–922.

Lucas, A.R., & Soundy, T.J. (1993). The rise of bulimia nervosa. In *Proceedings of the Ninth World Congress of Psychiatry*, Rio de Janeiro, Brazil, 6–12 June (Abstract 544, p. 139).

Lyons, A.S., & Petrucelli, R.J. (1978). *Medicine: An illustrated history*. New York: Harry N. Abrams.

Marshall, M.H. (1978). Anorexia nervosa: Dietary treatment and re-establishment of body weight in 20 cases studied on a metabolic unit. *Journal of Human Nutrition*, *32*, 349–357.

Martin, F. (1983). Subgroups in anorexia nervosa. In P.L. Darby et al. (Eds.), *Anorexia nervosa: Recent developments in research*. New York: Alan R. Liss.

Millican, F.K., Lourie, R.S., & Layman, E.M. (1956). Emotional factors in the aetiology and treatment of lead poisoning. *American Journal of Disorders of Childhood*, *91*, 144–150.

Minuchin, S. (1978). The psychosomatic family. In S. Minuchin, B.L. Rosman, & L. Baker (Eds.), *Psychosomatic families*. Cambridge, MA: Harvard University Press.

Morgan, H.S., & Russell, G.F.M. (1975). Value of family background and clinical features as predictors of long term outcome in anorexia nervosa: Four year follow up study of 41 patients. *Psychological Medicine*, *5*, 355–371.

Office of Population Censuses and Surveys. (1981). *OPCS Monitor* (Ref. SS 81/1).

Olmstead, M.P., Kaplan, A.S., & Rockert, W. (1984). Rate and prediction of relapse in bulimia nervosa. *American Journal of Psychiatry*, *151*, 738–743.

O'Neil, P.M., Currey, H.S., Sexaner, J.D., Riddle, F.E., & Molony-Sinnot, V. (1980). Persistence at three year follow up of male–female differences in weight loss. In *Abstracts of the Third International Congress on Obesity: Vol. 1. Alimentazione, Nutrizione, Metabolismo* (p. 333).

Orbach, S. (1979). *Fat is a feminist issue*. London: Hamlyn.

Parry-Jones, B. (1991). Historical terminology of eating disorders. *Psychological Medicine*, *21*, 21–28.

Patton, G.C. (1988). Mortality in eating disorders. *Psychological Medicine, 18*, 947–951.

Pyle, R.L., Mitchell, J.E., & Eckert, E.D. (1981). Bulimia: A report of 34 cases. *Journal of Clinical Psychiatry, 42*, 60–64.

Ratnasuriya, R.H., Eisler, I., Szmukler, G.I., & Russell, G.F.M. (1991). Anorexia nervosa: Outcomes and prognostic factors after 20 years. *British Journal of Psychiatry, 158*, 495–502.

Richardson, S.N. (1961). Cultural uniformity and reaction to physical disability. *American Sociology Review, 26*, 241–247.

Rimm, A.A., Werner, L.H., van Yserloo, B., & Bernstein, R.A. (1975). Relationship of obesity and disease in 73,532 weight-conscious women. *Public Health Report, 90*, 44.

Rosen, J.C., & Leitenberg, H. (1982). Bulimia nervosa: Treatment with exposure and response prevention. *Behaviour Therapy, 13*, 117–124.

Royal College of Physicians. (1983). Obesity: A report of the Royal College of Physicians. *Journal of the Royal College of Physicians, 17*, No. 1, January.

Russell, G.F.M. (1979). Bulimia nervosa: An ominous variant of anorexia nervosa. *Psychological Medicine, 9*, 429–448.

Russell, G.F.M. (1995). Anorexia nervosa through time. In G. Szmukler, C. Dare, & J. Treasure (Eds.), *Handbook of eating disorders* (pp. 5–17). Chichester, UK: John Wiley & Sons.

Schiele, B.C., & Brozek, J. (1948). "Experimental neurosis" resulting from semi-starvation in man. *Psychosomatic Medicine, 10*, 31–50.

Selvini-Palazzoli, M. (1974). *Self-starvation*. London: Chaucer.

Slimming foods face new curbs. (1980). *Marketing, 3*(4), pp. 20–21.

Sobal, J. (1995). Social influences on body weight. In K.D. Brownell & C.G. Fairburn (Eds.), *Eating disorders and obesity: A comprehensive handbook* (pp. 73–92). New York: Guilford Press.

Sontag, S. (1978). *Illness as metaphor*. New York: Farrar, Straus & Giroux.

Staffieri, J.R. (1967). A study of social stereotypes of body image in children. *Journal of Personality and Social Psychology, 7*, 101–104.

Stark, O., Atkins, E., Wolff, O.H., & Douglas, J.W.B. (1981). Longitudinal study of obesity in the National Survey of Health and Development. *British Medical Journal, 283*, 13.

Striegel-Moore, R.H. (1995). A feminist perspective on the etiology of eating disorders. In K.D. Brownell & C.G. Fairburn (Eds.), *Eating disorders and obesity: A comprehensive handbook* (pp. 224–229). New York: Guilford Press.

Stunkard, A.J., & Penick, S.B. (1979). Behaviour modification in the treatment of obesity: The problem of maintaining weight loss. *Archives of General Psychiatry, 36*, 801.

Stunkard, A.J., & Sobal, J. (1995). Psychosocial consequences of obesity. In K.D. Brownell & C.G. Fairburn (Eds.), *Eating disorders and obesity: A comprehensive handbook* (pp. 417–421). New York: Guilford Press.

Stuart, R.B. (1967). Behavioural control of overeating. *Behaviour, Research and Therapy, 5*, 357.

Theander, S. (1970). Anorexia nervosa: A psychiatric investigation of 94 female patients. *Acta Psychiatrica Scandinavica* (Suppl. 214), 1–194.

Theander, S. (1983). Long-term prognosis of anorexia nervosa: A preliminary report. In P.L. Darby et al. (Eds.), *Anorexia nervosa: Recent developments in research*. New York: Alan R. Liss.

Treasure, J., & Szmukler, G. (1995). Medical complications of chronic anorexia nervosa. In G. Szmukler, C. Dare, & J. Treasure (Eds.), *Handbook of eating disorders* (pp. 197–220). Chichester, UK: John Wiley & Sons.

Vincent, L.M. (1979). *Competing with the sylph: Dancers and the pursuit of the ideal body form*. New York: Andrews & McMeel.

Wardle, J. (1980). Dietary restraint and binge eating. *Behavioural Analysis and Modification, 4*, 201–209.

Wardle, J., & Beinart, H. (1981). Binge eating: A theoretical review. *British Journal of Clinical Psychology, 20*, 97–109.

Williams, E. (1958). Anorexia nervosa: A somatic disorder. *British Medical Journal, 2*, 190–195.

Williamson, D.F. (1995). Prevalence and demographics of obesity. In K.D. Brownell & C.G. Fairburn (Eds.), *Eating disorders and obesity: A comprehensive handbook* (pp. 391–395). New York: Guilford Press.

Williamson, D.A., Davis, C.J., Duchman, G.G., McKenzie, S.J., & Watkins, P.C. (1990). *Assessment of eating disorders: Obesity, anorexia and bulimia nervosa*. New York: Pergamon.

Wilson, G.T. (1989). The treatment of bulimia nervosa: A cognitive-social learning analysis. In A.J. Stunkard & A. Baum (Eds.), *Perspectives in behavioural medicine: Eating sleeping and sex*. Hillsdale, NJ: Lawrence Erlbaum Associates Inc.

Wilson, G.T. (1995). Behavioural approaches to the treatment of obesity. In K.D. Brownell & C.G. Fairburn (Eds.), *Eating disorders and obesity: A comprehensive handbook* (pp. 479–483). New York: Guilford Press.

CHAPTER SIX

Obsessive-compulsive disorder

Padmal de Silva
Department of Psychology, Institute of Psychiatry, London, UK

INTRODUCTION

Obsessive-compulsive disorder is one of the conditions traditionally considered as a neurotic disorder. In psychiatric classificatory systems, it is listed among anxiety disorders; the others in the category include phobias, generalised anxiety disorder, panic disorder, and post-traumatic stress disorder. The literature on obsessive-compulsive disorder is extensive and growing, and excellent clinical accounts and experimental reports are available. The features of the disorder are well recognised, and are in many ways fascinating.

Essentially, obsessive-compulsive disorder is characterised by *obsessions* (unwanted, intrusive and repetitive thoughts, images, or impulses) and/or *compulsions* (purposeful, stereotyped behaviours carried out with a sense of compulsion). For a person to be diagnosed as suffering from this condition, he or she would have either obsessions, or compulsions, or both. It is, however, not the mere presence of these that makes someone a candidate for this diagnosis; most people have obsessions and/or compulsions. Many people have fleeting unwanted thoughts that intrude into their consciousness. Studies have shown that over 75% of normal adults experience these. Equally, many have various compulsive behaviours such as checking light switches or door handles more than once. It is when the obsessions and/or compulsions are so intensive or pervasive that one is distressed by them, or they interfere with one's life and activities, that one is considered to be suffering from obsessive-compulsive disorder in the clinical sense. This highlights an important point: Obsessive-compulsive problems are not qualitatively different from normal behaviour. They are within the spectrum of normal behaviour, and become a problem only when excessive.

131

A brief word is necessary here about obsessional personality or character. The obsessional personality is generally considered as characterised by orderliness, meticulousness, parsimony, neatness, and perfectionism. Some consider obsessive-compulsive disorder to be necessarily related to obsessional personality (e.g. Reed, 1985). However, clinical evidence shows that many obsessive-compulsive patients do not have a premorbid obsessional personality (Lewis, 1965). Equally, a large majority of individuals with an obsessional personality do not develop the disorder at all (Pollak, 1979).

HISTORICAL AND CULTURAL ASPECTS

The nature and features of the disorder were described in detail by early European authors such as Freud (1895), Janet (1903), and Jaspers (1923/1963). Esquirol in 1838 and Westphal in 1878 had earlier given several descriptions identifying obsessions and compulsions. Historically, the phenomenon had been described or alluded to in much earlier times, though not recognised as a clinical entity. Shakespeare's description of Lady Macbeth's hand-washing rituals is well known and much quoted. John Bunyan, the author of *Pilgrim's Progress*, suffered considerably from obsessional thoughts of a blasphemous nature, by his own account. A similar example from a different part of the world is that of the Japanese Zen Buddhist master Hakuin (1685–1768), who is described as having had severe obsessional problems as a young man (Kishimoto, 1985). A very early Buddhist text describes a monk in the Buddha's time (563–483 BC), who repeatedly engaged in ritualistically sweeping the monastery, an activity that took priority over everything else (see de Silva & Rachman, 1998).

It is clear, then, that obsessive-compulsive problems are not a new phenomenon. Nor are they confined to the industrialised West. In fact, many descriptions of the disorder have come from such distant countries as Hong Kong, India, Israel, Pakistan, Sri Lanka, and Taiwan. The basic features are the same in all of these places. Yaryura-Tobias and Neziroglu (1997) have given a useful review of the cultural aspects of obsessive-compulsive disorder.

NATURE OF OBSESSIVE-COMPULSIVE DISORDER

It will be useful, at this stage, to give an account of the nature of obsessive-compulsive problems. This is best done in two ways: first, by looking closely at the phenomenology, and second, by describing the main clinical presentations.

Phenomenology

The major aspects of the disorder are obsessions and compulsions. As noted earlier, an obsession is an unwanted, intrusive cognition that is repetitive, persistent and generally resisted. It can take the form of a thought, an image, or an impulse, and is often a combination of two or all three of these. Here are some clinical examples:

• Thought that he was polluted by germs (male, 26 years).
• Thought, plus visual image, that he may have knocked someone down (male, 29 years).
• Thought, with vivid visual images, that her husband would die in a road traffic accident (female, 31 years).
• Image of her parents lying dead (female, 23 years).
• Impulse, with associated doubting thought, to shout obscenities during a church service (female, 19 years).
• Impulse, with visual images, to harm herself by burning her eyes with a lighted cigarette (female, 28 years).

Compulsions are repetitive and seemingly purposeful behaviours that are performed in a stereotyped way or according to certain rules. The compulsion is carried out because of a strong subjectively felt urge to do so, although the person often tries to resist this urge. Unlike the obsession, which is essentially a passive experience (it *happens* to the person), a compulsion is an active experience; the person *does* it, despite not wanting to. Here are some clinical examples:

• Checking door handles, gas taps, electric switches, etc. three times on every occasion he went past them (male, 29 years).
• Imagining sequence of photographs of family members (male, 38 years).
• Saying certain phrases silently four times (female, 26 years).
• Counting backwards from twenty-one (male, 21 years).
• Repeatedly and extensively washing hands, to "get rid of contamination by germs" (female, 18 years).

In most cases an obsession leads to a compulsion, although obsessions without an associated compulsion are not rare. Less frequent are compulsions without a preceding obsession. The relationship between the obsession and the compulsion is perhaps best understood in the context of all the key elements which may be involved in an obsessive-compulsive experience. These are presented in Fig. 6.1.

This scheme will fit many obsessive-compulsive episodes. This is not to say that all the elements given in Fig. 6.1 are found in every single obsessional experience; nor is there always an invariant sequence of them, although most would follow the order given under A (i to vi). A patient's main problem may be the recurrent intrusion (Aii) of the thought and associated visual image that he may have killed someone. This thought might be triggered (Ai) by the hearing or reading of news of murders and other violent acts (external trigger) and, less frequently, whenever he remembers a deceased relative (internal trigger). The

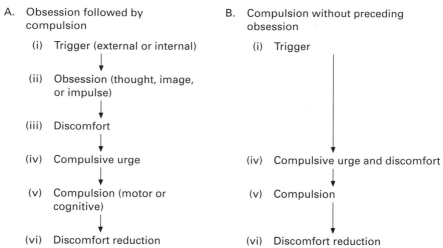

A. Obsession followed by
    compulsion

    (i)   Trigger (external or internal)

    (ii) Obsession (thought, image,
        or impulse)

   (iii) Discomfort

    (iv) Compulsive urge

    (v)   Compulsion (motor or
        cognitive)

    (vi) Discomfort reduction

B. Compulsion without preceding
    obsession

    (i)   Trigger

    (iv) Compulsive urge and discomfort

    (v)   Compulsion

    (vi) Discomfort reduction

FIG. 6.1   Elements of an obsessive-compulsive sequence. The figure illustrates two possible sequences: (A) in which an obsession is followed by a compulsion, and (B) in which a compulsion occurs without a preceding obsession. The elements are labelled A(i), A(ii), etc., in order to illustrate the similarities and differences between the sequence.

cognition is hard to dismiss and results in a strong feeling of discomfort, or even anxiety (Aiii). Associated with this may be a sharply felt urge (Aiv) to look at his hands. More often than not he will yield to this urge and so indulge in this compulsive behaviour (Av). The compulsion may well follow a set pattern with his looking first at the left hand and then at the right with the whole sequence being followed three times. Completion of the compulsion markedly reduces the feeling of discomfort (Avi). This marks the end of the obsessive-compulsive episode and the patient may then be relatively free of this experience for several hours until the whole sequence gets started once more.

In other examples, a trigger may lead to an intrusive image, and to discomfort, with a compulsive urge that is translated into cognitive compulsive behaviour. A woman complained of being assailed by images (Aii) of asymmetrical patterns or objects. In her case the compulsive behaviour (Av) was to imagine or visualise the offending patterns or objects in a perfect symmetrical form. Doing so brought relief (Avi). Other instances may only involve the distressing intrusive cognition without any compulsive act or urge. A young woman had intrusive and recurrent thoughts and images of her wedding (Aii). The cognitions particularly centred on the flower arrangements at the reception, which she felt were not right. These thoughts assailed her repetitively, they were hard to dismiss, and caused distress (Aiii). She had no associated compulsive behaviour, either overt or covert.

As also shown in Fig. 6.1, a small number of cases have a compulsive urge with resultant compulsive behaviour, but with no preceding obsession. An example is the case of a young woman who always had to look at the four corners (Bv) of any room she entered. Entering a room was the trigger (Bi) for this urge (Biv), but there was no intrusive cognition (obsession). Finally, there are a small number of cases where the carrying out of the compulsive behaviour does not bring about a reduction of the discomfort/anxiety and may even increase it.

The previous account and examples do not illustrate a number of factors which may be present in a good number of cases. Fears of disaster are common and can be manifest at the occurrence of the obsession, or even upon exposure to the trigger. They contribute to the discomfort felt by the person and thus to the strength of the compulsive urge. Many patients resort to reassurance seeking, which they usually receive from their family members. Often an obsessional thought in the form of a doubt (e.g. "Did I do it correctly?", or "Was it done the right way?") leads to this externally elicited form of relief. Avoidance is found in many cases where there is a clear external trigger to set off the whole experience. Thus, a woman who gets the thought that she might attack children with knives or other sharp objects, mainly in the presence of such items, may avoid knives, scissors, etc. when she is on her own. Patients who have obsessions about contamination by dirt or germs, usually leading to extensive cleaning and washing rituals if exposed to stimuli that they believe are contaminating, tend to avoid such situations as far as possible. Many with contamination fears avoid touching things handled by others, such as public telephones or door handles in public places. In extreme cases a patient may have only a small safe area in the home where he/she can move about freely. A patient may not wash in the morning because this behaviour requires a long, complicated ritual. Another may go to bed in his day clothes to avoid prolonged and exhausting compulsions involved in changing.

It has already been mentioned that both the obsession and the compulsion may be resisted by the sufferer. In his much quoted paper, Sir Aubrey Lewis (1936) argued that an essential feature of obsessive-compulsive disorder was the strong resistance that the patient had. More recent studies (e.g. Rachman & Hodgson, 1980; Stern & Cobb, 1978) have shown that, although resistance is very common, it is not found invariably. It is possible that in the early stages a patient may resist his or her obsessions and/or compulsive urges strenuously, but after repeated failures over a period of time may begin to show much less resistance. There are chronic obsessive-compulsive patients where resistance to symptoms is quite low (de Silva & Rachman, 1998; Rasmussen & Tsuang, 1986).

Two other terms used to describe aspects of obsessive-compulsive disorders need to be mentioned. A *ritual* in the present context is a compulsive behaviour, either overt or covert, which has a rigid set pattern or sequence of steps with a clear-cut beginning and end. An example is a checking ritual where a system of checks is carried out in an invariant sequence. Each step in the sequence may need to be repeated a fixed number of times. Most compulsive behaviours have

a ritualistic quality to them. A *rumination* is a train of thoughts, usually unpro-
ductive and prolonged, on a particular topic. A young man had complicated and
time-consuming ruminations on the question "Is everyone basically good?". He
would ruminate on this for long periods, going over various considerations and
arguments and contemplating what superficially appeared as evidence. A rumination has no satisfactory conclusion, nor is there a set sequence of steps with a
clear-cut end point, so it is different from a cognitive compulsive ritual. Not
surprisingly, ruminations are hard to classify as either obsessions or compulsions.
The decisive issue is whether they come as an intrusive experience, in which
case they would fall into the category of obsessions, or whether there is a compulsive urge to think through a topic, in which case they would be compulsions.
Clinically, it seems to be the case that most ruminations are compulsions and
that they are usually preceded by an obsession. To illustrate this, the intrusive
cognition "Am I genetically flawed?" would lead to the compulsive urge to think
through the subject. The muddled "thinking through" that follows is the rumination.

The content of obsessions and compulsions are characterised by a few common themes. Contamination and dirt, disease and illness, violence and aggression, death, and moral or religious topics are among them. Other themes include
order, numbers, symmetry, and sequence. Sexually related themes are also found.
One young woman complained of getting the recurrent thought: "Am I a lesbian?".
Sometimes the content of an obsession may be apparently senseless or totally
trivial. A middle-aged man, for example, complained of the repeated thought "these
boys when they were young". The content of ruminations may revolve around a
specific personal theme, or—quite often—a metaphysical or philosophical subject.

Clinical presentations

There are several major clinical presentations of obsessive-compulsive disorder.
A person may have more than one problem at a given time and/or may have had
different obsessions and/or compulsions over a period of time. Notwithstanding
this, there is usually a clear and predominant clinical picture when someone
presents for help. These clinical presentations are described next.

Contamination/washing/cleaning problems.   These patients have fear of contamination or pollution as their main obsessional concern, and usually have
extensive cleaning, wiping, or washing rituals. They are the largest sub-group of
obsessive-compulsive patients. Their cleaning is usually quite excessive and
may include the use of soap and detergents in large quantities. There can also be
extensive avoidance.

Checking.   Those with this problem check various things, such as gas taps,
electric switches, doors, etc. The aim of their checking is to ensure that no room
is left for any harm to come, either to themselves or to others. Sometimes they

fear that major disasters will happen if they do not carry out their checking rituals. Recent work has shown that checkers have a highly exaggerated sense of responsibility, and feel that they have to act to ensure safety (Lopatka & Rachman, 1995; Rheaume, Ladouceur, Freeston, & Letarte, 1995). These are the second largest sub-group.

Other overt rituals.   Many patients have other extensive ritualistic behaviours, usually including doing certain things in a highly stereotyped way and in a predetermined sequence. Repetition of the behaviour a certain number of times may be a feature, as indeed it can be with washers and checkers. These overt rituals include touching, arranging, straightening, looking, repeating, and many other behaviours.

Hoarding.   There are some patients whose main problem is hoarding. They compulsively hoard—collect and retain large numbers of articles that are useless or of limited value. In some cases the compulsive hoarding leads to an accumulation of piles of objects that occupy a steadily increasing amount of living space, with the patient and family members having to carefully navigate their way through mounds of clutter. Hoarders show a great inability to dispose of things, often believing that they may need them at some future time (see de Silva & Rachman, 1998).

Obsessions without associated overt compulsive behaviour.   A significant minority of patients with obsessive-compulsive disorder to not display overt compulsive behaviour. However, only some of this group are free of compulsions. Many do have compulsions, but their compulsions are cognitive or mental.

Primary obsessional slowness.   This is a relatively recently described condition, and those presenting with this clinical picture are small in number. In these most behaviour, especially self-care behaviour, is exceedingly slow. Each step is meticulously carried out, and in a set sequence. The slowness is not secondary to other compulsions such as checking or washing, or to mental rituals. The slowness of some of these patients with regard to their self-care and grooming behaviour is amazing. A man in his 50s got up at five each morning, but was not able to get ready to leave his home until well after ten. Obviously, primary obsessional slowness can handicap someone's functioning considerably.

SOME BASIC FACTS

Prevalence

Obsessive-compulsive disorder was considered to be quite rare until recently. The commonly accepted estimate for its prevalence in the general population was 0.05%. The National Epidemiology Catchment Area surveys in the United

States suggest a much higher rate (e.g. Karno, Golding, Sorensen, & Burnam, 1988). In Baltimore, for example, a life-time prevalence of 3% was found. This is a very high figure, considering earlier low estimates. In other areas, somewhat lower but still relatively high rates have been found. Because many obsessive-compulsives tend to be secretive about their problems and often successfully conceal their disorder for many years, the high figures unearthed by thorough and systematic epidemiological studies are perhaps not surprising. A life-time prevalence rate of 2% is considered by many authorities as a reasonable estimate.

Sex

There is no clear preponderance of males or females among clinical obsessive-compulsive patients. There are, however, clear sex differences in some of the sub-groups of these patients. Among washers/cleaners, there is a preponderance of women. Primary obsessional slowness is largely a male phenomenon.

Onset and course

The onset of obsessive-compulsive disorder is usually in adolescence or early adulthood (Rasmussen & Eisen, 1990). Onset after the age of 45 is rare, although a few cases have been reported recently of onset after 60. Most cases emerge by the age of 30. Recent data on childhood obsessive-compulsive disorder suggest that the age of onset in some cases can be quite early, even before the age of 5. Such early onset is more common in boys than in girls. In general, males have earlier onset than females.

The course of the disorder is a fluctuating one. Periods of severe problems may be followed by relatively symptom-free periods. In almost half of all cases, however, there is a steadily worsening course. It is well established that stressful experiences—such as illness, bereavement, redundancy, problems at work—make the obsessive-compulsive disorder worse, and can precipitate relapse. It is also known that depression is commonly associated with this disorder, and the problems tend to get exacerbated with significantly low mood.

THEORETICAL APPROACHES

There are many theories and models aimed at explaining obsessive-compulsive disorder. For the most part, the tendency has been to assume that the disorder represents a unitary phenomenon, with each theoretical model being offered to account for a diversity of symptoms and presentations. More recent reviews (e.g. de Silva, 1986; Jakes, 1996) suggest that such a unitary view may be mistaken. Apart from the fact that obsessions and compulsions are distinct phenomena, there are also differences between sub-groups of patients with compulsive rituals. Rachman and Hodgson (1980) and Foa and her team (Foa, Steketee, Turner, & Fischer, 1980; Steketee, Foa, & Grayson, 1982), amongst others, have documented important differences between those whose main compulsions are checking behaviours and those whose main problem consists of washing and cleaning rituals. It is important to recognise this diversity in proffering and evaluating theories for explaining these disorders. It must also be noted that the accounts offered for the aetiology of the disorders may not be adequate to account for the maintenance, and *vice versa*. These issues have been discussed recently by Jakes (1996).

The psychoanalytic approach

Historically, the oldest and best-known theoretical account of obsessive-compulsive disorder is the psychoanalytic one. Sigmund Freud's writings on obsessive-compulsive problems display different and changing views over time (e.g. 1895, 1913). What is loosely described as the psychoanalytic view is in fact a version of these as developed by later writers such as Fenichel (1945). Repressed memories, desires, and conflicts are held to be the source of neurotic anxiety, which manifests itself as various symptoms. Fixation ("getting stuck") at a particular stage of psychosexual development, caused by various factors during the formative years, determines the nature of the manifest problem when the neurosis appears in later life. Obsessive-compulsive disorder is assumed to be linked to the anal-sadistic stage of development in which toilet training is a major feature and with which anger and aggression are also associated. Those who do not successfully negotiate this phase of development are considered to be vulnerable to obsessive-compulsive problems in later years. The compulsive acts, obsessional thoughts, and so on are seen as defensive reactions that suppress the real, hidden anxieties.

More recent psychodynamic accounts have been given by some writers, for example Malan (1979), using the earlier notions but also adding to, or changing the emphasis of, them. In one detailed case example, Malan (1979) stresses that the obsessive-compulsive problems may "serve a purpose" in the patient's life. He also emphasises the possible symbolic nature of the problem behaviours. These notions have been discussed in some detail by Jakes (1996).

The learning approach

The behavioural/learning view has been more widely held and discussed in recent years. It derives from Mowrer's two-factor theory of learning (1939, 1960). Certain stimuli and situations may acquire anxiety-producing properties by a process of classical conditioning. On later occasions, the anxiety (conditioned emotional response) that results from exposure to the conditioned stimulus is terminated by an escape or avoidance response. This produces anxiety relief, thus reinforcing the response. This is a case of instrumental conditioning. Extending these views to obsessive-compulsive behaviour, it is assumed that the compulsive acts are performed in response to anxiety generated by certain stimuli, which may include the individual's own obsessions, and are strengthened as a result of the anxiety reduction that follows (Dollard & Miller, 1950). The model is essentially one of learned anxiety reduction.

Rachman and Hodgson (1980) have suggested that in these patients the critical negative emotion should be considered as discomfort rather than anxiety since in many cases patients report feelings other than those of anxiety. The view is, then, that discomfort reduction is the crucial element in the maintenance of obsessive-compulsive behaviour.

There is much evidence in support of this position. The studies of Rachman and his associates carried out in London in the 1970s provide appreciable corroboration (Hodgson & Rachman, 1972; Rachman, de Silva, & Roper, 1976; Rachman & Hodgson, 1980). In these experiments it was found that both checkers and cleaners show heightened anxiety/discomfort when exposed to certain situations and/or stimuli (cues), which normally generated their ritualistic behaviours. For example, a cleaner made to touch an item which he believed to be contaminated would typically report a marked heightening of anxiety or discomfort. When the compulsive behaviour, for example hand-washing, was carried out there was considerable reduction in discomfort. Associated with the discomfort, and following the same course, was the compulsive urge subjectively felt by the patient. In a small number of cases, the execution of the compulsive behaviour actually led to an increase in discomfort. Nevertheless, despite the exceptions, the model appears to be robust.

Further evidence supporting the model comes from two sources. First, Likierman and Rachman (1980) showed that repeated trials of exposure to cues in the same patient led to progressively lower levels of both discomfort and felt compulsive urge, and to progressively quicker dissipation of these under conditions of response prevention (i.e. the patient not being allowed to carry out his compulsive behaviour). This shows that there is a cumulative effect in repeated exposure to discomfort cues or, in other words, a habituation process. This fits well into the discomfort reduction model. If the compulsive behaviours were maintained by the reduction of anxiety/discomfort achieved by carrying out the behaviour, then the prevention of these behaviours in the presence of the relevant cues should have certain effects. With repeated exposures the urge to engage in the compulsive behaviours, and the behaviours themselves, should gradually reduce. This is exactly what the Likierman and Rachman (1980) experiment demonstrated. The second line of supporting evidence comes from the numerous treatment studies of obsessive-compulsive patients using the exposure and response prevention paradigm in which the patient's desire to engage in the compulsive behaviour is provoked, but he is persuaded not to carry it out. This is done in the context of a trusting therapeutic relationship. The success of this approach is well established and fits in well with the discomfort reduction model. These studies are summarised in detail elsewhere (e.g. Foa, Steketee, & Ozarow, 1985; Marks, 1987; Rachman & Hodgson, 1980).

The discomfort reduction aspect of this approach is thus supported by both experimental and treatment studies. On the other hand, the theory is on less sure grounds with regard to the aetiology of the disorder. Why is it that only certain types of stimuli tend to lead to these behaviours, as shown by de Silva, Rachman, and Seligman (1977)? Why is it that many patients do not have a traumatic (conditioning) experience as the starting point for their problem behaviours? The criticisms of the Mowrer two-factor theory as a model for neuroses are well known and need not be repeated here (see Chapters 1 and 3). Dollard and Miller (1950) proposed that certain behaviour patterns that previously led to anxiety reduction, such as hand-washing or checking, become exaggerated and take the form of compulsions. For example, washing in childhood is often associated with avoidance of, or escape from, parental criticism. However, how and why some behaviours turn into adult compulsions, or why only some individuals are subject to them, is not explained. Further, the learning model does not offer much help in understanding obsessions that are not accompanied by compulsive behaviours. Finally the elaborate, repetitive, and even bizarre nature of compulsive behaviour, which is best seen as active avoidance, unlike the passive avoidance found in phobias (see Gray, 1982; Rachman & Hodgson, 1980), needs to be explained more fully than the conditioning theory would allow.

Some writers have examined the animal-learning literature as a possible source of understanding of obsessive-compulsive disorders. In a key paper Teasdale (1974) suggested that compulsive behaviours may be considered as avoidance behaviours that are under poor stimulus control. They are reminiscent of the unnecessarily high frequency of responses shown by animals in experiments using the Sidman avoidance paradigm, where electric shocks are given to promote avoidance learning, but the delivery of the shock is unsignalled (Sidman, 1955). Compulsive rituals can also be seen as not having good feedback or safety-signal properties and hence their inefficiently high rate of occurrence (Rachman & Hodgson, 1980; Teasdale, 1974). For example, a patient will not know easily whether the germs he is trying to wash off have been effectively removed since there is no safety signal or feedback to indicate that this has happened. The same applies to many checking rituals intended to ward off future disasters.

Another aspect of the avoidance literature which has been cited as possibly relevant comes from the findings of Fonberg (1956, as cited by Wolpe, 1958, p. 65). In this study, she first trained dogs to make a response (e.g. leg-lifting) to avoid an aversive stimulus. They were then subjected to a second conditioning procedure aimed at inducing an experimental "neurosis" by making the required discrimination increasingly difficult. As the animals' behaviour became more and more "neurotic" it was observed that they began to show the previously learned avoidance response (leg-lifting) at a high frequency, although no more discriminative stimuli for this particular response were presented. What seemed to be happening was that a response learned to avoid aversive stimulation re-emerged in a different setting when anxiety was induced in a different way. The relevance of this to the present topic is that it appears to provide a parallel for the wide variety of situations in which compulsive behaviours are performed by the patient. For example, a patient may engage in repetitive hand-washing behaviour when under stress, although the hands are not in any way dirty or contaminated.

Thus, there are several findings from animal avoidance learning which have been considered as possibly relevant to the understanding of obsessive-compulsive disorders. None of these provides a full, or even closely approximate, analogy. However, they throw some light on the possible ways in which obsessive-compulsive behaviours may be acquired, why they occur in different settings, why some of them appear unrelated to the situation in which they are manifest, and why they are strongly persistent.

Cognitive deficit approaches

It has been suggested that obsessive-compulsive patients have a major difficulty in decision making, which may explain their symptoms (e.g. Beech & Liddell, 1974). Reed (1976, 1985) has also emphasised this aspect of obsessive-compulsive problems. There is some evidence of this (Volans, 1976), but it is not clear that it can be taken as an explanation of obsessive-compulsive phenomena. Emmelkamp (1982) has argued that the decision-making difficulty could equally well be a consequence of the symptoms. The proper evaluation of decision-making difficulties in these disorders must await further investigation.

Adopting a somewhat different approach, Carr (1974) has argued that obsessive-compulsive patients make very high subjective estimates of the probability of aversive outcomes. Compulsive behaviours develop to reduce the threat of these outcomes. The behaviours lead to the relief of anxiety and reduce the subjective threat. Further arguments along these lines are presented by McFall and Wollersheim (1979).

A more general cognitive theory has been offered by Reed (1985). According to Reed (1985, p. 220), the main problem is "that the obsessional finds difficulty in the spontaneous structuring of experience and attempts to compensate for this by imposing artificial, rigidly defined boundaries, category limits, and time markers. The rigidity and specificity of definition themselves lead to further uncertainty as to the 'appropriate' allocation of category items, schematization, completion times, etc." Reed attempts to explain all the major phenomena of the disorder in terms of this central concept. For example, checking may be seen as a failure in "terminating response" coupled with uncertainty. Rituals are an example of the imposition of artificial structure geared to the arbitrary definition of tasks and situations. A study by Persons and Foa (1984) provides some independent evidence of certain features of the thought patterns of ritualisers consistent with Reed's views. Ritualisers appeared to use "complex concepts", that is concepts that are excessively complex and over-specific. There are further data on the possible role of cognitive deficits in obsessive-compulsive problems. Sher and colleagues (e.g. Sher, Frost, Kushner, Crews, & Alexander, 1989; Sher, Mann, Frost, & Otto, 1983) found that non-clinical compulsive checkers had poorer memories for prior actions than non-checkers. They were also found to underestimate their ability to distinguish memories of real and imagined events ("reality monitoring"). Both these factors were considered to contribute to checking rituals. Despite this work, it is not yet possible to make a proper evaluation of Reed's position or of any other cognitive-deficit model. The postulated central deficit assumes too much uniformity in the phenomena. Both clinical and other data show too great a diversity. Such models also fail to take into account the selective nature of the content of obsessive-compulsive problems. A detailed discussion of cognitive approaches is found in Tallis (1995).

The explanation of obsessions

It is necessary at this point to discuss obsessions briefly. Many of the theoretical models address themselves to the origins and maintenance of compulsions, especially overt rituals. In theory they could apply equally well to cognitive rituals. If cognitive compulsive behaviour reduces discomfort, then it is likely that it is carried out to avoid impending discomfort. But what of the obsession, the intrusive cognition that in some cases occurs on its own and in others leads to a compulsion? In both these instances what is primarily needed is an explanation as to why the cognition occurs in the first place. This relatively neglected aspect of obsessive-compulsive disorder has only recently received systematic study. Following Rachman's (1971) view that such experiences may not be uncommon in the normal population, research has confirmed that normal people do have similar unwanted intrusive cognitions, or "normal obsessions" (Parkinson & Rachman, 1980; Rachman & de Silva, 1978). The amount of disturbance that they cause seems to determine how difficult they are to control (Rachman, 1982). The discomfort they generate may lead to anxiety reducing compulsions. It appears that their genesis may be related to stress, both naturally occurring and artificially induced. Studies by Horowitz (e.g. 1975) have shown that experimentally delivered traumatic input causes intrusions of related cognitions later on. Similar intrusions are found in those undergoing uncontrived stress experiences (Rachman & Parkinson, 1981). These common, normal experiences seem to be short-lived and removal of the stress dramatically reduces them. On the other hand, unresolved stress may cause them to become chronic. This would be especially so in cases where the initial stress is not clear-cut or where there are multiple stresses. Further, Sutherland, Newman, and Rachman (1982) have shown experimentally that induced dysphoria helps to evoke unwanted intrusive cognitions and also makes these difficult to remove. In the light of present knowledge, perhaps the best explanation for the persistence of obsessions, and of how normal intrusions become more chronic and achieve clinically significant levels of severity, lies with the broad concept of emotional processing as proposed by Rachman (1980). Elements of stressful material which have not been successfully processed emotionally, may appear in an intrusive way from time to time and cause distress. This can, and indeed does, happen to most people. The individual is more vulnerable to these when mood is low and when affected by fresh stresses. In those who are predisposed in certain ways (whether genetic, due to early social experiences, or whatever), such experiences are likely to become more persistent, more intense, more distressing, and more difficult to control. Whereas in some cases the intrusion directly reflects the stress, in others it may do so only indirectly or in a fragmented form. In numerous cases where the obsession is associated with a compulsion, the explanation of the compulsion is still plausible along the lines of discomfort reduction.

A more recent theoretical development is relevant at this point. Many patients complain of recurrent, persistent obsessions that are not historically linked to a stressful event, so the emotional processing explanation cannot plausibly apply to them. An account that appears to solve this problem has been proposed by Rachman (1997). Building on some of his previous theoretical views (e.g. Rachman, 1993) and those of Salkovskis (1985), Rachman (1997) argues that obsessions are caused by catastrophic misinterpretations of the significance of one's intrusive thoughts, images, and impulses. Most people have unwanted intrusive cognitions (Rachman & de Silva, 1978; Salkovskis & Harrison, 1984). The majority are neither distressed nor affected in any other way by them. Some, however, have a tendency to interpret these catastrophically; and this leads to clinically significant obsessions. Rachman (1997) gives the example of a 25-year-old computer analyst who had recurrent thoughts and images of harming the very young child of a friend. He interpreted this catastrophically: He took it to mean that he was a potential murderer and a fundamentally worthless human being. Another example given by Rachman (1997) is that of a devoutly religious woman who experienced recurrent obscene images about the church and Mary. These happened especially when she was in church or when she tried to pray. She interpreted these intrusive images to mean that she was a vicious, lying hypocrite, and that her religious faith and feelings were a sham.

According to Rachman's view (1997), obsessions will persist for as long as the misinterpretations continue.

This account appears to provide a plausible explanation for the genesis and persistence of obsessions. Experimental investigations are needed to test predictions from this theory, but it seems to fit a range of clinical observations.

Biological theory

The view that obsessive-compulsive disorder has a clear biological causation has been put forward by several authors in recent years. A few comments on this are in order.

The main biological theory proposes that the disorder is caused by a bio-chemical imbalance in the brain. In particular, it is claimed that obsessive-compulsive disorder arises from an inadequate supply of serotonin. (Serotonin is a neuro-transmitter—that is, a chemical substance which carries messages between cells in the brain. It is known that serotonin plays quite an important part in brain functioning.) This theory originally emerged from the finding that an antidepressive drug, clomipramine, which blocks the natural loss of serotonin, can produce therapeutic effects in these patients. A useful discussion is available in Gross, Sasson, Chopra, and Zohar (1998).

This theory has gained some support, but has also been criticised. Therapeutic effects of equal or greater magnitude than produced by clomipramine or similar drugs have been achieved through purely psychological treatment methods—when the serotonin level is ignored. There is no evidence that people suffering from obsessive-compulsive disorder have serotonin levels that differ from those of people suffering from other comparable psychological disorders, especially other anxiety disorders, or levels that differ from people free of any such disorder. Further, there is no relationship between the amount of clomipramine absorbed and the degree of therapeutic change. Even with high doses of the drug, and hence high levels of serotonin, relatively few patients are free of obsessive-compulsive symptoms. Some patients simply do not improve, even with high doses of serotonin bolstering drugs such as clomipramine. It has also been found in recent research that the patient's initial response to clomipramine does not provide a good basis for predicting the longer-term effects of this medication. Another criticism of the biological theory is that the attempt to decide the cause of a disorder from a therapeutic effect is risky. For example, the fact that aspirin relieves a headache tells us little about the cause of the headache, and it certainly does not tell us that the headache occurred because the person was short of aspirin. The fact that clomipramine often reduces obsessive-compulsive symptoms does not mean that the disorder was caused by a shortage of clomipramine, or of serotonin which clomipramine bolsters. A further problem is that there are serious inconsistencies in the empirical literature on serotonin involvement in obsessive-compulsive disorder. Several authors have suggested a neuroanatomical basis for obsessive-compulsive disorder (e.g. Behar et al., 1984; Scarone et al., 1992). This emerging field, however, has not produced a consistent picture, and at present the evidence is far from conclusive.

CONCLUDING COMMENTS

None of the theories outlined here offers a fully convincing and comprehensive account of obsessive-compulsive disorder. It is possible that different aspects of the disorder need different explanations. Several of the theoretical approaches proposed have some validity in explaining some aspects of the disorder, but do not provide a comprehensive account. It is likely that there is some biological predisposition that may be genetically transmitted. Personal experiences and social learning are also likely to be implicated. The role of the stressful experiences in triggering and worsening obsessive-compulsive disorder is well known. Stresses that are not satisfactorily emotionally processed and absorbed may well be the major cause of obsessions. Individual proneness to catastrophically misinterpret commonly occuring intrusive cognitions also appears to be a key factor in recurrent, persistent obsessions. Compulsions may be seen as anxiety-reducing behaviours which have been well established and ritualised. Their maintenance can be understood as the result of their efficacy in anxiety reduction. In other words, anxiety reduction may be said to reinforce the compulsive behaviour and thus perpetuate it. In this specific sense, the learning theory approach appears to have clear support. Whether there is a causal role for cognitive deficits or style is at present doubtful.

Despite much clinical and experimental research, our understanding of obsessive-compulsive disorder is still incomplete. There is no doubt that it will continue to generate much empirical research. Such research is likely to enhance our understanding of this fascinating disorder, and to help develop testable theoretical accounts.

RECOMMENDED READING

Barlow, D. (1988). *Anxiety and its disorders*. New York: Guilford Press.

A comprehensive book on the whole range of anxiety disorders, with a particularly useful chapter on obsessive-compulsive disorder.

de Silva, P., & Rachman, S. (1998). *Obsessive-compulsive disorder—the facts* (2nd ed.). Oxford, UK: Oxford University Press.

This brief text gives a concise account of the nature of the disorder.

Jakes, I. (1996). *Theoretical approaches to obsessive-compulsive disorder*. Cambridge, UK: Cambridge University Press.

This gives a full discussion of theoretical approaches.

Jenike, M.A., Baer, L., & Minichiello, W.E. (Eds.). (1990). *Obsessive-compulsive disorders: Theory and management* (2nd ed.). Chicago: Yearbook Medical Publishers.

This edited volume gives useful up-to-date information on many aspects of the disorder.

Rachman, S.J., & Hodgson, R.J. (1980). *Obsessions and compulsions*. Englewood Cliffs, NJ: Prentice-Hall.

This book provides a description and discussion of the field of obsessive-compulsive disorder. It describes what is known about obsessions and compulsions, gives an account of the authors' research, and comments on theoretical issues. Still the best single text on the subject.

REFERENCES

Beech, H.R., & Liddell, A. (1974). Decision-making, mood states and ritualistic behaviour among obsessional patients. In H.R. Beech (Ed.), *Obsessional states* (pp. 143–160). London: Methuen.

Behar, D., Raport, J.L., Berg, C.J., Denckla, M., Mann, L., Cox, C., Fedio, P., Zahn, T., & Wolfman, H. (1984). Computerized tomography and neuropsychological test measures in adolescents with obsessive-compulsive disorder. *American Journal of Psychiatry, 141*, 363–369.

Carr, A. (1974). Compulsive neurosis: A review of the literature. *Psychological Bulletin, 81*, 331–318.

de Silva, P. (1986). Obsessional-compulsive imagery. *Behaviour Research and Therapy, 24*, 333–350.

de Silva, P., & Rachman, S. (1998). *Obsessive-compulsive disorder: The facts* (2nd ed.). Oxford, UK: Oxford University Press.

de Silva, P., Rachman, S.J., & Seligman, M.E.P. (1977). Prepared phobias and obsessions: Therapeutic outcome. *Behaviour Research and Therapy, 15*, 65–78.

Dollard, J., & Miller, N.E. (1950). *Personality and psychotherapy: An analysis in terms of learning, thinking and culture.* New York: McGraw-Hill.

Emmelkamp, P.M.G. (1982). *Phobic and obsessive-compulsive disorders.* New York: Plenum.

Fenichel, O. (1945). *The psychoanalytic theory of neurosis.* New York: Norton.

Foa, E.B., Steketee, G., & Ozarow, B. (1985). Behavior therapy with obsessive-compulsives: From theory to treatment. In M. Mavissakalian (Ed.), *Obsessive-compulsive disorder: Psychological and pharmacological treatment* (pp. 49–129). New York: Plenum Press.

Foa, E.B., Steketee, G., Turner, R.M., & Fischer, S.C. (1980). Effects of imaginal exposure to feared disasters in obsessive-compulsive checkers. *Behaviour Research and Therapy, 18*, 449–455.

Freud, S. (1895). Obsessions and phobias. In J. Strachey (Ed.), *Standard edition of the complete psychological works of Sigmund Freud* (Vol. 3, pp. 45–61). London: Hogarth.

Freud, S. (1913). The disposition to obsessional neurosis. In J. Strachey (Ed.), *Standard edition of the complete psychological works of Sigmund Freud* (Vol. 12, pp. 317–326). London: Hogarth.

Gray, J.A. (1982). *The neuropsychology of anxiety.* Oxford, UK: Clarendon.

Gross, R., Sasson, Y., Chopra, M., & Zohar, J. (1998). Biological models of obsessive-compulsive disorder. In R.P. Swinson, M.M. Antony, S. Rachman, & M.A. Richter (Eds.), *Obsessive-compulsive disorder: Theory, research, and treatment* (pp. 141–153). New York: Guilford Press.

Hodgson, R.J., & Rachman, S.J. (1972). The effects of contamination and washing in obsessional patients. *Behaviour Research and Therapy, 10*, 11–17.

Horowitz, M. (1975). Intrusive and repetitive thoughts after experimental stress. *Archives of General Psychiatry, 32*, 145–163.

Jakes, I. (1996). *Theoretical approaches to obsessive-compulsive disorder.* Cambridge, UK: Cambridge University Press.

Janet, P. (1903). *Les obsessions et la psychasthenie.* Paris: Alcan.

Jaspers, K. (1963). *General psychopathology* (J. Hoenig & M.W. Hamilton, Trans.). Chicago: University of Chicago Press. (Original work published 1923)

Karno, M.G., Golding, J.M., Sorensen, S.B., & Burnam, A. (1988). The epidemiology of obsessive-compulsive disorder in five US communities. *Archives of General Psychiatry, 45*, 1094–1099.

Kishimoto, K. (1985). Self-awakening psychotherapy for neurosis: Attacking unimportance to oriental thought, especially Buddhist thought. *Psychologia, 28*, 90–100.

Lewis, A. (1936). Problems of obsessional illness. *Proceedings of the Royal Society of Medicine*, *29*, 325–336.

Lewis, A. (1965). A note on personality and obsessional illness. *Psychiatria et Neurologia*, *150*, 299–305.

Likierman, H., & Rachman, S.J. (1980). Spontaneous decay of compulsive urges: Cumulative effects. *Behaviour Research and Therapy*, *18*, 387–394.

Lopatka, C., & Rachman, S. (1995). Perceived responsibility and compulsive checking: An experimental analysis. *Behaviour Research and Therapy*, *33*, 673–684.

Malan, D.H. (1979). *Individual psychotherapy and the science of psychodynamics*. London: Butterworths.

Marks, I.M. (1987). *Fears, phobias and rituals*. Oxford, UK: Oxford University Press.

McFall, M.G., & Wollersheim, J.P. (1979). Obsessive-compulsive neurosis: A cognitive-behavioural formulation and approach to treatment. *Cognitive Therapy and Research*, *3*, 333–348.

Mowrer, O.H. (1939). A stimulus-response theory of anxiety. *Psychological Review*, *46*, 553–565.

Mowrer, O.H. (1960). *Learning theory and behaviour*. New York: Wiley.

Parkinson, L., & Rachman, S.J. (1980). Are intrusive thoughts subject to habituation? *Behaviour Research and Therapy*, *18*, 409–418.

Persons, J.B., & Foa, E.B. (1984). Processing of fearful and neutral information by obsessive-compulsives. *Behaviour Research and Therapy*, *22*, 159–165.

Pollak, J.M. (1979). Obsessive-compulsive personality: A review. *Psychological Bulletin*, *86*, 225–241.

Rachman, S.J. (1971). Obsessional ruminations. *Behaviour Research and Therapy*, *9*, 229–235.

Rachman, S.J. (1980). Emotional processing. *Behaviour Research and Therapy*, *18*, 51–60.

Rachman, S.J. (1982). Obsessional-compulsive disorders. In A.S. Bellack, M. Hersen, & A.E. Kazdin (Eds.), *International handbook of behaviour modification and therapy* (pp. 749–766). New York: Plenum.

Rachman, S. (1993). Obsessions, responsibility and guilt. *Behaviour Research and Therapy*, *31*, 149–154.

Rachman, S.J. (1997). A cognitive theory of obsessions. *Behaviour Research and Therapy*, *35*, 793–802.

Rachman, S.J., & de Silva, P. (1978). Abnormal and normal obsessions. *Behaviour Research and Therapy*, *16*, 233–248.

Rachman, S.J., de Silva, P., & Roper, G. (1976). The spontaneous decay of compulsive urges. *Behaviour Research and Therapy*, *14*, 445–453.

Rachman, S.J., & Hodgson, R.J. (1980). *Obsessions and compulsions*. Englewood Cliffs, NJ: Prentice Hall.

Rachman, S.J., & Parkinson, L. (1981). Unwanted intrusive cognitions. *Advances in Behaviour Research and Therapy*, *3*, 89–123.

Rasmussen, S.A., & Eisen, J.L. (1990). Epidemiology of obsessive-compulsive disorder. *Journal of Clinical Psychiatry*, *51* (Suppl.), 10–13.

Rasmussen, S.A., & Tsuang, M.T. (1986). Clinical characteristics and family history in DSM-III obsessive-compulsive disorders. *American Journal of Psychiatry*, *143*, 317–322.

Reed, G.F. (1976). Indecisiveness in obsessional-compulsive disorder. *British Journal of Social and Clinical Psychology*, *15*, 443–445.

Reed, G.F. (1985). *Obsessional experience and compulsive behaviour*. London: Academic Press.

Rheaume, J., Ladouceur, R., Freeston, M.H., & Letarte, H. (1995). Inflated responsibility in obsessive-compulsive disorder. *Behaviour Research and Therapy*, *33*, 159–169.

Salkovskis, P.M. (1985). Obsessive-compulsive problems: A cognitive-behavioural analysis. *Behaviour Research and Therapy*, *23*, 571–583.

Salkovskis, P.M., & Harrison, J. (1984). Abnormal and normal obsessions: A replication. *Behaviour Research and Therapy*, *22*, 549–552.

Scarone, S., Columbo, C., Livian, S., Abbruzzese, M., Ronchi, P., Cocatetti, M., Scotti, G., & Smeraldi, E. (1992). Increased right candidate nucleus size in obsessive-compulsive disorder: Detection with magnetic resonance imaging. *Psychiatry Research*, *45*, 115–121.

Sher, K.J., Frost, R.O., Kushner, M., Crews, T.M., & Alexander, J.E. (1989). Memory deficits in compulsive checkers: A replication and extension in a clinical sample. *Behaviour Research and Therapy*, *27*, 65–69.

Sher, K.J., Mann, B., Frost, R.O., & Otto, R. (1983). Cognitive deficits in compulsive checkers: An exploratory study. *Behaviour Research and Therapy*, *21*, 357–363.

Sidman, M. (1955). Some properties of warning stimulus in avoidance behaviour. *Journal of Comparative and Physiological Psychology*, *48*, 444–450.

Steketee, G., Foa, E.B., & Grayson, J.B. (1982). Recent advances in the behavioural treatment of obsessive-compulsives. *Archives of General Psychiatry*, *39*, 1365–1371.

Stern, R.S., & Cobb, J.P. (1978). Phenomenology of obsessive-compulsive neurosis. *British Journal of Psychiatry*, *132*, 233–239.

Sutherland, G., Newman, B., & Rachman, S.J. (1982). Experimental investigations of the relation between mood and intrusive unwanted cognitions. *British Journal of Medical Psychology*, *55*, 127–138.

Tallis, F. (1995). *Obsessive-compulsive disorder: A cognitive and neuropsychological perspective*. Chichester, UK: Wiley.

Teasdale, J. (1974). Learning models of obsessional-compulsive disorders. In H.R. Beech (Ed.), *Obsessional states* (pp. 197–229). London: Methuen.

Volans, P.J. (1976). Styles of decision-making and probability appraisal in selected obsessional and phobic patients. *British Journal of Social and Clinical Psychology*, *15*, 430–450.

Wolpe, J.R. (1958). *Psychotherapy by reciprocal inhibition*. Stanford, CA: University of Stanford Press.

Yaryura-Tobias, J.E., & Neziroglu, F.A. (1997). *Obsessive-compulsive disorder spectrum*. Washington, DC: American Psychiatric Press.

CHAPTER SEVEN

Couple and sexual problems

Patricia d'Ardenne
Department of Clinical Psychology, City & Hackney Community Services NHS Trust, London, UK

This chapter will be looking at the difficulties experienced by people who live in intimate sexual partnerships. The difficulties can be those that arise when one or both parties experience unhappiness about the relationship in general, or about their sexual functioning in particular. Much of the psychological work in the field has historically been with heterosexual couples, and especially marriage; previous texts have therefore referred to marital problems and marital therapy. Nowadays significantly more couples are living together without marrying, including of course same-sex relationships. Many of the difficulties described as well as some of the therapeutic solutions are applicable to more informal relationships, and it is for this reason the term "couple" therapy is used.

Other difficulties around couples, for example those around their children or their wider family, will be addressed in Chapter 8 on family problems. This chapter will consider specifically disorders within the couple relationship, and sexual difficulties that arise for either partner within the context of that relationship. No psychological problem exists outside its social or cultural contexts, and some consideration will be given to these.

How couples first recognise that they have problems and seek help are described, together with some major therapeutic models that have been found effective in dealing with them. These will include behavioural, cognitive, systemic, and psychodynamic approaches. In addition, issues specific to helping same-sex couples will also be described, together with couples from minority ethnic communities, and those with specific needs, especially long-term illness or disability. The next subject is that of specific sexual problems and dysfunctions, their presumed causes, assessments, and the methods that have been found effective in helping people with them. A reading and resource list is intended to guide the reader for further direction.

HOW PROBLEMS PRESENT THEMSELVES

Couples today have high expectations of intimate relationships, enjoy greater greater economic and social mobility, and more flexible gender roles, brought about by the Women's Movement. In addition, the breakdown in formal religious, familial, and legal supports for couples may account for the very high rates of breakdown of marital and other cohabiting relationships in the UK today (Clulow, 1995; Clulow & Mattison, 1989). Women—three times more often than men—will complain that there is something wrong with the relationship itself, and will endeavour to seek some kind of external help when internal resolution has failed. This can be something very general—a sense of misery, or anxiety, or failure with each other. It may be behavioural, for example an inability to negotiate solutions with the partner, uncontrolled verbal or physical violence, or "circular" problems, e.g. provocative behaviour followed by a jealous reaction, followed by provocative behaviour. A problem may also be specific to one individual; failures within the relationship may lead to a fear that it will break down altogether. Such a fear in turn may include a loss of self-esteem, fear of poverty, loneliness, failure, loss of family life, or ridicule, and may be seen by the individual as not only being caused by the dysfunction, but maybe determining current behaviour within the partnership, for example increasing withdrawal of affection or trust.

Occasionally couples will present with a difficulty about their children, or indeed another member of the family, or there may be a problem presented as a physical complaint, a contraceptive problem, or an individual who has a range of neurotic or behavioural difficulties which can then be contextualised within the couple's relationship. Since it is the couple themselves who have to make a decision to undertake treatment, or intervention, a recognition that the difficulty lies with them will be the first therapeutic task. Getting both parties to attend an initial assessment may be the most difficult hurdle to jump. It is possible to treat dysfunctional relationships with only one partner (Bennun, 1991), especially if one of the partners has specifically requested it, but most of the techniques described in this chapter as couple therapies refer to working with the couple in therapy.

APPROACHING THE COUPLE

All of the models described here come from different theoretical bases, but it may be worthwhile considering first, what different therapies have in common when couples first recognise that they have a difficulty and go to a third party to seek help.

First, all effective couple work is aimed at creating a *therapeutic alliance*—a term first used in psychodynamic literature and now applied widely. This describes the network of attachments, understandings, and activities undertaken by both the therapist and couple in helping that couple deal with their relationship difficulties. Both therapist and the couple have to make contributions to this alliance. The therapeutic alliance can usually be seen to be made up of three components: bonds—or the quality of the relationship between all parties; goals—which arise from a common understanding of the purpose of therapy; and tasks—the necessary activities to achieve these goals. There is some evidence that the more the couple are active in this alliance, the better the therapy outcome will be.

Second, all couple work entails an important and detailed *initial assessment*. The purpose of this is to gather historical information about a couple's difficulties, both from interviewing the couple conjointly, and from seeing each separately. The assessor is seeking a picture that is cogent and comprehensive, and will be looking for discrepancies between the two stories as a means of understanding something about the nature and history of the disordered relationship. Separate interviews also give each partner the time to give a personal biography, a space for themselves, and an opportunity to reveal to the therapist information that may be confidential, for example an extramarital affair. The assessment also "sets the stage", where the therapist is able to acknowledge the couple's difficulties with optimism and constructive realism.

Third, couple work is *contractual*—the couple and therapist have explicit and reciprocal obligations. These will concern the core purpose of therapy, e.g. goals and assignments, as well as the practicalities of therapy, e.g. duration, frequency, and, where applicable, fees. Increasingly, contracts include agreed outputs—a means of ascertaining explicit and measurable benefits from therapy. Contract may be verbal and/or written, but it is agreed by all parties after the initial assessment, and serves in part to remind the couple that their relationship (even if non-marital) is also contractual and contains reciprocal rights and responsibilities.

Fourth, all of the therapies outlined will introduce to the couple the idea of *collaborative set*, which affirms that what couples have in common, and undertake in common, is likely to be more helpful than identifying guilt, blaming each other, or attributing power of external factors beyond the control of the couple. Again, this aspect of therapy echoes in part the nature of the original couple partnership, and is intended to introduce a more positive and rewarding experience for the pair, as well as achieve an attitudinal change early on in assessment and therapy.

BEHAVIOURAL MODELS FOR THE COUPLE

The basic assumption behind any approach using behavioural approaches is that all partnerships work best on reciprocal positive reinforcement (Stuart, 1969, 1980). Each partner thus reinforces the behaviour of the other, positively or negatively. Successful partnerships will, therefore, be those where each party is able to derive the maximum gain for both of them, whilst incurring minimum cost. In the unhappy partnership, the equation is reversed, each partner incurs maximum cost for minimum gain, or at least the expectation of minimum gain. Partners in such relationships do not find each other attractive, and have low trust, fewer strategies for change of resolution, and have substantial communication difficulties. They may seek their rewards in other relationships, thus adding more cost to the existing partnership.

Behavioural theorists have argued that couples who have had experience of many rewarding relationships, may be able to tolerate low or little reward within their current partnership (more trust). On the other hand, couples who have had few rewards in previous personal relationships, will have less tolerance (trust) within the current partnership of delay in receiving reward. "Trust" in the behavioural sense becomes the time delay that can be supported between instances of reward from the partner. "Skills", in the behavioural sense, will mean any behaviour that is deemed to increase the possibility of achieving reciprocal reinforcement ("contingency contracting") and may also include communication and problem-solving abilities, all of which can be learnt in therapy.

Behavioural analysis

This is both assessment and therapy, and represents the cornerstone of the behavioural therapist's approach with the couple. The couple will describe the antecedents, behaviour, and consequences of their troubled exchanges, and the therapist will establish hypotheses which will be systematically tested as the intervention is undertaken. Nothing will be left to infer; the couple will be told to make explicit their intentions and to communicate this to their partner in the presence of the therapist.

Increasing the probability of positive behaviour

The next stage of the intervention involves the therapist and the couple in identifying those behaviours that each identifies as pleasing to the other, and either increasing its frequency, or ensuring that other pleasing behaviours are included in the partners' behavioural repertoire. The couple is encouraged to be explicit and concrete about these, and to monitor how their satisfaction in response to behavioural changes begins to affect the whole quality of the relationship. For example, Jack may identify that Jill telephoning from the office when she is late from work, makes him feel more valued, and more generous about her wanting time with him when she returns. Both would be required to monitor how often Jill calls, and Jack to assess his feelings as a direct result of this.

Interpersonal skills training

At this stage the therapist or therapists teach a model and provide feedback to each partner regarding the skills of effective listening, taking turns to speak, making positive and affectionate statements in response to each other, and negotiating directly for more frequent desirable behaviours. Couples will be scripted and rehearsed with their own material and shown how to be unambiguous in reinforcing and shaping what it is they most want from each other.

An example of this is where Jack says that he feels undermined by Jill in his relationship with their children, and Jill feels that Jack shouts at them and frightens them. In training, they will agree beforehand how the children are to be controlled through negotiation. When Jack is confronted with inappropriate behaviour from a child, he wants Jill literally to stand beside him while he speaks, and show by her words and nods that she supports Jack. In turn, he will consciously speak in talking tones to the child, and any disagreements will only be discussed when the children are out of earshot.

Training in problem solving

Research shows that couples who report greater satisfaction in their lives are those who are able to negotiate problems in a reciprocal and mutually acceptable way (Crowe & Ridley, 1990). Compromise and mutuality are required, and changes are required to be agreed formally and in writing. Training involves giving the couple specific and time-limited agendas.

Contingency contracting

As the last part of this training, couples are shown how to "give to get" in achieving mutual responsibility for changes in their relationship. An example of this might be: If Jack undertakes to shop for the family without prompting, Jill will greet him at the house with a hug and kiss, and express appreciation of his value as a worker in the home.

COGNITIVE APPROACHES FOR THE COUPLE

Behavioural approaches to couple distress have been used for nearly three decades. In the last decade, greater emphasis has been placed on a wider view of the couple's needs, which would increase not just a change in positive behaviours and skills, but would restructure *harmful or distorted thinking* that partners have and help them to circumvent conflict escalation.

Cognitive behaviourists argue that couples in distress have a chain of *reciprocated negative behaviour*. Furthermore, each partner might have an *expectation* of being criticised by the other. For example, if Jack asks Jill about a task, even in a neutral tone, Jill—expecting criticism—may respond with a critical attack. Jack, sensing a critical tone, also feels attacked, and criticises in turn—leading to an escalation of the distress.

A cognitive behavioural assessment is similar to that of a behavioural approach, targeting problem behaviours at the initial conjoint session, and taking a relationship history. The difference, however, is that the therapist will emphasise during the history taking the positive aspects of their relationship. This will include how they met, courtship, mutual attraction, the "good times", and how and when they decided to commit to each other. The purpose of this is to reorientate the couple to the wider historical context of their relationship, and to remind them about the strengths of it. The cognitive behaviourist also seeks to instil a sense of hopefulness—a significant cognition—about how matters may seem for the future.

Following joint and individual history taking—a round-table discussion is held with the therapist who formulates the couple's strengths and needs, their problems, a cognitive treatment plan, and a space for concerns to be raised by the couple. As with behavioural approaches, the couple will be introduced to the collaborative set—a construct that sees the couple as partners who move from mutual blame to mutual responsibility and solution seeking.

Treatment

The cognitive behavioural therapy session is a highly structured event. Schmaling, Fruzzetti, and Jacobson (1989) suggest the following plan for a 90-minute session:

(1) Setting the agenda—exact allocation of tasks (5 minutes)
(2) Evaluating progress to date—by 12 formal ratings (10 minutes)
(3) Debriefing—informal and explorative (15 minutes)
(4) Business—new topics and skills (45 minutes)
(5) Assigning homework tasks (15 minutes)

Cognitive therapists structure time and material to ensure a steady progress with the couple. They instigate and direct that progress, they educate and provide feedback to the couple, they create optimism and enthusiasm, they predict setbacks and share this with the couple, and they help to create an alliance of equal partners.

Above all, the accurate expression of feeling by each party is encouraged. During cognitive therapy such emotions are dependent on the thoughts they have about each other's behaviour and the meaning they give to it. The primary purpose of cognitive therapy is to look out for any *distorted* or *maladaptive* thinking and to help the couple identify other meanings that would hurt less, or break the vicious cycle of reciprocated negative behaviour.

Negative attributes, of course, may be accurately applied to a partner and, in this case, the therapist will try both to identify the intent of the partner who misbehaves, as well as help each to understand the *impact* of such conduct on the other. Additionally, therapists will explore behaviour that is seen as ambiguous and help the puzzled partner offer alternative explanations for why the behaviour might have more than one meaning. An example of this is Jack's habit of delaying joint trips to the pub, seen by Jill as an example of his not wanting to share her company. Jill becomes irritated and sarcastic about the delay, and Jack will delay their departure further, or even cancel the outing. Jill and Jack may be able to offer another explanation; for example, that Jack feels self-conscious in pubs because he can't hear conversations with background music. Or he may be worrying about money—his self-consciousness in any event would only be aggravated by Jill's sarcasm.

PSYCHODYNAMIC APPROACHES FOR THE COUPLE

The most important of these approaches is the *psychoanalytic* model, whose central tenet is that it is the inner worlds of the partners that interacts with the external reality which causes relationships either to prosper or flounder. Our earliest experiences of being loved and cared for (or not, as the case may be) are the means by which our unconscious life develops and helps to shape our choice of partner (Bowlby, 1980). In the couple, each adult has had an experience of attachment, which both unconsciously and consciously shapes the individual's pattern of emotional bonds in intimacy (Ruszczynski, 1993; Ruszczynski & Fisher, 1995; Shapiro & Emde, 1995).

The therapist is there to *define* these processes to the couple and to provide them with an *interpretation* of what is causing and maintaining the problem. As well as dealing with the past, the therapist will use the feelings that the couple project onto the therapist, *transference*, to understand more about their projections and defences within their partnership (Chapter 1). The therapist also provides containment—in other words, a safe place to express feelings that have previously felt unsafe.

In psychodynamic couple therapy, as with behavioural and cognitive-behavioural approaches, the assessment of the couple and the emphasis on joint responsibility for conflict rather than blaming each partner is the starting point. Thereafter, the individual or the couple may be seen by the therapist. There has been some debate about when and how an individual or couple should be seen. Pincus (1973) has suggested that when one of the pair has a borderline or narcissistic personality, that it might be more appropriate to see the individual and to use the therapeutic relationship at a preverbal stage. In one-to-one work, the therapist can accept and affirm the individual and prepare the person for conjoint collaborative work at a later stage of therapy.

Conjoint psychotherapy, as with other approaches, requires the couple to share their personal understanding of the relationship with their partner in the presence of the therapist, who interprets, reformulates, encourages, feeds back, and works within the therapeutic alliance for the couple.

Not all psychodynamic approaches incorporate psychoanalytic theory. Client-centred Rogerian models applied to the couple are useful in providing the couple with a safe place to meet each other and be accepted by the therapist in a non-judgemental fashion. Here again, there is emphasis on the reciprocal role of the spouses or partners, but the agenda is driven more by the couple than the therapist (Clulow & Mattison, 1989; Daniel, 1985). A client-centred approach may be more effective when problems are neither severe nor longstanding, and has been widely used by RELATE (previously National Marriage Guidance Council) in the UK (Clulow, 1995; Lewis, Clark, & Morgan, 1992).

SYSTEMIC APPROACHES

Theoretical approaches to family therapy based on General Systems Theory (GST) have applications for couple and sexual problems (but see also Chapter 8). Developed in the early 1950s, GST was seen as a means of helping to broaden the focus from individuals or couples to the families and networks of which they were members. In this approach, a couple in a nuclear family system would be construed by the therapist as a *marital or parental sub-system*, and their children would be described as the *sibling sub-system* of the family. In turn, the *supra-system* would include the wider world of families of origin, friends, neighbours, and employers (Minuchin, 1974).

This method of thinking has been found useful in practice, and represents an important theoretical perspective that can be integrated with other therapeutic approaches for the dysfunctional couple. Implicit in this model is the notion that couples do not function in isolation, but influence and are influenced by other systems. Not only this, but couples and families are rule-bound structures with regard to their conduct, and the way in which they see each other and their reciprocal roles. Couples who come together bring the rules from their families of origin and have to negotiate (or not, as the case may be) a new set of rules for the new system, itself in a constant state of developmental flux.

The process by which people leave a parental system and achieve their own is called *individuation*, as is made more or less easy by the rigidity or fluidity of the family's rules.

In systemic work, there is an assumption of circularity between cognitive and behavioural processes; and that changing behaviour will change the beliefs that individuals have about each other, and *vice versa*.

BEHAVIOURAL SYSTEMS THEORY

Crowe and Ridley (1990) have devised an elegant hierarchy of Alternative Levels of Intervention (ALI) for working with couples in the contexts of their families, using a behavioural-systems approach. The ALI hierarchy is very flexible and allows the therapist to devise a "horses for courses approach", from a behavioural approach for problems of communication and negotiation to more systemic approaches for more individually focused or more difficult problems. The hierarchy allows the therapist to judge when it may be necessary to cease therapy altogether, or to refer for other forms of treatment, and enables the clinician to deal with a wide range of couple and sexual difficulties in clinical settings.

COUPLE THERAPY FOR SAME-SEX PARTNERS

Little has been written on this topic, and there have been unwarranted assumptions that gay and lesbian couples face similar issues to heterosexual couples in therapy. Butler and Clarke (1991) and Simons (1991) have summarised some features for therapists, which include:

- being positive about gay and lesbian relationships
- helping couples to find positive role models, within a history of the couple having none from their families of origin
- dealing with homophobia in the therapist, and the tendency to marginalise if not pathologise same-sex relationships
- dealing with internalised homophobia within the couple themselves
- dealing as individuals and in partnership with "coming out" issues
- dealing with low expectations and overemphasis on problem areas.

COUPLES IN TRANSCULTURAL SETTINGS

There remains little literature on transcultural or inter-racial marriages in the UK. Studies on the differing ethnic communities since the 1991 census have centred on inter-generational conflict, not those between spouses or couples. There is, however, a slowly growing field of published work on ethnicity and mental health, and some themes are emerging (Bhugra & de Silva, 1993; Kareem & Littlewood, 1991; Sue & Sue, 1991). It is clear that the effects of racism, alienation, and prejudice, combined with economic hardship, are likely to be aggravating couples from minority cultures, and that their needs are unlikely to be fully met within the existing services for couples (d'Ardenne, 1991). There is also little information about what happens to inter-racial partnerships, and the specific stressors that apply to them. This is all the more surprising in a context of increasing global social mobility. Therapists themselves have to begin by examining their own prejudices and assumptions in therapy, and the amount of cultural baggage they themselves bring into the therapeutic relationship. There is some evidence from the American mental health literature (Sue & Sue, 1991) that the attitudes and optimism of white therapists may be critical in supporting black and ethnic clients through crisis. Transcultural skills are pertinent to all psychological therapy; what is needed for the future is an organised, proactive, and integrated assessment of cultural and crosscultural needs of all members of the community, and a commitment to recruit a more representative cohort of therapists from a diverse population.

COUPLES WITH LONG-TERM HEALTH NEEDS

Couples who suffer from enduring physical or mental illness or disability remain another marginalised group, whose needs have been very under-represented in the therapeutic literature. Hawton (1985) and Bancroft (1989) provide an extensive review of the impact of gynaecological, urological, general surgical, oncological, and medical conditions, and in particular sexually transmitted diseases and AIDS, whose psychological sequelae can be devastating on the couple relationship. The sexual needs of the disabled are in part addressed by an organisation called SPOD (Sexual Problems of the Disabled), but the relationship needs of couples coping with disability, as with so many other aspects of their lives, are rarely given the attention they merit. Disabled people are perceived as asexual, or invisible, and despite recent changes in legislation remain stigmatised. They suffer significantly higher levels of unemployment, poorer housing, and social isolation, and census data has shown that their partnerships are likely to be more at risk of breakdown than those without disability (McAllister, 1995).

SEXUAL PROBLEMS

Hawton (1985) has defined sexual dysfunction as the persistent impairment of the normal patterns of sexual interest or response. This of course begs a further question about what is a normal pattern, which will be discussed later. Until the middle of the 20th century, psychoanalytic accounts of sexual disorders prevailed, and problems were deemed to have originated in childhood relationships, notably with parents. The work in the United States, of Kinsey (Kinsey, Pomeroy, & Martin, 1948; Kinsey, Pomeroy, Martin, & Gebhard, 1953), and, more importantly, of Masters and Johnson in the 1960s and 1970s, did much to promote a more scientific and epidemiological account of the actual sexual behaviour of larger populations. They published *Human Sexual Response* in 1966 and defined a four-stage model, which has now been widely accepted in defining patterns of desire in men and women, and formed the basis of their clinical work, described in *Human Sexual Inadequacy* (1970). These two works have been seminal in providing therapists with demonstrably effective, behavioural interventions for some very common sexual problems, and, though they have been much criticised, provided an important landmark in our understanding of sexual functioning and dysfunction.

Sexual Behaviour in Britain—The National Survey of Sexual Attitudes and Lifestyles (Wellings, Field, Johnson, & Wadsworth, 1994) is the most recent and comprehensive account of practice in the UK, and probably the only reliable one. Although it was commissioned largely in response to the AIDS crisis in the 1980s, it does describe in some detail the earliest sexual practices and attitudes of 20,000 respondents by age, class, ethnicity, and marital status. Its usefulness lies in allowing clinicians to define what is currently normal sexual behaviour in the UK.

Regrettably, we have no equivalent survey of the prevalence of sexual problems, between heterosexual or same-sex couples. Bancroft (1989) has discussed the limited data and methodological problems in some detail, but it is worth comparing his small-scale figures with the American figures of Kinsey et al. (1948, 1953) and Hite (1978)—both large-scale questionnaires. The system of classification of sexual disorders widely used (DSM-IV) is phenomenological and is based on the four-stage model of sexual arousal proposed by Masters and Johnson, with minor amendments. The four stages are known as excitement, plateau, orgasm, and resolution.

(1) *Excitement* is the phase characterised by the onset of erotic feelings and the development of arousal to a real or imagined stimulus. In men, the primary physical change is penile erection; in women it is vaginal lubrication, and the expansion and distension of the inner two-thirds of the vaginal barrel, and clitoral swelling.

(2) The *plateau* phase describes a more intense state of sexual tension which levels off over time. In men the penis is distended fully by peak blood flow, the erection has become firm, and is physiologically ready for penetration. In women, the vagina distends and the outer third now swells, thus narrowing the entrance, and the clitoris retracts into the clitoral hood.

(3) *Orgasm* is preceded immediately by a sense of orgasm or *ejaculatory inevitability*. Women's orgasm consists of rhythmic contractions around the vagina and surrounding tissues, for about a second—anywhere from five to fifteen times. Masters and Johnson challenged the Freudian distinction between vaginal and clitoral orgasm, and showed that the clitoris is always implicated as the main organ of sexual sensation. They also showed that women are not always conscious of these changes, and the accompanying psychological changes will vary enormously according to the individual.

   For men, semen is emitted into the urethra and seminal fluid expelled by rhythmic contraction of the prostrate gland, the perineal muscles, and the shaft of the penis. The psychological experience varies enormously, and men also may be uncertain about whether or not ejaculation has actually occurred, though this is less common than in women. Pleasure is affected by both internal and external factors, but men are especially influenced by performance anxiety, and how much control they have over both the arousal and ejaculatory phases.

(4) During *resolution* the sexual organs of both sexes return to their pre-excitement phase. Men experience a rapid loss of initial erection, and then a slower detumescence. During this time—known as the *refractory period*—men cannot ejaculate, although there is considerable individual variation, from minutes to hours. In men, the refractory period increases with age. Women do not have a refractory period, which means that a woman can return to orgasm immediately after resolution.

CAUSES OF SEXUAL DYSFUNCTION

There are many causes of sexual problems, but emphasis in this book will of course centre on psychological causes. In recent years, however, there has been substantial research into the many physical factors that contribute to the problem, and which interact with psychological or psychosocial difficulties, and aggravate them further. These can include injury, illness, surgery, and medication, and it is worth noting that the vast majority of psychotropic medication has a tendency to inhibit sexual desire or sexual performance (Bancroft, 1989; Hawton, 1989). It is important not to adopt an either/or approach. Human beings are complex and a physical experience, such as loss of erection following onset of diabetes, will produce anxiety and the expectation of failure again. These psychological problems will in turn aggravate the physical cause, and create a higher probability of failure, unless there is an intervention that breaks that cycle. Harland and Huws (1997) estimate that 20–25% of diabetic patients had psychological disturbance associated with their sexual dysfunction, which could be appropriately managed by counselling; this was particularly true for women. Similarly, Schiavi (1996) indicates that older people, who experience loss of sexual function, have neglected emotional needs and that clinicians are too quick to pathologise change of function in older people.

Psychological causes

Hawton (1985) has described psychological causes as predisposing, precipitant, and maintaining.

Predisposing factors—those that make a person vulnerable to dysfunction—include poor parenting, especially lack of affection and physical contact, disturbed family relationships, particularly abusive or incestuous ones, restrictive attitudes to sex, and poor or non-existent sex education. These causes are in part speculative; for example, many women who are sexually dysfunctional have an early history of abuse (Jehu, 1988), but it has not been proven that everyone who has been abused becomes sexually dysfunctional in adult life.

Precipitant causes—those that lead to the appearance of the problem—include those difficulties within the current relationship, including dysfunction in the other partner, sexual trauma, childbirth, depression, anxiety, ageing, random failure, organic factors, and the psychological response to a perceived sexual failure.

Maintaining factors—those in the relationship that cause the problem to persist or worsen—include performance anxiety, fear of failure, poor communication, guilt, loss of attraction, inadequate information, or insufficient foreplay.

For example, a 25-year-old woman had never been relaxed or confident about her sexuality since a restrictive and unaffectionate upbringing which led her to feel guilty about sex (predisposing factors). She suffered depression after the birth of her first child, and no longer had any desire for sex with her husband (precipitant). Although her husband was sympathetic, she felt guilty and anxious and tried to have sex as quickly as possible with no foreplay in an attempt to placate him (maintaining factor).

Types of sexual dysfunction

Table 7.1 represents current nomenclature for disorders, and it is worth mentioning that these apply to individuals, to those in heterosexual relationships, and those in same-sex relationships. Impaired sexual interest, or disorders of sexual desire (Kaplan, 1974), affect either sex, and describe a situation where the individual avoids situations likely to have been erotic in the past, and reports a lack of erotic feelings and fantasy. Impaired sexual interest is not about a loss of attraction to one partner; nor is it about an absence of sexual response altogether. Typically, the client will say that with enough stimulation, it is possible to reach orgasm, but the quality of that response is poor. This problem is often secondary to depression, or a crisis within the relationship, and may be successfully treated if the causes are dealt with. It can also be a sign of more serious psychological difficulty, stemming from childhood experiences, and reflecting ambivalence towards sexuality in general.

Erectile dysfunction is the most common of male sexual disorders. It is still called impotence, especially within medical settings, but this term is now avoided (Bancroft, 1989) because of its emphasis on powerlessness. Erectile dysfunction is any failure of the erectile reflex to pump enough blood into the cavernous sinuses, to make it erect enough for penetration. Erection and ejaculation are separate functions, and men will sometimes have one without the other. Erectile dysfunction can be partial or complete; it can also be continuous or spasmodic, or situational, for example with a certain partner, or in a particular setting.

TABLE 7.1
Classification of sexual dysfunction

Category	Women	Men
Interest	Impaired sexual interest	Impaired sexual interest
Arousal	Impaired sexual arousal	Erectile dysfunction
Orgasm	Orgasmic dysfunction	Premature ejaculation
		Retarded/absent ejaculation
Other	Vaginismus	Painful ejaculation
	Dyspareunia	Dyspareunia
	Sexual phobia	Sexual phobia
	Panic states	Panic states

Primary erectile dysfunction is a serious disorder, and means that a man has never had an erection. It is mainly associated with physical causes, neurological diseases, trauma, diabetes, or with severe and longstanding psychological disturbance, and has a poorer prognosis than secondary dysfunction. Secondary erectile failure, where erections have previously occurred, is far more common; indeed, most men experience it from time to time. The most common psychological causes are anxiety, especially about performance, fear, guilt, shame, duress, and ambivalence about sex.

Premature ejaculation is a complaint where a man experiences little voluntary control over his ejaculatory reflex, and reaches orgasm too quickly. It can be a transient or longstanding problem, and is associated with failure to recognise the sensations immediately before ejaculating, and gaining conscious mastery over them. It can occur as a result of very stressful early sexual experiences, for example with a prostitute, or any anxiety that interferes with learning to perceive such sensations. It is the second most common sexual disorder seen in clinical settings, but the true prevalence is unknown, since only those who cannot achieve penetration or experience a serious loss of pleasure for themselves or their partners are likely to seek help.

Retarded ejaculation is less common, and refers to a man's inability to ejaculate when fully aroused (and erect) and desirous of orgasmic release. Retarded ejaculation (or ejaculatory incompetence as it is sometimes called) can be situational or total, and is frequently associated with psychological causes, especially conscious and unconscious difficulties in relinquishing control. Less commonly, it may be caused by hostility or ambivalence towards a particular partner or towards sexual intimacy in general.

Women's sexual dysfunctions are less connected to performance and more to the quality of the sexual experience. The most common in women is known as low libido or inhibited sexual desire. There is only one method of ascertaining inhibited desire, and that is that the woman subjectively experiences it, often in relation to past levels of desire. Primary problems, where the woman reports that she has never experienced desire, may be associated with depression, as well as more general difficulties in her current relationship. More commonly, secondary difficulties will develop, sometimes in relation to life cycle changes, such as late pregnancy, childbirth, postpartum, or menopause, or it may be related to depression, either endogenous or reactive.

Difficulties with sexual arousal, such as the physiological changes of vaginal engorgement and lubrication, are usually associated with inhibited sexual desire, but, exceptionally, may occur at times of significant physical change, such as childbirth and menopause. According to Kaplan (1983, 1988) they may occur in women with major inhibitions about their own sexuality.

Orgasmic dysfunction requires a careful assessment to distinguish here women who are non-orgasmic with their partners, but who can masturbate to orgasm, from those who have never had an orgasm under any kind of stimulation—what

Kaplan (1983) calls *pre-orgasmic*. Women who can reach orgasm by masturbation but not with their partner may also experience difficulties with communication, trust, and intimacy with their partner.

Vaginismus refers to spasm in the outer third of the vaginal barrel when anything—penis, finger, or tampon—is introduced into the vagina. This is not an uncommon problem, and it is usually primary and effectively prevents intercourse from occurring, although it can more rarely occur secondarily, following infection or sexual trauma. Women may present as feeling that they have no control over their sexuality, and may also have unusual ideas about the capacity of their own vaginas. Many describe a phobia of being ripped open by penile penetration, an "as if" feeling which is amenable to exploration and education.

Dyspareunia refers simply to pain during intercourse, and affects both sexes, although it is more frequently reported by women. Its causes and presentations are many. Gynaecological assessment should always be sought, especially as organic factors are often implicated. Presentation may be located in the outer vagina—superficial or mild symptoms, often characterised by a stinging, burning, or tearing experience. The most common causes are lack of arousal, local infection, or scarring. The deeper dyspareunia—which may be connected to pelvic infections, endometriosis, or psychological and/or physical trauma, is described as a deep pain—often a kicking sensation—and is usually unconnected with sexual interest, arousal, or orgasm.

ASSESSMENT FOR SEXUAL PROBLEMS

Couples often present with sexual dysfunction and will be assessed conjointly and separately, psychologically and physically, before a decision can be made about whether therapy is possible or desirable. Couples who attend for the first time for an assessment of their problem will need to be listened to and reassured about the nature of the work of therapy. Assessment allows four main aims to be achieved:

- a definition of the problem and the changes that are sought
- detailed information about the history and causes of the problem
- to assess the type of therapy indicated on the basis of the formulation
- to begin therapy, and to encourage partners to think and to formulate for themselves

as well as considering other aspects of their relationship where change could or should be possible. Where the dysfunction is secondary to mental disorder, it may be more appropriate to deal with the mental disorder first, since it has a complex relationship with self-esteem, emotional reflexivity, mood, and reality testing (Birley & Hudson, 1991). There is little research in this neglected field, but estimates of up to 50% of clinically presenting sexual disorders have major mental illness as a component.

SEXUAL COUNSELLING

Couples will present with difficulties of recent onset where it is clear that there is a lack of information or awareness about sexual process, which is amenable to education. In these cases, sex counselling, directed to choices and simple changes, may be the treatment of choice. The huge success of agony aunts in magazines and newspapers, together with the abundance of self-help literature available at most bookstores, testifies to the fact that many individuals and partners find the provision of advice and information helpful in dealing with some emotional distress. These resources are usually responsible in advising people also when a different kind of intervention is required, such as a behavioural approach. Counselling also challenges the beliefs and attitudes that couples have—notably common sexual myths (Zilbergeld, 1978) that raise false expectations about performance, such as a man is only aroused if he has an erection, nice women do not initiate sex, etc.

SEX THERAPY

Indications for behavioural sex therapy are usually the following:

(1) The problem is of longer duration.
(2) Efforts by the couple have failed, including counselling.
(3) The problem is being maintained primarily by psychological factors.
(4) The problem is threatening the overall relationship.

Behavioural sex therapy, developed from the original work of Masters and Johnson incorporates assessment and formulation of the problem (which is shared with the couple). The therapist then provides behavioural homework assignments which are agreed and undertaken throughout therapy, with records of that homework often brought back to the consulting room by both partners. Counselling and cognitive strategies may also be used when resistance to homework is met, and education both specific to the session, and generally. Termination of therapy is critical and sexual partners will be given strategies and ideas to prevent relapse, together with follow-up at least three months later.

Central to the behavioural model is the concept of anxiety as a maintaining factor in the dysfunction, and the importance of removing the need to perform from the couple. It is common practice to request after formulation, and prior to homework tasks, a complete and voluntary ban on intercourse. This curious and paradoxical requirement, especially for partners who may not be having intercourse anyway, achieves two purposes. First, it removes, in an explicit and equal way, the requirement to perform, and relieves the couple of the fear that any intimacy they might share will inevitably lead to expectations of lovemaking and possible failures around that. Second, it allows partners to return to non-genital intimacy and to undertake in homework a series of graded tasks intended to increase their awareness of their own and their partners' sensual needs. Masters and Johnson called this *sensate focus*.

Couples are invited to *pleasure* each other in a non-demanding way, in turn, on a "give to get" principle. Sensate focus is used with all behavioural interventions in sex therapy, and allows the couple to learn to be more relaxed and more sexually aroused with each other. They begin with non-genital contact, progressing to genital contact, and then to orgasm and/or penetration depending on the nature of the dysfunction and the agreed goals of therapy.

An example of a specific intervention is the Semans or *squeeze* technique for premature ejaculation. The aim of therapy here is to provide the man with an opportunity to increase his awareness of the sensations leading inevitably to orgasm, so that he can learn to hold back and thus control his ejaculatory reflex. His partner is instructed to squeeze his penis when he has an erection just below the glans between the forefinger and thumb, and press hard until most of the erection is lost. This process is repeated several times, and the man is asked to concentrate on "the point of inevitability" and then allowed orgasmic release. Intercourse is not attempted until this has been learnt and when he is ready.

Vaginismus sufferers are treated by desensitising the woman to penetration with its associated pain and fear. She is taught relaxation and self-exploration initially, together with education about the capacity of the vagina, and the nature of the involuntary reflex. Some therapists will demonstrate the reflex to the woman in the presence of her partner to relieve both of them of the guilt and anxiety about her "excluding" him, and show that the reflex occurs when *any* penetration is attempted.

The woman is then provided with either a set of graded dilators and asked to insert the smallest of these into her vagina very gently, and to contain it until the pain or discomfort has passed. She then moves into the next size until she can accommodate a dilator that approximates to the size of an erect adult penis. Many clinicians now offer the woman a choice between dilators and using her own fingers, and then those of her partner, to increase her sense of control and allow digital exploration of her own body. Penile penetration is attempted when the woman is ready, usually with her on top, and initially without thrusting—a process called *vaginal containment*. This *in vivo* desensitisation only works when the woman is highly motivated and has a partner who can explicitly work with her at her pace.

There remain other behavioural interventions, all based on the principle of reducing anxiety, increasing arousal, and improving communication between the partners. Couples are set tasks and may be asked to keep notebooks or diaries, and to use them in therapy to help create a graded programme suitable to their needs. There is evidence that behavioural techniques such as these are well suited to crosscultural settings, especially where there may be language and cultural barriers (d'Ardenne, 1986).

PSYCHODYNAMIC APPROACHES

Psychoanalytic theory rests on the principle of incomplete psychosexual development. It is deemed more appropriate for individuals or couples whose difficulties extend beyond performance anxiety or lack of education about sexuality. Helen Kaplan (1974) described an integrated behavioural and analytic approach that allows clinicians to deal with a sexual problem in a more flexible way. She recommends a behavioural structure at the start of the therapeutic exchange, and when resistance encountered by the couple in the completion of assignments is met, that they work on their deeper conflicts and anxieties about sexuality within a dynamic framework.

Nevertheless, this is a very different use of psychodynamic psychotherapy to the way it is expounded in feminist analytic thinking, for example, Maguire (1995). She argues that male power is the source of many psychosexual difficulties in people, and that analytic writers can and do perpetuate that power difference. Influential male analysts may pathologise the behaviour of their clients (mainly women) directly as a result of their own sexual anxieties, and the patriarchal culture of neo-Freudian thinking, which is neither universal nor timeless.

COGNITIVE MODELS FOR SEXUAL THERAPY

All psychosexual therapy has an educational and counselling component to it, which is aimed at correcting false attitudes and information about sexual responsiveness, as well as improving communication between partners. There are occasions, however, when a resistance to homework assignments, sabotage of bans on intercourse, or a negative reaction to the assignments can be dealt with by using a cognitive model (Hawton, 1995; Hawton, Catalan, Martin, & Fagg, 1986), which goes deeper than counselling.

A model is proposed that a couple's previous or current experiences create attitudes which in turn lead to automatic negative thoughts or images about sex. These directly interfere with the homework assignment, where the task will evoke sometimes a fleeting and barely conscious negative response, leading to avoidance or outright rejection of the task in hand.

Hawton (1995) proposes that the therapist asks the individual or couple to generate as many possible explanations for the refusal as possible, to look at the evidence for these explanations and then identify the most likely account. This process helps them to achieve greater awareness, and to use evidence as a recognition task for attitudes and beliefs held. The therapist then asks the individual to generate alternative attitudes based on education, listening, or a rational view of the evidence, that are more likely to achieve the explicit goals of therapy. An example might demonstrate this: A man with erectile dysfunction became very tense during sensate focus therapy when he and his wife progressed from non-genital touching to having his wife touch his penis and attempt to give him pleasure. He ended up sabotaging or avoiding homework sessions but continued to attend sex therapy. He was able to generate the following four explanations for his behaviour, with the help of his therapist:

(1) He believed his wife found his genitals repulsive to touch and was merely trying to please him.
(2) He believed that if his wife touched him, and he did not become erect, that his wife would feel she was no longer attractive to him.
(3) He believed his problems were physical in nature and that a psychological approach was a waste of time.
(4) He believed that if touched, he would ejaculate immediately and feel even more inadequate than before.

Once this man could see these explanations in front of himself and his wife, it became clearer that the second explanation was the most valid. This client had always felt unattractive to his wife, but this was compounded by his fearfulness of his wife feeling unattractive as well. He saw each episode of a failed erection as evidence that there might be something in her that was "Turning him off" and that he had no control over this. His therapist and his wife were able to address with evidence to the contrary; for example, he had had a good erection during non-genital contact. In fact, he lost his erection only when he experienced performance anxiety prior to an expectation that intercourse was likely to occur. The client agreed to try genital contact with his wife in a non-demanding exchange, and the erections resumed.

EFFECTIVENESS

The NHS review of psychological therapies (Roth & Fonagy, 1996) does not provide overwhelming evidence for the effectiveness of sexual and relationship therapy. This is in part because no large controlled studies have been carried out to compare this kind of intervention with less specific therapies, but also because most clinicians use a range of interventions with couples who themselves present with a range of difficulties, and cause and effect become more difficult to demonstrate. Treatment approaches aimed at reducing sexual anxiety and improving communication and the quality of relationships appear to be most successful particularly where couples have established motivation and treatment compliance, and results suggest long-term success in 60–65% of cases. Cognitive and communications skills training are best for these kind of difficulties. The best success for behavioural interventions appears to be for premature ejaculation and vaginismus. Hawton et al. (1986) examined the outcome of 200 couples and found that the original Masters and Johnson figures were harder to replicate. They had an ordinary clinical sample in the UK, compared to highly motivated couples willing to undertake the original 2-week residential course provided in the original Mid-West setting. Roth and Fonagy concluded that the role of anxiety in sexual and relationship disorders needs to be identified and treated distinctly; that organic factors, especially for erectile disorders, have been under-recognised until the 1990s; and lastly, that there remain no large, well-designed controlled trials that examine the effectiveness of specific therapies for specific dysfunctions.

In conclusion, the basic research on intereventions, both *individual* and *integrated*, is lacking in the field of sexual and relationship work. The era of medical treatments for male sexual disorders (Riley, 1998), and the impact this will have on existing relationships (Barnes, 1998), will require a fundamental reappraisal of specific psychological therapies for couple and sexual problems. The pharmaceutical industry has recognised the significance of psychological issues in the clinical effectiveness of its products. It remains to be seen whether psychotherapeutic practitioners, trainers, and researchers are equally motivated to seek partnerships in providing couples with integrated and informed care. Notwithstanding, there remains much for the psychotherapist to do that is rewarding and useful with couples. Sexual and relationship psychological problems continue to provide one of the more significant and fast-growing areas of therapeutic need in the clinical population.

RECOMMENDED READING

Couple problems and therapy

Crowe, M., & Ridley, J. (1990). *Therapy with couples: A behavioural-systems approach to marital and sexual problems*. Oxford, UK: Blackwell Scientific Publications.

This remains the best text in the field for behavioural and systems approaches to the couple.

Ruszczynski, S. (Ed.). (1993). *Psychotherapy with couples: Theory and practice at the Tavistock Institute of Marital Studies*. London: Karnac Books.

An excellent edited text describing psychotherapeutic interventions with couples with a range of complex problems.

Stuart, R.B. (1980). *Helping couples change: A social learning approach to marital therapy*. New York: Guilford Press.

A clear account of applied learning theory to couples' communications dysfunction.

Sexual problems

Bancroft, J. (1989). *Human sexuality and its problems* (2nd ed.). Edinburgh, UK: Churchill Livingstone.

This remains the definitive text for any student of sexual disorders. Broad based and scholarly.

Hawton, K. (1985). *Sex therapy: A practical guide*. Oxford, UK: Oxford University Press.

A very clear "how to do it" book for clinicians of all backgrounds.

USEFUL ORGANISATIONS

The British Association for Sexual and Relationship Therapy is an organisation that trains, supervises and accredits sexual and marital therapists and their trainers in the UK. It provides practitioners with UKCP registration, and is affiliated to the World Congress of Sexology. It produces *Sexual and Relationship Therapy*, an international refereed journal for all professionals concerned with sexual and couple dysfunction, and places a strong emphasis on multidisciplinary research and practice. Information from The Administrative Assistant, BASMT, PO Box 13686, London SW20 9ZH, UK. Tel: 0181 543 2707; Email: BASMT@demon.co.uk; Website: www @basmt.co.uk

RELATE—National Marriage Guidance, Herbert Gray College, Little Church St., Rugby CV21 3AP, UK. Tel: 01788 573241; Email: info@relate.org.uk; Website: www.relate.org.uk. A national organisation offering sexual therapy and other services to help people with difficulties in marriage or couple relationships.

The Tavistock Marital Studies Institute (TMSI) is a psychoanalytically informed and practice-based organisation, committed to studying marriage and the couple relationship. Information from Patricia Harrington, Information Officer, TMSI, The Tavistock Centre, 120 Belsize Lane, London NW3 5BA, UK. Tel: 0171 447 3273; Email: tmsi@tmsi.org.uk

One Plus One, The Marriage and Partnership Research Charity, 14 Theobalds Rd., London WC1X 8PF, UK. Tel: 0171 831 5261; Email: 106006.705@compuserve.com. A research charity concerned with the causes, effects, and prevention of marital breakdown. One Plus One translates its research into practical projects for couples and families.

REFERENCES

Bancroft, J. (1989). *Human sexuality and its problems* (2nd ed.). Edinburgh, UK: Churchill Livingstone.

Barnes, P. (1998). The female partner in the treatment of erectile dysfunction: What is her position? *Sexual and Marital Therapy, 13*(3), 231–238.

Bennun, I. (1991). Working with the individual from the couple. In D. Hooper & W. Dryden (Eds.), *Couple therapy: A handbook* (pp. 110–124). Milton Keynes, UK: Open University Press.

Bhugra, D., & DeSilva, P. (1993). Sexual dysfunction across cultures. *International Review of Psychiatry, 5*, 243–252.

Birley, J., & Hudson, B. (1991). The family, the social network, and rehabilitation. In F. Watts & D. Bennett (Eds.), *Theory and practice of psychiatric rehabilitation* (pp. 171–188). Chichester, UK: Wiley.

Bowlby, J. (1980). *Attachment and loss: Loss, sadness and depression*. New York: Basic Books.

Butler, M., & Clarke, J. (1991). Couple therapy with homosexual men. In D. Hooper & W. Dryden (Eds.), *Couple therapy: A handbook* (pp. 196–206). Milton Keynes, UK: Open University Press.

Clulow, C. (Ed.). (1995). *Women, men and marriage: Talks from the Tavistock Marital Studies Institute.* London: Sheldon Press.

Clulow, C., & Mattison, J. (1989). *Marriage inside out: Understanding problems of intimacy.* Harmondsworth, UK: Penguin.

Crowe, M., & Ridley, J. (1990). *Therapy with couples: A behavioural-systems approach to marital and sexual problems.* Oxford, UK: Blackwell Scientific Publications.

Daniel, D. (1985). Marital therapy: The psychodynamic approach. In W. Dryden (Ed.), *Marital therapy in Britain.* Harper & Row.

d'Ardenne, P. (1986). Sexual dysfunction in a transcultural setting: Assessment, treatment and research. *Sexual and Marital Therapy, 1,* 23–34.

d'Ardenne, P. (1991). Transcultural issues in couple therapy. In D. Hooper & W. Dryden (Eds.), *Couple therapy: A handbook.* Milton Keynes, UK: Open University Press.

Harland, R., & Huws, H. (1997). Sexual problems in diabetes and the role of psychological intervention. *Sexual and Marital Therapy, 12*(2), 147–158.

Hawton, K. (1985). *Sex therapy: A practical guide.* Oxford, UK: Oxford University Press.

Hawton, K. (1989). Sexual dysfunctions. In K. Hawton, P.M. Salkovskis, J. Kirk, & D.M. Clark (Eds.), *Cognitive behaviour therapy for psychiatric problems* (pp. 374–405). Oxford, UK: Oxford University Press.

Hawton, K. (1995). Treatment of sexual dysfunctions by sex therapy and other approaches. *British Journal of Psychiatry, 167,* 307–314.

Hawton, K., Catalan, J., Martin, P., & Fagg, J. (1986). Long term outcome of sex therapy. *Behaviour Research and Therapy, 24,* 665–675.

Hite, S. (1978). *The Hite report.* London: Talmy Franklin.

Jehu, D. (1988). *Sexual abuse and beyond.* Chichester, UK: Wiley.

Kaplan, H. (1974). *The new sex therapy.* New York: Bruner Mazel.

Kaplan, H. (1983). *Disorders of sexual desire.* New York: Bruner Mazel.

Kaplan, H. (1988). Sexual panic states. *Sexual and Marital Therapy, 3*(1), 7–9.

Kareem, J., & Littlewood, R. (Eds.) (1992). *Intercultural therapy: Themes, interpretation and practice.* Oxford, UK: Blackwell.

Kinsey, A.C., Pomeroy, W.B., & Martin, C.F. (1948). *Sexual behaviour in the human male.* Philadelphia: Saunders.

Kinsey, A.C., Pomeroy, W.B., Martin, C.F., & Gebhard, P.H. (1953). *Sexual behavior in the human female.* Philadelphia: Saunders.

Lewis, J., Clark, D., & Morgan, D. (1992). *Whom God hath joined together: The work of marriage guidance.* London: Routledge.

Maguire, M. (1995). *Men, women, passion and power: Gender issues in psychotherapy.* London: Routledge.

Masters, W.H., & Johnson, V.E. (1966). *Human sexual response.* Boston: Little Brown.

Masters, W.H., & Johnson, V.E. (1970). *Human sexual inadequacy.* Boston: Little Brown.

McAllister, F. (Ed.). (1995). *Marital breakdown and the health of the nation.* London: One Plus One.

Minuchin, S. (1974). *Families and family therapy.* London: Tavistock.

Pincus, L. (Ed.). (1973). *Marriage: Studies in emotional conflict and growth.* London: Institute of Marital Studies.

Riley, A. (1998). Integrated approaches to therapy in integrated interventions—physical and psychological treatments. *Sexual and Marital Therapy, 13*(3), 227–230.

Roth, A., & Fonagy, P. (1996). *What works for whom? A critical review of psychotherapy research.* New York: Guilford Press.

Ruszczynski, S. (Ed.). (1993). *Psychotherapy with couples: Theory and practice at the Tavistock Institute of Marital Studies.* London: Karnac Books.

Ruszczynski, S., & Fisher, J. (Eds.). (1995). *Intrusiveness and intimacy in the couple.* London: Karnac Books.

Schiavi, R.C. (1996). Sexuality and male ageing: From performance to satisfaction. *Sexual and Marital Therapy*, *11*(1), 9–14.

Schmaling, K.B., Fruzzetti, A.E., & Jacobson, N.S. (1989). Marital problems. In K. Hawton, P.M. Salkovskis, J. Kirk, & D.M. Clark (Eds.), *Cognitive behaviour therapy for psychiatric problems: A practical guide* (pp. 339–369). Oxford, UK: Oxford Medical Publications.

Simons, S. (1991). Couple therapy with lesbians. In D. Cooper & W. Dryden (Eds.), *Couple therapy: A handbook* (pp. 207–216). Milton Keynes, UK: Open University Press.

Stuart, R.B. (1969). Operant interpersonal treatment for marital discord. *Journal of Consulting and Clinical Psychology*, *33*, 675–682.

Stuart, R.B. (1980). *Helping couples change: A social learning approach to marital therapy*. New York: Guilford Press.

Sue, D.W., & Sue, S. (1991). *Counseling the culturally different*. New York: John Wiley.

Wellings, K., Field, J., Johnson, A.M., & Wadsworth, J. (1994). *Sexual behaviour in Britain: The national survey of sexual attitudes and lifestyles*. Harmondsworth, UK: Penguin.

Zilbergeld, B. (1978). *Male sexuality*. Boston: Little Brown.

CHAPTER EIGHT

Family problems

Karen Partridge
Kingston District Community NHS Trust, Richmond Healthcare
Hamlet, London, UK

INTRODUCTION: FROM PROBLEMS TO RELATIONSHIP

Problems presented as family problems may include the full range and diversity of symptoms presented in clinical practice from anxiety and bedwetting to sexual abuse, anorexia, and schizophrenia. This raises the question of what makes something a "family problem" and what distinguishes it from an individual or marital problem. In fact, any presenting symptom can be seen as a family problem if you choose to view it in relational terms, that is, if a problem is seen as a communication that affects and organises relationships. This means that there can be no specific definition of what constitutes a family problem without asking the question of who chooses to describe a particular behaviour or series of behaviours as a problem and what their relationship is to those they describe as having the family problem. So the problem is in the eyes of an observer.

The observer may be a family member observing his or her own behaviour or that of other family members. Since relatively few clients present themselves for treatment explicitly requesting help for family problems, the observer is frequently someone outside the family unit such as a relative, neighbour, or friend, or a health care professional such as a GP or health visitor. There are a number of situations where an observer to the family unit is likely to describe the family as having family problems. First, when more than one member of a family appears to be very involved in the presenting problem. Second, when there are a number of different presenting problems affecting different family members. And third, when previous attempts at help have failed. Finally, a family may be described as having family problems or even as being a "problem family" when a number of different therapeutic, legal, or statutory agencies are involved with them, as for example in the case of domestic violence or disclosure of sexual abuse.

These problems of definition mean that it is not possible to identify and categorise family problems according to the presenting problem, nor to talk about their prevalence and epidemiology as if they were a separate class of problems from any other presented in clinical practice. It is more meaningful to talk in terms of a family approach to problems. Then one is able to talk about which problems are more frequently addressed by using a family approach and which problems have been found to be more effectively treated in this way.

Many clinicians might argue that by taking family relationships into account when they approach a problem they are taking a family approach. Behavioural approaches may, for example, include parents in implementing a behaviour programme for a child, whereas psychodynamic approaches may focus on an individual's relationships. However, the three main approaches that this chapter will outline take a further step than this, which identifies them as family therapy approaches. They conceptualise the family system as the main target for treatment and see the individual who is labelled as having the problem as the designated patient, that is, the family "elects" an individual to present the symptom on behalf of the system. This can be described as a family systems approach. The first model of family therapy to be outlined in this chapter is an example of a family systems approach.

The second and third approaches to be described take a further step from the family systems approach. These approaches remove the boundary from the group of persons described as a "family" to include the wider system. This may include for example, friends, work relationships, the referring network, other helping agencies, and, in the case of the third approach to be outlined, will always include the therapist and the therapeutic agency of which he or she is a part.

The three approaches to be described represent the three most distinct and influential current developments in the field. The first approach is Salvador Minuchin's Structural Therapy. The second is the Brief Therapy Model of Steve de Shazer, and the third is the Milan Associates approach and Post-Milan developments arising out of the work of Gianfranco Cecchin and Luigi Boscolo. The chapter will not cover in detail the Strategic approach to family therapy, which is most clearly articulated by Jay Haley (1963) and the Palo Alto group on the West Coast of America, that is, Watzlawick, Weakland, and Fisch (1974), since few currently practising family therapists now identify themselves purely with this approach (Madanes, 1981). The work of those practitioners who have not sought to be or have actively resisted being defined in a particular school, such as Milton Erikson, Carl Whitaker, and Virginia Satir, will not be covered in this chapter. Their unique and charismatic style has made these approaches difficult to describe and to teach, although much can be learnt from them at an abstract, creative level. Compared to the systemic approaches discussed here, behavioural and psychodynamic approaches to family therapy have far less influence in the field. These approaches will not be outlined in detail but will be briefly compared and contrasted with the approaches presented here. The interested reader should refer to the work of the Adolescent Department at the Tavistock Clinic (Box, Copley, Magagna, & Moustaki, 1981) and to the work of Ian Falloon (1988) for detailed accounts of the psychodynamic and behavioural family therapy approaches.

THE HISTORICAL CONTEXT: FROM SYMPTOM TO SYSTEM

Since the early 1960s when R.D. Laing (Laing & Esterson, 1964) first started looking at the family relationship, in particular the relationships that his schizophrenic patients had with their mothers, a quiet revolution has been taking place within the field known as family therapy. This revolution is tantamount to what Kuhn (1962) described as a paradigm shift. Prior to these developments any family work that did take place was usually conceived of from a psychodynamic perspective. Crucial to this shift, which began in the early 1970s, was the work of Gregory Bateson (1972) and Von Bertalanffy's General Systems Theory (1968). A number of key ideas can be seen as fundamental in the ensuing developments: first, Bateson's use of communication theory, which he used to differentiate between different levels of meaning, for example between the verbal and non-verbal; second, his use of the term *context*, which he saw as providing meaning to behaviour; and, third, the idea of punctuation. Bateson described causality as a circular process and it is a matter of punctuation where one chooses to draw the distinction between cause and effect. The shift from punctuating our experience in terms of cause and effect to describing the form and pattern of organisation of behaviour is what is termed a cybernetic approach.

These ideas fitted closely with the shift towards general systems theory that was happening in general science. Systems were seen as being structured by feedback, reaching a stable state as the opposing focus for change and stability balance each other out. Like a central heating system regulated by a thermostat, any change in one part of the system was seen as necessitating a corresponding change in every other part, that is if you turn off a radiator without adjusting the thermostat all the other radiators will become hotter.

In observing a system Bateson described information as a "difference" and "difference" as a relationship. So family therapists became interested in mapping the differences in relationships between family members (Bateson, 1972). These ideas led to a development that further distinguishes family therapy from other approaches. That is, the use of teamwork. Bateson noted that by observing from two different perspectives, a third dimension, that of depth, could be observed. Using this idea family therapists began to use a one-way screen with a therapy team behind the screen observing the therapist and family interaction.

These ideas were developed by the Palo Alto group on the West Coast of America and the Milan Associates in Italy. This era in family therapy is described as first-order cybernetics, that is, the observer stands outside the system in order to describe its characteristics. Around the mid/late 1970s a further change took place. Instead of emphasising the stability of systems, more emphasis was placed on their constantly evolving nature and the observer was seen as being part of the system rather than standing outside it. This is described as a second-order cybernetic approach.

One of the implications of expanding the system to include the observer is that the proponents no longer describe themselves as family therapists but as systemic therapists or systemic consultants. Since the system is created by the observers, a therapist/consultant may decide to define the system as an individual, a couple, a family, a work group, an organisation, or any mixture of these. The shift from a first- to second-order cybernetic view also has implications for the way in which a symptom is viewed. For example, alongside the earlier view is the idea of symptom functionality, that is, that the system leads to the production of the symptom as a solution to a problem. In contrast, the idea of Problem Determined Systems (Anderson, Goolishian, & Windermand, 1986) describes problems creating systems around them rather than the other way round. Lynn Hoffman (1981) graphically uses the analogy of the golden goose in the fairy tale to describe this process. In the fairy tale everybody who touches the golden goose sticks to it until a whole chain of people are stuck together around the golden goose. In a problem determined system everybody who touches the problem "sticks" until a system is created. This more dynamic view of systems is extremely helpful in working with multi-agency families or clients who have received a lot of previous help because it allows one to consider the way in which the helping agency has become part of the system.

In the 1980s a further significant influence in the field was von Foerster and von Glaserfeld's constructivist ideas (Hoffman, 1988). The central tenant of the constructivist position is that reality is socially constructed. This means that there are as many versions of reality as there are observers to draw the distinction and we cannot "know" reality independently of our perception of it (Von Foerster, 1981; Von Glaserfeld, 1984). The work of the Chilean biologist Humberto Maturana introduced the notion of a "multiversa" to describe the multiple constructions of reality by observers. He also introduced the idea that systems exist in language (Maturana & Varela, 1980). The corollary of this stance is that there is no right way to be or to live but that some constructions may be more useful than others. This stance lay itself open to criticisms of a radical relativist position from a moral and ethical perspective, and in the 1990s gave way to Social Constructionism. This shift has begun to be described by some writers as "third-order cybernetics" (Dallos, 1991). Unlike a constructivist perspective, social constructionism does not seek to deny the "reality" of the physical world but instead sees action in the world as an attempt to maintain coherence and coordination between observers. That is, we connect or coordinate with each other in such a way so as to maintain the coherence of our beliefs or "stories" about the world. Whereas constructivism saw the individual as primary, social constructionism sees the social as primary so that individual identity is seen as a social construction. From this frame every action is seen as political with moral and ethical dimensions. The social constructionist perspective has led to a focus on narrative and the "storying" of experience akin to Wittgenstein's notion of "language games" (Wittgenstein, 1953). Action and meaning are seen as recursively connected, "stories lived" inform "stories told" about those lived experiences, so therapy becomes an attempt to create alternative "stories told" or narratives, and hence different lived experiences for people who present with problems (Pearce, 1989).

In embracing these ideas the field of "family" or systemic therapy has made the paradigm shift from a modernist to a postmodern perspective in common with moves in literature, art, science, and the humanities. This has major implications not just for the theory and practice of systemic therapy but for psychology as a whole which are yet to be fully explored (Shotter, 1993). Here there is a divergence between family therapists working in this way with other therapists, including for example David Smail, Miller Mair, and the psychoanalyst Lacan, who are interested in narrative and the meaning of language.

To summarise, it seems that the wheel has come full circle in terms of working with individuals or whole families. From a focus on the individual there was a shift to a family perspective. For a period there was rigid adherence to working with the whole family who were sometimes even turned away if all did not attend. With the advent of second-order cybernetics the system was enlarged to include the observer, referring agents, and other networks. Once again it became possible to address the relationship between the client and the therapist, this time not in terms of transference but in terms of "fit", circularity, and feedback. With the focus on linguistic systems it became less important to see the whole system and much work is now carried out with parts of a system or with individuals. Many current developments in the field embrace the narrative metaphor and focus on the construction and development of alternative stories in a move coined by some as third-order cybernetics.

To some extent the approaches that will be described in this chapter are presented in a developmental and historical sequence but there has been much crossfertilisation. Each of the three approaches to be described in some detail have made major contributions to the field that have been taken up and developed by the other schools, such that current practice in family therapy is becoming more blurred in its origins.

STRUCTURAL FAMILY THERAPY

Structural family therapy is perhaps the most well known of all family therapy approaches. As its name suggests, it is interested in family structure. Salvador Minuchin's approach is best represented in *Families and Family Therapy* (1974).

Minuchin has a view of how a healthy family would appear in terms of a clear organisation hierarchy and well-defined permeable boundaries between sub-systems, as illustrated in Fig. 8.1. For example, the parental sub-system should be hierarchically at a higher level than the sibling sub-system in terms of duties, rights, and responsibilities. Boundaries ensure privacy, autonomy, and individuality. The marital sub-system will have closed boundaries to protect the privacy of the marital couple but the boundary will be permeable enough to allow children to move in and out of the parental sub-system. The marital and parental sub-systems will be distinct. The sibling sub-system will have its own boundaries and will be organised hierarchically with children being given tasks and privileges appropriate to their age and sex. Individuals will also have boundaries in terms of respect for privacy and individuality. Finally, the boundary round the family system will also be respected, although this will depend to some extent on cultural, social, and economic factors. According to these factors there may be great variety in the extent to which other family relationships and other agencies may be allowed into the family system.

The life-span view of development has influenced all family therapy approaches and in particular the structural approach. Development is seen as continuing throughout the life cycle and can be marked by a series of normative transitions that characterise each life stage. This shifting scenario is known as the Family Life Cycle, which will be described in some detail because of its importance to

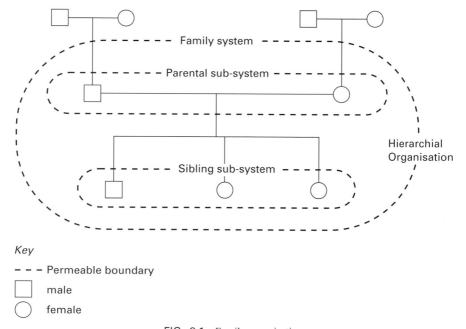

FIG. 8.1   Family organisation.

the other models outlined. At each transition point in the life of the family, relationships are renegotiated with subsequent shifts in alliances between family members as the family structure changes. The idea of the family life cycle embodies a central idea in therapeutic practice, that is, that there is a normative developmental sequence in relationships (see also Chapter 2). Problems are seen as likely to arise at points of transition if the family has difficulty adjusting its relationships to a new structure more appropriate to its stage of development. This means that many interventions in family therapy are seen as attempts to "unblock" or "unstick" obstacles which may have arisen in the normal developmental process.

There are many possible versions of the family life cycle. The example given here can be described as following four major structural changes in family organisation, as illustrated in Fig. 8.2.

At the first stage of the cycle, birth of a child, the primary care giver (usually the mother) is primarily occupied with the baby and the secondary care giver (father or close friend or family member) can be seen as containing the mother/child dyad and acting as a bridge to the outside world. If available, grandparents may become much more involved with the new family at this stage. According

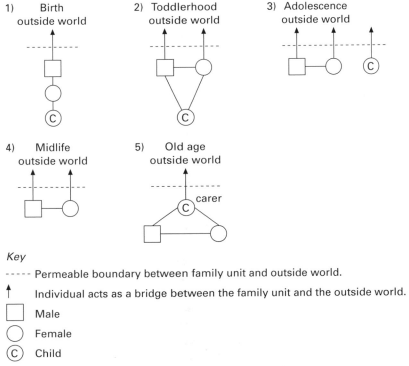

Key

----- Permeable boundary between family unit and outside world.

↑ Individual acts as a bridge between the family unit and the outside world.

☐ Male

◯ Female

Ⓒ Child

FIG. 8.2   Stages of family organisation.

to the past history of relationships, the involvement of grandparents may be experienced as helpful/supportive, unhelpful/intrusive, or unhelpful/rejecting.

In the second stage, between the ages of 1 and 3, the child takes its first steps both physically and metaphorically towards independence. As the child begins to establish a stronger relationship with its father or a secondary carer, and becomes less dependent on the mother, a realignment occurs in the marital couple or primary dyad from the vertical organisation of the first stage to a triangular organisation where both parents or carers relate in a different but equal capacity to the child, as shown in Fig. 8.2. This shift is highlighted when the child starts school or full-time child care and the mother's role with respect to the outside world is re-established. Difficulties in negotiating these stages in the family life cycle often result in the child presenting problems such as night-time waking, bedwetting, soiling, and temper tantrums.

The third stage begins with adolescence, which can be viewed as the second major thrust of the child towards independence. Families who have difficulties negotiating toddlerhood may experience even greater difficulties during adolescence when the whole atmosphere is highly charged with the adolescent's emerging sexuality. During this stage the influence of the peer group on the adolescent increases as the child struggles against parental values in the attempt to establish an autonomous sense of self. Difficulties in negotiating this stage of the life cycle may result in behaviour problems in adolescence such as smoking, drinking, school refusal, and, at the severe end of the continuum, anorexia/bulimia and emergence of schizophrenic symptoms.

The third stage of the cycle culminates in the young person leaving home and finding a partner. This establishes the adolescent as a young adult able to make his or her own relationships separate from the family of origin. This stage gives rise to what is often referred to as the "empty nest syndrome" where the original marital couple are turned back on themselves after years of relating to a third party in the form of children or dependent parents. Difficulties in re-establishing themselves as a couple as well as forging new roles with respect to the outside world may result in referral for anxiety, agoraphobia, depression, and sleep problems, as well as for sexual or marital problems.

Depending on the age of the parents, the fourth stage, that of midlife, may overlap with the previous one. Issues of midlife include the end of childbearing years for women, and fears of waning attractiveness in both sexes. This is often coupled by the need to acknowledge that one has reached the peak in career terms and that the future holds old age and decline, although alternatively many women start a new career at this stage. This parental "midlife crisis" is often exacerbated by the decline of grandparents, who may become more dependent through illness and disability, and by their eventual death.

The second half of life brings with it increased awareness of one's own mortality. This is highlighted with "retirement", literally a retirement from the world, when issues around one's self-worth, and past achievements come to the fore with the realisation that one is unlikely to further achieve in external terms. Difficulties in negotiating retirement are emphasised by a reversal in sex roles in the marital couple. Men frequently become more home loving and internally focused, whereas women who may have been restricted by childcare or caring for dependent relatives may use their new-found freedom and confidence to become efficient and busy members of the local community. If one's children produce grandchildren a new link to the future can be made, perhaps giving a sense of immortality; otherwise issues of mortality and the finite nature of life may be more keenly felt. Family pets may take on an important role, especially for childless couples.

Stage five brings old age, and with it a greater likelihood of illness, disability, and greater dependence. This will require another realignment of relationships and may place different demands on sons and daughters, women being expected to take on more of a caring role with respect to elderly parents and relatives. Religion may increase in importance as a way of creating meaning for life and in cushioning the fears of one's own mortality. The final stage, death and mourning, results in a family transition during which the younger generation are faced with succession to the final generation. The reality of the death of parents may highlight issues of dependence and ambivalent relationships between generations which may complicate normal grief reactions requiring professional help at this time.

In describing the life cycle, cultural context is a fundamental issue. The sequence described is essentially a white, middle-class Western pattern. Stages will be different and have different meanings associated with them within a different cultural context. This means that the life cycle must be considered in its cultural and political context; by reifying the life cycle as the way in which a family "should" behave, cultural, class, and gender bias will be reinforced.

The genogram or "family tree" is an essential tool in structural family therapy that is used in other family therapy approaches. It can be described as a map of the family structure which includes major life stages including births, marriages, separations, and deaths. It illustrates the stage of the life cycle that the family is currently negotiating and provides the therapist with useful ideas about the interactions that may be occurring around a problem. An example of a three-generational genogram for the Smith family is illustrated in Fig. 8.3. The Smith family were referred for family therapy by Stella's individual therapist. Stella presented the problem as her feeling of isolation and difficulty in dealing with her three children, Simon, James, and Isobel. Her husband Ian is a freelance journalist very involved in his work. The genogram illustrates that Ian and Stella have been together for 12 years, they left South America to come to this country 10 years ago. Ian is the eldest of four children, Stella the eldest of three children. All their relatives live in South America. Stella's father died 4 years ago and 1 year ago Ian's grandmother died—she was seen as having had a "traumatic life" and had a great influence on the family.

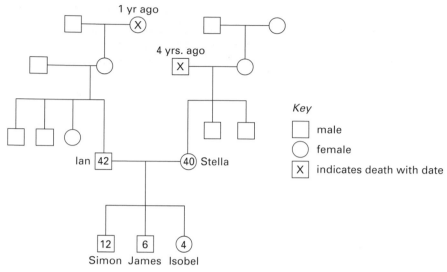

1 yr ago

4 yrs. ago

Key

[square] male

[circle] female

[X] indicates death with date

Ian 42 ———— 40 Stella

12   6   4
Simon James Isobel

FIG. 8.3   Genogram for Smith family.

Similarly, Stella's maternal grandmother was also seen as a very important figure in the family. The structural family therapist may construct a genogram with the family in one of the first sessions of therapy as a way of "joining" with family members. Together with the family the therapist might then look for patterns between and within generations and use the genogram as a means of highlighting these patterns; for example, the therapist might note the pattern of powerful and influential women on both sides of the family and two family deaths in the last 4 years, which are related in time to Ian and Stella seeking individual therapy.

Given the view of normative family functioning proposed by the structural school, the therapist's task is to note to what extent the presenting family adheres to this structure. If it does not, the aim of therapy is to create a new structure which is more appropriate for the life stage the family has reached, so development can continue in a normative way. The therapist does this by initially "joining" or "engaging" with all family members as she attempts to understand the family structure and the role of each family member within it (Minuchin & Fishman, 1981). This is done by mapping the family terrain. The therapist notes important factors such as membership of alliances and coalitions. Alliances are overt close relationships between family members, whereas coalitions are covert and are directed against a third party. Membership and structure of sub-systems and the location and permeability of boundaries are also included. Family organisation is described as "chaotic" if there is no clear hierarchical structure, or "rigid" if this is so fixed that there can be no flexibility, for example, if parents are so remote that children do not have full access to them. Relationships are described as "disengaged" if they are so distant that creative communication cannot occur, or "enmeshed" if individuals have no personal space. Any of these polarities of organisation may result in problems at points of transition if the family lacks the flexibility to adapt its structure readily to the new life stage.

In mapping family structure the therapist takes on the role of an active intruder within it. Taking the example of the Smith family, the therapist might note from the genogram that the family is reaching the stage in the life cycle when the youngest child will soon start school. This means that the couple must renegotiate their relationship and Stella must re-establish a role with respect to the outside world. The therapist might note that in this case the marital and parental sub-systems are not distinct and that a coalition against Ian exists between Stella and the two boys. Within the sibling sub-system there is no hierarchical organisation because all the children enjoy the same status and privileges irrespective of age.

The next phase of therapy involves the therapist challenging the family structure and the way that things are done using a variety of verbal and non-verbal techniques including "enactment" and "sculpting". Enactment involves acting out patterns in the here and now, for example, the therapist might ask the Smith family children to "go on the rampage" and for Ian and Stella to behave as they would normally. In sculpting, the therapist asks the family to position themselves physically, to make a family sculpture, in terms of certain criteria, for example who is closest to who and most involved in the problem. The therapist may unbalance the family structure by changing seating arrangements or by siding with a member who has been scapegoated against other family members. For example, she might side with Ian since he is being excluded from the family or with Simon who is being labelled as being unpopular and difficult at school.

Third, the therapist restructures the family by offering different alternative ways of operating. Minuchin sees change as coming about by challenging the family's perception of reality, offering alternative ways of interacting and by bringing these about by providing a new experience within the family which will reinforce new structures and relationships. She might for example instruct Ian and Stella in setting limits for the children and give them the experience of putting these into practice during the session by enacting a different scenario. The therapist will set clear goals for therapy and takes on an educative position in bringing these about.

The structural model of family therapy provides the field with many key ideas and although still widely practised, especially in services working with children, it is declining in influence. The normative model it presents does not sit easily with the "zeitgeist" of the postmodern age. It remains in a first-order cybernetic paradigm where the observer remains outside the system, there is one universal view of reality, and the therapist is viewed as the expert. A major deficiency in Minuchin's model of change is that although he describes the structure of families and their organisation in great detail his theory is not comprehensive enough to include the idea of "resistance" or an explanation of the so-called paradoxical techniques that deal successfully with it, especially with those families Minuchin would label as enmeshed. Nevertheless, the method is probably the most well researched of all family therapy models and in particular has been shown to be effective with psychosomatic problems in children (Minuchin, Rosman, & Baker, 1978).

THE BRIEF THERAPY MODEL

The history of the brief therapy approach can be traced back to Milton Erickson (1963). He saw the key to brief therapy as utilising what clients bring with them to help them meet their needs in such a way that they can make satisfactory lives for themselves. The brief therapy model proposed by Steve de Shazer et al. (1986) developed alongside the strategic approach until 1972 and has since built on and extended these ideas especially those put forward in Jay Haley's later work, as articulated in *Problem Solving Therapy* (1976) and Watzlawick, Weakland, and Fisch's book *Change* (1974). Whereas the strategic group focused on problems, the way in which they are maintained and how to solve them, De Shazer focuses on solutions; like the cheer leaders who warm up audiences in the United States, De Shazer sees himself as cheering on solutions. The approach is focused and goal directed. It is based on the idea that if something works do more of it, if not do something different.

Like other models of family therapy the brief therapy model sees problems being developed and maintained in the context of human interactions. To emphasise that a problem is a particular distinction made by an observer, the brief therapy model refers to problems as "complaints". In order to construct solutions it is important to understand as much as possible about the constraints of what is termed the complaint situation and the interactions involved, so that the solution will "fit" the situation. Like a key in a lock, the idea is to fit sufficiently to turn the lock and to open up the possibilities for solutions. This means that some keys might be sufficient to operate a number of different locks. Using this model only a small change is necessary no matter how complex and difficult the situation appears, since change in one part of the system leads to change in the system as a whole. This means that the brief therapy model will often work with a part of a system and frequently with an individual client. The aim of brief therapy, like structural family therapy, is to help clients do something different by changing the way they interact with each other, or like the Milan Associates, to change the way that they interpret their situation, so that a solution to their problems can be achieved. The model is not concerned with the structural organisation of the family system and has no normative view of how a healthy family would function.

There are a number of unique terms in the brief therapy model which differentiate it from other models of family therapy. For example, De Shazer defines difficulties as "the one damn thing after another of everyday life" (Shazer et al.,

1986, p. 210); these include such things as the car not starting, the tin opener not working, an argument now and again, and so on. Clients often present these as problems. A complaint is a difficulty plus a recurring, ineffective attempt to overcome it and/or a difficulty plus the perception on the part of the client that nothing is changing so "one damn thing after another becomes the same damn thing over and over" (Shazer et al., 1986, p. 210). Solutions are the behavioural and/or perceptual changes that the client and therapist construct to alter the difficulty or the ineffective way of trying to overcome it and/or the construction of an acceptable alternative perspective that allows the client to experience the situation differently.

De Shazer locates his work in a social constructionist framework although the tightly prescribed framework echoes a more reality-based approach. The brief therapy model approach is very simple and very focused because it is built around the idea that clients already know what to do to solve problems, they just do not know that they know. The brief therapist's role is to help them construct for themselves a new use for the knowledge that they already have. The approach is narrow, focused, and goal directed and it is seen as achieving good results within its scope (Shazer et al., 1986). It is gaining in popularity, perhaps because its clear specifications make it easy to describe, to teach, and potentially to evaluate. It fits comfortably with current preoccupations in the Health Service for evidence-based practice and brief treatment approaches.

THE MILAN ASSOCIATES AND POST-MILAN DEVELOPMENTS

The Milan approach, or systemic approach, as it is sometimes called, refers to the work of four Italian psychiatrists and psychoanalysts—Palazzoli, Prata, Boscolo, and Cecchin. They had been greatly influenced by Watzlawick, Beavin, and Jackson (1967) from the Mental Research Institute and their approach adheres closely to Bateson's (1972) systemic ideas. The approach was initially developed with families containing a designated anorexic or schizophrenic member but it is now applied to a wide range of problems, especially to those seen as chronic. The most well-known early publication is their book *Paradox and Counterparadox* (Palazzoli, Boscolo, Cecchin, & Prata, 1978a), which outlines the method. At this point in their development they viewed systems as reaching a stable organisation around a central point, which might be a double bind or paradoxical injunction. For example, parents might give a son two mutually exclusive instructions simultaneously, one verbally and one non-verbally. Placed in this double bind and therefore being unable to act, the son may respond by producing schizophrenic symptoms. The aim of therapy was to direct an intervention or "counterparadox" (i.e. against paradox) towards this central point with the intention of changing the rules that organise the system and thereby eliminating the symptom.

The early Milan team laid great emphasis on the role of the therapy team to provide an overview or "meta-perspective" on the client–therapist system and the therapist's role was at times relegated to being a messenger of the team. The language used to describe the interactions between the team and therapist/family system in their early work is almost adversarial in nature. This may in part be due to the challenging families, with anorexic and schizophrenic members, that they were treating, but it also illustrates that although they were beginning to look at wider systems, in particular the role of the referring person in maintaining the problem, their view of systems remained more in line with a first-order cybernetic paradigm. In fact, their early work has more in common with a Strategic approach than with subsequent developments.

The Milan Associates proposed a five-stage session, which remains relatively unchanged in later developments. It is made up of a pre-session discussion, the session, an intersession break, delivery of an intervention, and a post-session discussion. Three guiding principles—Hypothesising, Circularity, and Neutrality (Palazolli, Boscolo, Cecchin, & Prata, 1980)—inform therapist activity throughout these stages. Hypothesising takes place primarily in the pre-session discussion where the therapist and team put together the information they have about the clients. The Milan approach advocates a telephone intake interview with the designated patient in which factual information about the family structure and the presenting problem is gathered. On the basis of this information, and any communication from the referring person, a genogram will be constructed in the pre-session discussion. This together with all other information is used to hypothesise about the family and the presenting problem. A number of alternative possible hypotheses will be created. During hypothesising a wealth of ideas from other therapeutic approaches may be incorporated, including for example attachment theory, psychodynamic ideas, and psychosocial transitions. The hypothesis that is chosen to guide the therapist should connect as many of the family members as possible. The hypothesis is systemic rather than linear in that it does not attempt to identify a cause–effect relationship but to punctuate a circular pattern. For example, on the basis of a telephone intake interview with the Smith family the team's original systemic hypothesis was that the children were creating problems in order to pull professionals into the family to provide them with a new extended family; first, Stella's individual therapist, next the children's school, then Ian's individual therapist, and now via this referral a family therapist and team. Via therapy sessions and discussions Ian is pulled back into the family, so preventing Stella from being isolated, but at the same time this maintains some distance between Stella and Ian so the children create problems to pull them together, and so on.

The second part of the session, the interview with the family, is carried out using circular questioning, which is the main tool of the Milan Associates. It illustrates the second guiding principle of circularity. Circular questioning makes connections between people, between events, and between ideas. Circular questions encourage what is often termed "gossiping in the presence of" by asking one family member about the relationship between another two. For example, "When Simon decides not to do his homework do Stella and Ian argue more or less?", "If Stella were to feel competent in managing the children who would notice first, Ian or her therapist?" The Milan team also makes use of questions to track patterns of behaviour surrounding a problem as in the brief therapy model, for example "When Isobel has a tantrum what does Stella do? Where are Simon and James? Do they talk more to their father or less? and then what happens?" etc. In tracking behaviour patterns it is seen as important to continue questioning until a circular pattern emerges. So the family begins to shift from a linear to a circular view of the problem.

Circular questions are the means by which the therapist tests out the team's hypothesis. If in the series of questioning the hypothesis clearly does not fit, the therapist takes a break in order to formulate a new guiding hypothesis with the team. The aim of the hypothesis is to guide the therapist to ask questions that make a difference. If the hypothesis is too far away from the family's own belief system about the problem, they will not accept the new ideas that emerge. Similarly, if the hypothesis fits too well with the family's own ideas about the problem, there will be no "news of difference". So the hypothesis needs to be continually revised throughout the session on the basis of information generated by the questioning.

In asking circular questions and in managing the session as a whole the therapist needs to be actively aware of the third guiding principle, neutrality. By the end of the session all family members should feel equally engaged with the therapist. Unlike the Structural therapist who might make a strong alliance with a scapegoated family member, the Milan therapist promotes an equal alliance with each family member. The notion of neutrality extends beyond neutrality to persons to include neutrality to ideas and even to change itself. The concept emphasises that no one piece of information is any more important than any other, but that it is the process or pattern that is important. In fact, the concept of neutrality has drawn much criticism to the Milan team's work. The neutral therapist has been accused of being cool and detached and it has been argued that since no one can ever be truly neutral the term masks implicit racism, sexism, etc. on the part of the therapist. In later developments this notion has subsequently been reworked in terms of Curiosity (Cecchin, 1987) and Irreverence (Cecchin, Lane, & Ray, 1992), that is, the therapist must continually remain active and curious and maintain a gentle irreverence to all ideas, however sacred, especially those held by the therapy team. If therapists lose their curiosity then the potential for developing new perspectives is lost.

The message to the family in Stage 4 of the session was originally referred to as the Intervention, which was put together by the team in the intersession break. The Milan team became well known for their dramatic, largely strategic interventions, which were often paradoxical in nature. Paradoxical interventions may include prescribing the symptom or prescribing "no change". Prescribing the symptom involves asking the client to carry out what has been described as the problem behaviour at a designated time and place, thus shifting the context of the problem behaviour from one in which the problem is seen as uncontrollable to one in which it is predicted and therefore controlled. Prescribing "no change" within the context of therapy, which is about change, is similarly paradoxical. These elements were often included as a part of a ritual task.

The most well-known task of the early Milan team is the "odd days, even days" ritual (Palazolli, Boscolo, Cecchin, & Prata, 1978b) in which parents who were unable to control their children were told to take sole control of the children on alternative days. The other parent was instructed to observe and make notes on the difference it made. Ritual tasks act by introducing a third dimension, that of time, into the double bind so that the mutually exclusive injunctions are no longer happening concurrently. Traditionally the therapist delivered the message and left very promptly so that the family left with the message foremost in their minds. In more recent developments the intervention has been viewed as less significant in itself; instead it has been viewed as a message from the team to the family with the aim of cementing the new connections that have been made in the session.

The team found that in order for the repercussions from the intervention to filter throughout the system and for the system to reorganise itself, a month's gap between sessions was most beneficial. Milan-style therapy has often been described as "long short-term therapy", since the number of sessions is unlikely to exceed 12 but these may take place over a year or more in duration. The last part of the session, the post-session discussion, involves the therapist and team hypothesising about the effect of the intervention on the family. Any reaction whether positive or negative is treated as information about the system to inform future action by the therapy team. Contact from the family between sessions is treated similarly.

After the publication of *Paradox and Counterparadox* (Palazzoli et al., 1978a), the Milan team underwent a shift in their view of the system and they began to include themselves as observers as part of the system. Around this time the team split and the two women, Palazolli and Prata, continued to pursue their research interests with anorexic and schizophrenic families. Meanwhile, Boscolo and Cecchin have led what has been termed the Post-Milan developments. Karl Tomm (1984) has acted as a spokesman for their approach.

The most exciting developments have come about, as outlined earlier, via the influence of constructivism and social constructionism (see Leppington, 1991). This has led to a much more dynamic view of systems, as they are seen as being socially constructed in language by observers (Hoffman, 1990). In turn this has led to a more egalitarian co-evolutionary model of therapy, which is concerned with opening up possibilities and alternatives rather than trying to change the system strategically. This narrative or "discursive turn" also has implications for the therapy team, which may take a more active role in the therapy, for example by Anderson's (1987) use of the "reflecting team" in which the family is invited to listen while the team discuss their ideas. Therapists currently using these ideas include Peter Lang and Martin Little (Lang, Little, & Cronen, 1990) at Kensington Consultation Centre in London, David Campbell at the Tavistock Clinic in London, and Michael White at the Dulwich Centre in Australia and David Epston in New Zealand (White & Epston, 1990). Michael White's Narrative approach in particular focuses on the development and elaboration of alternative stories around what he terms a "Unique Outcome" or exception to the problem story. He describes the therapist as a conversational architect whose skills lie in the ability to story build. His unique approach has been used with a wide range of presenting problems including schizophrenia, violence, and sexual abuse. Since his therapeutic approach includes an analysis of power from a social constructionist perspective, his approach has been applied to problems where there are power imbalances, for example in the setting up of the "Just Therapy" approach in New Zealand, a culturally sensitive way of working with Maori, Samoan, and English people (Tapping, 1993; Waldegrave, 1990).

EVALUATION AND CRITIQUE

The number of studies reported in the literature evaluating family therapy approaches is sparse. This reflects the relatively recent popularity of the approach. The research literature raises some major epistemological issues in the evaluation of family therapy approaches. The main debate centres around the issue of using a positivistic research methodology to evaluate approaches that are based on a non-positivistic paradigm. The two sides of the argument are articulated by those who have been termed "old hatters" versus those who have been termed "new wavers" (Gurman, 1983). The "old hatters" advocate the use of standard research procedures as currently the best available. The "new wavers" on the other hand argue that new means must be evolved to evaluate work that is based firmly within a second-order cybernetic framework.

Probably the most comprehensive analysis of the literature to date was carried out by Gurman and Kniskern (1979) who surveyed over 200 studies. They tentatively concluded that overall 61% of individual cases and 73% of family cases improved using a systemic family therapy approach and that most studies found family therapy to be more effective than individual treatment, although this was not exclusively so. Individual schools are beginning to produce results, although at present these remain limited in number and often based on clinical impression. On the basis of client self-report as a way of evaluating the brief therapy model, de Shazer et al. (1986) have concluded that their model can be effective within a short period of time and within a limited number of sessions. Out of 1600 cases seen on average for six sessions, 72% either met their goals for therapy or felt that significant change had occurred such that they did not require further sessions.

The Milan team states that it finds improvement in 68% of its cases (Tomm, 1984). Since the Milan team sees families who may be regarded as some of the most difficult, this figure is particularly significant. Tomm (1984) also states that using the Milan approach change occurred in fewer sessions allowing the same number of staff to increase the number of cases seen by 25% over a 4-year period after having introduced this approach. A number of outcome studies are currently in progress and clearly much research still needs to be done.

The main criticisms of family therapy centre around the issue of power. The most clearly articulated is the feminist critique (Mackinnon, 1987). The feminist position sees family therapy as supporting patriarchal society in reifying the nuclear family as the "right" way to live. It argues that the nuclear family subjugates women and requires their submission in order to maintain white male middle-class supremacy. This is institutionalised by society in governmental structure to which women have little access. Similarly, family therapy has been criticised as upholding middle-class, white Western values and not addressing issues of race, sexual orientation, disability, or ageing, and so implicitly upholding societal structures and values that oppress members of these minority groups. Further criticisms of the approach are levelled against the position of power assumed by the therapy team. Family therapists have been accused of objectifying families and of being manipulative social engineers often using deceit to achieve their dubious aims.

Criticisms of family therapy tend not to differentiate between the different approaches and, although many of the previous criticisms might justifiably be levelled at approaches based on a first-order cybernetic thinking, more recent approaches can theoretically encompass the issue of power. Most criticisms of family therapy are based on a view of power as a linear concept consisting of unilateral control over another person. Maturana and Varela (1980) describe this as the "myth of power" and argues that one part of a system cannot have unilateral control over another part of a system. This more circular view, however, has further fuelled feminist criticism, which sees circular causality as blaming victims of incest/child abuse/wife battering and not addressing the issues of responsibility and the wider social context. With the move to a social constructionist perspective a greater diversity of definitions of power have begun to emerge, including for example Michael White's analysis of power based on the philosophy of Foucault (White, 1991), ideas from Derrida (1981), and discourse analysis. These approaches view power as lack of access by certain social groups to privileged social discourses and analysis of patterns of rights, duties, opportunities, and constraints derived from the theory of the Coordinated Management of Meaning, a social constructionist theory that sees every action as having ethical, moral, and political implications (Pearce, 1989). Therapeutic approaches based on narrative ideas bring issues of power into the centre of the therapeutic endeavour; however, not all systemic approaches have embraced these ideas. As Mackinnon (1987) argues, although systemic approaches can address the issue of power from a theoretical perspective, the application of these ideas will be constrained by the conservatism of its proponents. This remains an issue of debate and a challenge for the field to address.

COMPARISON AND INTEGRATION

The aim of this section is to compare and contrast the three models of family therapy that have been described in this chapter, together with behavioural and psychodynamic family therapy approaches. These approaches have not been addressed in detail because they represent a relatively minor influence in the field. Behavioural family therapy is best outlined by one of its major proponents, Ian Falloon (1988). As he states in his overview, behavioural family therapy is still in its infancy but has undergone major change since its inception 20 years ago. Growing out of the pioneering work of Patterson, McNeal, Hawksin, and Phelps (1967), Liberman (1970), and Stuart (1969), the shift was made from focusing on the patient to complex behavioural analyses of the whole family environment. The aim of therapy was to restructure the reciprocal exchange of rewards in family relationships and to maximise exchanges of positive behaviour, often using written contracts between family members. In the 1970s a major transformation took place with the introduction of packages for parent retraining of deviant children (Falloon & Liberman, 1983), behavioural marital therapy (Liberman, 1970; Stuart, 1969), and sex therapy, which was made well known by the work of Masters and Johnson (1970). The most recent developments in the field have aimed at addressing limiting features of the approach. The most striking inclusions are consideration of the therapeutic alliance and of resistance, that is, those families who do not improve as readily or easily as one might expect, and approaches to reconstruct family members' subjective experiences using cognitive strategies. As Falloon (1988) states, the approach is very much in its infancy and lacks a clear theoretical framework, but crossfertilisation between behavioural and systemic family therapy approaches is beginning to occur.

Psychodynamic family therapy is best represented by the work of the Adolescent Department at the Tavistock Clinic in London (Box et al., 1981). Its members share an interest in applying psychoanalytic principles to the understanding of groups and institutions and in particular to families. The approach is based on two particular developments, that of object relations psychoanalytic practice derived from the work of Freud and Melanie Klein, and the application of this to the understanding of group relations following the work of W.R. Bion (1961) and others. The approach embraces the idea of a family as a system and attempts to understand the processes involved in such a system, but unlike other family therapy approaches it implies working with the group dynamics of the family, including unconscious processes, especially in terms of the way in which the family members perceive and engage the therapists. The aim is to create a space for the family to re-live and think about conflicts as they emerge in the therapeutic setting.

Table 8.1 compares the three main family therapy approaches along with psychodynamic and behavioural approaches according to five distinguishing features. The view taken of the family system, the view of the problem, the model of change, the role of the therapist, and the main skills and techniques employed by that approach. The most fundamental of these features is the view of the family system, which informs all other features. The structural model takes its view of systems from organisational theory, whereas the brief therapy and post-Milan/systemic approaches are based on a cybernetic model. The behavioural approach derives from learning theory and thus sees behaviour as being environmentally determined, whereas the psychodynamic approach sees intrapsychic factors as being most important. The differing views of systems have implications for the way in which change is seen to take place and therefore for the stance of the therapist.

One possible way of integrating the approaches covered in this chapter is in terms of levels of psychotherapy. This idea is borrowed from Cawley (1977) and elaborated by Brown and Pedder (1991) but will be used in a modified form by the present author. Psychotherapy can be seen as operating at the three different levels, as illustrated in Fig. 8.4. Outer levels include support and counselling; intermediate levels include more focused therapeutic approaches, which begin to use the relationship with the therapist; deeper levels include exploratory work addressing unconscious processes. This involves working through the relationship with the therapist as in psychoanalytic psychotherapy and analysis. The triangle is presented standing on its apex so that the areas within the triangle bear an approximate relationship to the comparative size of the population of people who may best be helped by each approach.

According to the severity of the problems, different people may require deeper levels of psychotherapy. For example, many people who present asking for help have less severe problems and may be best helped by outer levels of support and counselling. This might include people who have experienced life events such as bereavement/illness/redundancy, and so on. A smaller proportion of people will require further help in terms of intermediate levels of therapy. An even smaller proportion of people, who have more severe difficulties or may wish to explore their problems further, will seek deeper levels of psychotherapy. Moving from the base of the triangle to its apex the therapeutic approaches tend to move from a greater focus on process, from being active to reflective, supportive to exploratory, and directive to non-directive.

The approaches described here can be best placed at the intermediate level and could be described as comparable in level to other short- to medium-term focused therapeutic approaches, such as brief psychotherapy, cognitive analytical therapy, and short- to medium-term group work. Out of the five approaches presented here, the structural, brief therapy model, and behavioural family therapy approach could be described as being located towards the outer levels.

TABLE 8.1
Comparison of different models

	Structural	Brief Therapy Model	Post-Milan/Systemic	Behavioural	Psychodynamic
View of family system	System is clearly structured Hierarchically organised Boundaries between sub-systems	System is structured on feedback System maintains a steady state	System is evolving Constructed in language, co-ordinated through action	Family is formed when sufficient potential for mutual reinforcement is perceived in spouse Chains of behaviour are set up and maintained	Family shares an internal world
View of problem	Structure inappropriate for life stage of family Structure does not adapt freely to change Inappropriate alliances between sub-systems	Too many repeating samenesses Failed attempts at solution	Brought forth in language Stories become too limiting and restrictive	Individual behavioural repertoires no longer elicit appropriate reinforcement within family environment and may become punishing to other family members Negative chains of interaction are set up and maintained	Unconscious conflicts are acted out as recurring problems in the family
Model of change	Force a change and system will reorganise New relational realities become self-reinforcing	Focus on solutions Interruption of vicious circles of mishandled attempted solutions	Dissolve problem-determined system through co-evolution of new story in language	Construct more appropriate behaviours	Unconscious is made conscious, therefore allowing increased choice, growth and differentiation of family members
Role of therapist	Active intruder, joins, challenges and restructures family system	Cheer-leader for solutions Tracks sequences around exceptions to problems in order to construct solutions	Co-creator of new stories Triggers reflexivity between levels of meaning Looks for "fit": how historical and current pieces of puzzle "fit" together	Active and educative Problem solver Constructor of new sets of behaviours	Facilitative Containing Providing space for exploration and understanding
Skills and techniques	Sculpting Enactment Goals set	Reframing Focusing on strengths Goals set Tasks	Circular questioning Circularity neutrality/ curiosity Hypothesising Rituals and tasks	Behavioural monitoring Behavioural analysis Communication skills training Problem solving and training Contingency contracting	Containment Making links through interpretation Providing space for emergence of hidden attitudes and internal relationships Working through these in therapeutic relationship

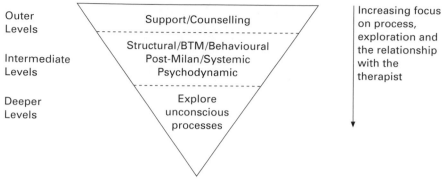

FIG. 8.4   Family therapy and levels of psychotherapy.

With the exception of the psychodynamic approach, all other models take an active stance. The structural, brief therapy model, and behavioural approaches are all directive in terms of setting explicit goals for therapy and in determining the direction and nature of change to occur. The post-Milan and psychodynamic approaches both focus more explicitly on process, and directly address the relationship between the clients and the therapist. The psychodynamic approach is the only approach outlined that views the working through of conflicts as a part of the therapeutic process. The other approaches see the aim of therapy as bringing about a change, which is then worked with by the clients after therapy has ended. This means that these approaches tend to be more focused and short term in nature than the psychodynamic approach. So the psychodynamic approach is represented as spanning the boundary between intermediate and deeper levels of therapy.

The value of this integrating model is that it clearly illustrates that, rather than one approach being better or preferable to another, each approach has something different to offer in terms of its aims and appropriateness for a particular portion of the population. The behavioural, structural, and brief therapy models could be seen as focusing directly on the production of explicit agreed changes and are more supportive in nature, whereas the post/Milan systemic and, to an even greater extent, the psychodynamic models focus more on exploration. This would imply, as the research evidence confirms, that the former may be most valuable in treating more frequently occurring less-complex problems that are already well defined, whereas the latter may most usefully address more complex and potentially chronic difficulties. Unfortunately, however, such an integration is at present lacking in the field of family therapy and perhaps, as one might expect in such a relatively young field, proponents of the different models tend to have a combative and competitive relationship. One hopes that as the field matures greater communication within the field will lead to creative and challenging new developments.

RECOMMENDED READING

Burnham, J.B. (1986). *Family therapy*. London: Tavistock Publications.

Dallos, R. (1991). *Family Belief systems: Therapy and change*. Milton Keynes, UK: Open University Press.

McNamee, S., & Gergen, K.J. (Eds.). (1992). *Therapy as social construction*. Guildford, UK: Sage Publications.

Street, E., & Dryden, W. (Eds.). (1988). *Family therapy in Britain*. Milton Keynes, UK: Open University Press.

White, C., & Denborough, D. (Eds.). (1998). *Introducing narrative therapy: A collection of practice based writings*. Adelaide, Australia: Dulwich Centre Publications.

REFERENCES

Anderson, H., Goolishian, H.A., & Windermand, L. (1986). Problem determined systems: Towards transformation in family therapy. *Journal of Strategic and Systemic therapies*, 5, 1–13.

Anderson, T. (1987). The reflecting team: Dialogue and metadialogue in clinical work. *Family Process*, 4, 415–428.

Bateson, G. (1972). *Steps to an ecology of mind*. San Francisco: Chandler.

Bion, W.R. (1961). *Experiences in groups*. London: Tavistock Publications.

Box, S., Copley, B., Magagna, J., & Moustaki, E. (1981). *Psychotherapy with families: An analytic approach*. London: Routledge & Kegan Paul.

Brown, D., & Pedder, J. (1991). *Introduction to psychotherapy* (2nd ed.). London & New York: Tavistock Publications.

Cawley, R.H. (1977). The teaching of psychotherapy. *Association of University Teachers of Psychiatry Newsletter*, Jan., 19–36.

Cecchin, G. (1987). Hypothesising, circularity and neutrality revisited: An invitation to curiosity. *Family Process*, 26, 405–413.

Cecchin, G., Lane, G., & Ray, W.A. (1992). *Irreverence: A strategy for therapist's survival*. London: Karnac.

Dallos, R. (1991). *Family belief systems, therapy and change*. Milton Keynes, UK: Open University Press.

Derrida, J. (1981). *Positions*. Chicago: University of Chicago Press.

Erickson, M. (1963). *Advanced techniques of hypnosis and therapy*. In J. Haley (Ed.), *Strategies of psychotherapy* (pp. 395–397). New York: Grune & Stratton.

Falloon, I.R.H. (1988). *Handbook of behavioural family therapy*. London: Hutchinson.

Falloon, I.R.H., & Liberman, R.P. (1983). Behavioural therapy for families with child management problems. In M.R. Texor (Ed.), *Helping families with special problems* (pp. 121–147). New York: Jason Aronson.

Gurman, A.S. (1983). The old hatters and the new wavers. *Family Therapy Networker*, 7, 37.

Gurman, A.S., & Kniskern, D.P. (1979). Research on marital and family therapy progress: Perspective and prospect. In S.L. Garfield & A.S. Bergin (Eds.), *Handbook of psychotherapy and behavioural change* (2nd ed., pp. 817–901). New York: Wiley.

Haley, J. (1963). *Strategies of psychotherapy*. New York: Grune & Stratton.

Haley, J. (1976). *Problem solving therapy*. San Francisco: Jossey Bass.

Hoffman, L. (1981). *Foundations of family therapy: A conceptual framework for systems change*. New York: Basic Books.

Hoffman, L. (1988). A constructivist position for family therapy. *Irish Journal of Psychology, 9*(1), 110–129.

Hoffman, L. (1990). From system to discourse. *Human Systems, 1*, 5–7.

Kuhn, T. (1962). *The structure of scientific revolutions*. Chicago: University of Chicago.

Laing, R.D., & Esterson, D. (1964). *Sanity, madness and the family*. London: Tavistock Publications.

Lang, P., Little, M., & Cronen, V. (1990). The systemic professional: Domains of action and the question of neutrality. *Human Systems, 1*, 39–57.

Leppington, R. (1991). From constructivism to social constructionism and doing critical therapy. *Human Systems, 2*(2), 79–105.

Liberman, R. (1970). Behavioural approaches to family and couple therapy. *American Journal of Orthopsychiatry, 40*, 106–118.

Madanes, C. (1981). *Strategic family therapy*. San Francisco/Washington/London: Jossey-Bass.

Mackinnon, L.K. (1987). The new epistemology and the Milan approach: Feminist and sociopolitical considerations. *Journal of Marital and Family Therapy, 13*(27), 139–155.

Masters, W.H., & Johnson, V.E. (1970). *Human sexual inadequacy*. London: Churchill.

Maturana, H.R., & Varela, F.J. (Eds.) (1980). *Autopoesis: The realization of the living*. Boston: Reidel Press.

Minuchin, S. (1974). *Families and family therapy*. Cambridge, MA: Harvard.

Minuchin, S., & Fishman, H.C. (1981). *Techniques of family therapy*. Cambridge, MA: Harvard University Press.

Minuchin, S., Rosman, B., & Baker, L. (1978). *Psychosomatic families*. Cambridge, MA: Harvard.

Palazzoli, S.M., Boscolo, L., Cecchin, G., & Prata, G. (1978a). *Paradox and counterparadox*. New York: Jason Aronson.

Palazzoli, S.M., Boscolo, L., Cecchin, G., & Prata, G. (1978b). A ritualised prescription in family therapy: Odd days and even days. *Journal of Marriage and Family Counselling, 4*(3), 3–9.

Palazzoli, S.M., Boscolo, L., Cecchin, G., & Prata, G. (1980). Hypothesizing, circularity, neutrality: Three guidelines for the conductor of the session. *Family Process, 19*, 3–12.

Patterson, G.R., McNeal, S., Hawksin, N., & Phelps, R. (1967). Reprogramming the social environment. *Journal of Child Psychology and Psychiatry, 8*, 181–195.

Pearce, W.B. (1989). *Communication and the human condition*. Carbondale, IL: Southern Illinois University Press.

Shazer, S. de, Berg. I.K., Lipchik, E., Nunnally, E., Mulnar, A., Gingerich, W., & Weiner-Davies, M. (1986). Brief therapy: Focused solution development. *Family Process, 25*, 207–222.

Shotter, J. (1993). *Conversational realities*. London: Sage Publications.

Stuart, R.B. (1969). Operant-interpersonal treatment for marital discord. *Journal of Consulting and Clinical Psychology, 33*, 675–682.

Tapping, C. (1993). Other wisdoms other worlds. *Dulwich Centre Newsletter, 1*.

Tomm, K. (1984). One perspective on the Milan systemic approach: Pt. I. Overview of development, theory and practice. *Journal of Marital and Family Therapy, 10*(2), 113–125.

Von Bertalanffy, L. (1968). General systems theory—a critical review. In W. Buckley (Ed.), *Modern systems research for the behavioural scientist* (pp. 11–35) Chicago: Aldine.

Von Foerster, H. (1981). *Observing systems*. Seaside, CA: Intersystems.

Von Glaserfeld, E. (1984). An introduction to radical constructivism. In P. Watzlawick (Ed.), *The invented reality*. New York: W.W. Norton.

Waldegrave, C.T. (1990). "Just therapy". *Dulwich Centre Newsletter, 1*, 5–46.

Watzlawick, P., Beavin, J.H., & Jackson, D.D. (1967). *Pragmatics of human communication*. New York: Norton.

Watzlawick, P., Weakland, J., & Fisch, R. (1974). *Change*. New York: W.W. Norton.

White, M. (1991). Deconstruction and therapy. *Dulwich Centre Newsletter, 3*, 21–40.

White, M., & Epston, D. (1990). *Narrative means to therapeutic ends*. New York/London: W.W. Norton.

Wittengstein, L. (1953). *Philosophical investigation*. Oxford, UK: Basil Blackwell.

CHAPTER NINE

Schizophrenia

Tony Lavender
Salomons, Centre for Applied Social & Psychological Development,
Canterbury Christ Church University College, Kent, UK

INTRODUCTION

This chapter provides an overview of the major issues and approaches that are currently of importance in schizophrenia. It is perhaps most useful to begin with a brief description of what life can be like for an individual suffering from what have come to be regarded as the symptoms of schizophrenia.

John is a 26-year-old man who lives at home with his mother and two sisters. John describes how he had always been something of a loner even at primary school. He never seemed able to mix very well with his peers and says he was bullied by some of the boys at secondary school. He describes how he had a girlfriend for a brief period at school but this only lasted a couple of months. His initial contact with psychiatric services came three months after he had left home to take up a place at a higher education college to study to be a teacher.

During the period at college he found he was unable to cope with either the academic work or living in a student house with five new people. When he began to experience difficulties he withdrew to his room for long periods, which led to him becoming something of an outcast in the house. During these periods alone he began to think and feel that people were against him; continually talking about him and plotting to get him moved out of the house. As he became more isolated so his anxieties about the others grew to the point where he thought both the people within the house and indeed the college lecturers were planning to get him out of the country. These thoughts gradually developed to the point where John was concerned that M15 had become involved and had placed microphones in the wall.

John did, however, have one friend in the house, a young woman who had always been friendly, whom he tried to tell about the plot. She actually became quite frightened by his story, especially when he described people outside his door talking to each other about him and shouting abuse at him, which she knew was not the case. She eventually decided to talk to the college counsellor who contacted John's GP and he was persuaded to see a psychiatrist.

The psychiatrist saw John when he was 22 and diagnosed him as suffering with schizophrenia. The psychiatrist prescribed a small dose of a major tranquilliser and John returned to his family home under the care of a local GP and psychiatrist. Since that time John has remained very dependent on his mother, is unemployed, has made two unsuccessful attempts to start evening classes, and appears rather frightened about contact with people outside the home. He remains convinced that the students plotted against him. His medication has recently been increased. He now describes himself as having little energy, lacking any particular interests, but remains hopeful that things will improve given a bit of time.

Any overview of schizophrenia that attempts to describe the efforts that have been made to explain the occurrence of such problems can only provide a brief summary and the reader will need to pursue the references to gain a fuller understanding. This rider is perhaps particularly important with schizophrenia because of the vast amount of research and associated literature available about the subject. The present chapter begins with the historical background and in this context presents the major problems involved in establishing "schizophrenia" as a reliable and valid concept. This is followed by a discussion of what is known about the genetic and biological basis of the condition. The remaining two sections are devoted to a presentation of the main psychological and family approaches that have been applied to schizophrenia.

HISTORICAL BACKGROUND: DEFINING THE CONDITION

In 1898 Emil Kraepelin first presented the term *dementia praecox* to classify those severe mental disturbances that were not clearly organic in origin. Kraepelin (1905) originally thought that dementia praecox occurred in young people and was associated with a progressive emotional and intellectual deterioration, although he recognised that occasionally it occurred in later life and/or was associated with complete recovery. The common symptoms included auditory hallucinations (hearing voices when there is nobody there), delusions (a set of beliefs obviously discordant with reality), thought disorder (obvious lack of logical thinking), stereotypies (repetitive movements or actions), and flattened affect (lack of clear emotional response). Kraepelin separated this condition from paraphrenia in which there was less marked intellectual deterioration but pronounced delusions and hallucinations and paranoia (feeling persecuted without any objective evidence or persecution) in which the major feature was non-hallucinatory delusions.

Eugen Bleuler in 1908 proposed the term *schizophrenia* to cover dementia praecox, paraphrenia, and paranoia. Bleuler (1950) was much influenced by the newly developing psychoanalytic theory and attempted to define the core underlying psychological process that accounted for the disorder. He described this key process as the breaking or loosening of the associative threads which linked thoughts together. The effect of this breaking or loosening of associations led to severe difficulties in communication, an inability to respond appropriately to the surroundings, and finally to withdrawal. Bleuler considered this loosening of associations not as a categorical distinction between abnormality and normality but as a dimension along which people varied and to which different physicians would apply different cut-off points. This conceptual change allowed Bleuler to classify all the types of disorder identified by Kraepelin under the one diagnostic label, "schizophrenia".

Kraepelin and Bleuler disagreed somewhat over the progressive nature of the disorder, with Kraepelin emphasising the progressive deterioration of the condition, whereas Bleuler remained optimistic about the chances of recovery. Warner (1994) has pointed out that this difference may have been due to differences in the management approaches adopted by the two clinicians. Kraepelin's work was largely undertaken in the large asylums where the conditions and practices advocated were likely to have had a deteriorating effect on patients. Bleuler on the other hand may have seen less-disabled people because of his broader definition and his progressive management approach, which attempted to remove people from hospital conditions as soon as possible and emphasised the importance of regulated work.

The original phenomena identified by Kraepelin and Bleuler have remained at the heart of what clinicians have referred to when using the label schizophrenia. During the rest of the first half of the 20th century there was a tendency to expand the definitions of the condition. Langfeldt (1937) distinguished between a core group of process or nuclear schizophrenics who showed an insidious onset and a deteriorating course and reactive schizophrenics who showed more acute onset, better premorbid social functioning, and a better prognosis. This expanding of the definition of schizophrenia was more pronounced in certain countries. For example, Kuriansky, Deming, and Gurland (1974) pointed out that in the United States 20% of patients at the New York State Institute were diagnosed as schizophrenics in the 1930s, but that this had risen to 80% in the 1950s. In contrast, only 20% of patients were diagnosed as schizophrenic at the Maudsley Hospital, London, throughout this period (Cooper et al., 1972).

From the late 1950s until the present day, the most rigorous approach to developing a sound philosophical and empirical base for the classification of psychiatric conditions in general, and schizophrenia in particular, has been the phenomenological approach of Karl Jaspers (1962). Phenomenology is essentially concerned with the description and classification of observable phenomena. Jasper's approach involved going beyond a simple description of the phenomena, that is, the signs and symptoms, to produce a system of describing the phenomena that built on the clinicians' ability to understand the meaningful connections between the patients' experiences in the world and their current behaviour, thoughts and emotions (i.e. ability to empathise). In Jasper's system of classification, what marked the schizophrenic experiences from others was the difficulty or inability of the clinician to understand those experiences empathically. The case of John, described earlier, being convinced that there were microphones in the wall illustrates this point.

Schneider (1959) in his description of the first-rank symptoms appears greatly influenced by Jaspers' thinking. Schneider identified a number of phenomena that he regarded as essential to the diagnosis of schizophrenia, and these included:

(1) hearing one's thoughts spoken aloud
(2) voices talking to each other
(3) voices that comment on one's behaviour
(4) a conviction that external forces are interfering with bodily functions or interfering with or removing or broadcasting thoughts
(5) the experiences that emotions or behaviour or volition are under the control of an external agency.

The essence of this definition was a description of the phenomena which, in a Jasperian sense, were not understandable. This definition, unlike those of Kraepelin, Bleuler, and others, was not based on notions of age of onset, prognosis, and cause, but on both a description of the phenomena that were considered as "primary", that is not reducible to other psychological components, and the extent to which they were understandable to the psychiatrist.

Before describing the current systems of classification, it is important to note that, since the research into the effects of social conditions in psychiatric institutions carried out in the 1960s (Wing & Brown, 1970), it has become common to distinguish between the positive (i.e. hallucinations, delusions, thought/speech disorder, etc.) and negative (i.e. emotional blunting, slowness of speech and movement, lack of motivation, social withdrawal) symptoms of schizophrenia (Wing, 1989). These different types of symptoms have been incorporated into the current diagnostic systems described later. These systems have somewhat lost Jasper's notions of understandability in the attempt to establish reliable diagnostic criteria (Farmer, McGuffin, & Bebbington, 1988).

Currently the most widely adopted systems are the fourth edition of the American Psychiatric Association Diagnostic and Statistical Manual (DSM-IV: APA, 1994) and the World Health Organisation's International Classification of Mental and Behavioural Disorders (ICD-10: WHO, 1992). These systems are both categorical and provide lists of similar, although not identical, signs and symptoms. In addition, each system has a series of sub-types of schizophrenia with definitions of the signs and symptoms required for each. The major difference, however, between the two systems is that in DSM-IV, the important symptoms must be present for at least 6 months, whereas only 1 month is required by ICD-10. The evidence indicated that within these well-developed systems interdiagnostic reliability can be achieved (Farmer et al., 1988) when applied rigorously, for example, with well-trained researchers and clinicians using the standard interviewing technique known as the Present State Examination (PSE). The problem, however, remains that although different but reliable diagnostic systems exist, the level of agreement between these systems is relatively poor (Brockington, Kendell, & Leff, 1978). Reliability, however, does not guarantee validity because two or more people might agree that specific symptoms are present but this does not mean that it is valid to call a group of them schizophrenia. It is the doubts about validity that remain most potent (Bentall, 1993).

VALIDITY OF SCHIZOPHRENIA

During the 1960s a number of radical workers involved in mental health services began to question the validity of conceptualising mental health problems generally, and schizophrenia in particular, as diseases caused by organic malfunctioning (Laing, 1965). The roots of their disquiet can be traced to the research and their clinical experience concerned with the effects of family relations on identified patients. What emerged from this work was that the identified patients' difficulties appeared to be expressions of severe problems in their relationships with parents. Further it was the difference between how these problems were expressed rather than the similarities, which was crucial to understanding patients' difficulties. Consequently, the need for a concept, schizophrenia, to link or group these people was thought of not only as invalid but also harmful.

Given this historical background, recent researchers have attempted to take a more traditional scientific approach to the problem of validity. Bentall, Jackson, and Pilgrim (1988) suggest that there are three ways of assessing the validity of schizophrenia. First, symptoms included in the syndrome should go together, that is, people suffering with one symptom should have a high probability of suffering with other symptoms included in the syndrome. Second, from the diagnosis it should be possible to predict onset, outcome, and response to treatment. Third, diagnosis should be related to aetiology. It is helpful to summarise the major arguments they put forward.

The first validity problem is that the symptoms thought to be crucial to the diagnosis of schizophrenia are found in patients with other psychiatric conditions. For example, thought disorder is common amongst people suffering with mania (Andreasen, 1979; Warner, 1994), delusions are found in people with affective disorders, and hallucinations are found in numerous conditions including depressive disorders and abnormal grief reactions. Further studies utilising the statistical techniques of factor analysis and cluster analysis to identify common groups of symptoms have generally failed to produce clusters and proved flawed on methodological grounds in that they have used hospitalised samples and as such are unlikely to include patients with few psychotic symptoms (Blashfield, 1984; Slade & Cooper, 1979).

The second problem concerns predictive validity, that is, the onset and outcome for patients diagnosed as schizophrenic is extremely variable. Kraepelin's original theory of insidious onset and deteriorating course has been largely disproved. Ciompi (1980) in his study of 228 schizophrenics over a period of 35 years found the onset was either acute or, conversely, insidious in approximately half the cases. With regard to the course of the condition equal numbers had an episodic and continuous course, whereas with outcome (that is, symptomatology) only half were left with a moderate or severe disability and more than a quarter showed full recovery. Other studies attempting to predict outcome have proved equally inconclusive (Kendell, Brockington, & Leff, 1976). In addition, Strauss and Carpenter (1977) found that social factors, including work performance and social contacts, were better predictors of outcome than symptomatology. Similarly, Vaughn and Leff (1976) and Ciompi (1984) have found family variables (see later discussion) to be good predictors of relapse. Indeed, Bentall et al. (1988, p. 310) agree that "it is possible that these factors are all sufficient to account for the marginal differences in outcome". Finally, the extent to which a diagnosis of schizophrenia enables prediction about response to treatment has proved problematic and will be discussed later in the chapter.

The third validity problem concerns the lack of a clear relationship between diagnosis and aetiology (cause of schizophrenia). Thus far it has proved impossible to discover a clear genetic, biochemical, neurological, cognitive, familial, or psychodynamic cause or causes of schizophrenia. This is perhaps not surprising given the difficulties of establishing the validity of schizophrenia. If it is not a valid concept, then it is somewhat odd to expect to find a cause.

It is important to note that none of the writers on schizophrenia deny the distressing nature of the experiences that people given that label suffer. The doubts concern the usefulness of grouping those experiences, or, in diagnostic terms, symptoms, into an illness concept, namely "schizophrenia". However, the factors implicated in the aetiology need to be examined in order to understand what is currently known about schizophrenia and to evaluate whether it remains a valid concept.

THE GENETIC EVIDENCE

The vast majority of psychiatric and psychological texts concerned with schizophrenia (e.g. Gottesman & Shields, 1982) accept that there exists a convincing body of evidence that a predisposition for schizophrenia is transmitted genetically.

This evidence falls into three categories: family, twin, and adoptee studies, with the work with twins and adoptees providing the most powerful support for the genetic case.

Family studies

The prevalence of schizophrenia in the general population is less than 1% (Jablensky, 1986) although there is some variation according to which diagnostic criteria are used. Relatives of schizophrenics have a higher chance of developing the condition than others. Gottesman (1991), in summarising the evidence, claims that the children of two schizophrenic parents have a 46% chance, children of a single schizophrenic parent a 17% chance, siblings a 9% chance, and grandchildren a 5% chance of developing the condition. With regard to whether this supports a genetic or environmental hypothesis about the aetiology of schizophrenia, the data are ambiguous in that they support both views. The risk of developing the condition increases with the closeness of the genetic relationship, but also the relatives will have shared similar familial and social experiences.

Twin studies

The earliest and most widely quoted twin study is that of Kallmann (1946). Kallmann sought to test the genetic hypothesis by demonstrating that monozygotic twins (MZ) who had the same genetic material were more likely to develop schizophrenia than dizygotic (DZ) twins who have different genetic material. His sample was larger than any study before or since in that he located 174 MZ twins, at least one of whom was schizophrenic, and 517 DZ twins. Kallmann reported an MZ concordance rate of 86.2% and for DZ twins of 26.3%. As Marshall (1984) points out, it is useful to analyse this study in some detail as it illustrates many of the methodological problems that beset all twin studies.

The first problem involves the definition of the phenotype, that is, the observable characteristics of the disorder and how reliably this was applied. There has been considerable variability in the definitions of schizophrenia and, as McGuffin (1988) points out, the different definitions produce different concordance rates. The general point emerges from reviews (Gottesman & Shields, 1972; Marshall, 1990; McGuffin, 1988) that the stricter the definition the lower the concordance rates. McGuffin, Farmer, Gottesman, Murray, and Revely (1984), in a study reanalysing case abstracts and comparing concordance rates when using different definitions, found when Schneider's first-rank symptoms were used the estimate of heritability was zero, whereas DSM-IV definitions give a higher heritability estimate. Kallmann (1946) provided little evidence about how schizophrenia was defined or how reliable his diagnosis proved (Boyle, 1994).

The second problem concerns the difficulty of defining zygosity, that is, Kallmann never presented information about how this was diagnosed and at that time this was problematic technically (Jackson, 1960). Advances in genetic research have made this less of a problem for more recent studies, although the reliability of the diagnosis of zygosity should be checked and raters of zygosity should always remain blind to information concerned with concordance. This has not always been the case (Marshall, 1984).

The third problem concerns the variability in terms of how concordance is calculated. The simplest method is pairwise concordance, where if out of a sample of 100 schizophrenics who are also twins, 40 pairs are diagnosed as schizophrenic, this will give a concordance of 40%. Gottesman (1991) argues, however, the best and certainly the most commonly quoted way of calculating concordance is probandwise although this, it can be argued, inflates the concordance rates. The argument for using this is that if the twin pair who are diagnosed as schizophrenic are identified independently they are added to the number of concordant pairs. Using the figures in the previous example this would give a concordance of 45%. Finally, the casewise method involves counting both members of the affected pair. Thus, the 40 pairs identified previously could be represented as 80 individuals with an affected partner. Using this method this would give a concordance rate of 57.1%. Thus, when presenting concordance data as well as making clear which definitions of schizophrenia have been used it has also become customary to quote the method employed to calculate concordance (McGuffin, 1988).

Kallmann (1946) was never particularly explicit about how concordance was calculated and used a number of other methods that had the effect of inflating his concordance rates (Jackson, 1960; Marshall, 1984; Shields, Gottesman, & Slater, 1967). The criticisms of Kallmann's work are so profound that it is somewhat surprising that his results are still frequently quoted in standard texts (Gottesman, 1991); such uncritical acceptance gives credence to Boyle's (1994) and Rose, Kamin, and Lewontin's (1984) arguments that the "existence of a genetic factor in the aetiology of schizophrenia has been treated as an axiom rather than a hypothesis" (Boyle, 1994, p. 403).

Other twin studies have been carried out since Kallmann's (1946) study (Fischer, 1973; Gottesman & Shields, 1972, 1976; Kringlen, 1967; Slater, 1953; Tienari, 1975). Gottesman (1991) in reviewing this later evidence quotes pairwise concordance rates for MZ twins of between 0 and 50% (probandwise concordance 35–38%) and for DZ twins between 4 and 19% (probandwise concordance 13–27%). As Marshall (1990) points out, the size of the concordance rate appears to be related to the scientific rigour of the studies. Quite simply, the more controlled the studies, the lower the concordance rates. Many reviews summarising the evidence are often quoted (Gottsman, 1991; Rosenthal, 1970) but when the original evidence is subject to rigorous investigation (Schiff, Cassou, & Stewart, 1980), the support for a genetic effect is less convincing.

Adoptee studies

There have been two major adoptee studies. Heston (1966) traced 47 people who had been born to schizophrenic mothers while they were in hospital and who had been brought up, since shortly after their birth, either by relatives or in children's homes. Fifty control children brought up in similar homes were then identified. Five of the forty-seven children (10.6%) were diagnosed as schizophrenic and none of the control children. The study still provides the strongest adoptee evidence for the genetic hypothesis.

Kety, Rosenthal, Wender, and Schulsinger (1968), in the USA–Danish adoption studies, located all the children who had been adopted at an early age in Denmark between 1927 and 1947. All adoptees who were admitted to a psychiatric hospital were located and the biological parents, siblings, and half siblings were then traced. A control group without a psychiatric history was identified. A group of 150 biological relatives and 156 controls were selected. Kety et al. (1968) claim that there was a 10% prevalence rate for schizophrenia in the families of the naturally reared schizophrenics, but this depended on a broad definition of schizophrenia. Lidz and Blatt (1983) point out that in fact only one "chronic schizophrenic" was found in both groups, which clearly provides little support for a genetic aetiology. Kety, Rosenthal, Wender, Schulsinger, and Jackson (1975) interviewed the families of 33 schizophrenic adoptees and found 12.6% of biological parents were schizophrenic or latent schizophrenics. This study has been critically reviewed by Rose et al. (1984), who found problems similar to earlier studies with shifting diagnostic boundaries, a selective adoptive placement effect, and cases where pseudo interviews were compiled from hospital records for a number of interviews where the relatives were dead.

Molecular genetics

In more recent years attempts have been made using techniques from molecular genetics to detect whether there is a single or multiple genetic loci for the disorder (Reed, Potter, & Gurling, 1992). These techniques have proved very successful in locating the genetic loci for a number of diseases including insulin-dependent diabetes mellitus (IDDM) and premature coronary heart disease. However, the initial optimism attached to using this approach with schizophrenia (Sherrington et al., 1988) has been tempered by the complexity of the problems in both defining the disorder and the apparent complexities of its genetic transmission (Owen, 1992). A number of major studies are due to report their results soon but so far studying schizophrenia using molecular genetic approaches remains in its infancy.

In summary, the evidence that genetic factors are involved in the aetiology of schizophrenia is a good deal more problematic than is usually presented in standard psychiatric and psychological texts. Marshall (1990) interestingly points out that, throughout the history of investigations into a genetic basis for schizophrenia, researchers have perhaps been influenced by the desire to establish the link rather than adhere to the more conservative rules of scientific method. This position is, however, not surprising given the reliability and validity problems associated with the condition.

BIOLOGICAL METHODS

There remains a fundamental problem involved in examining the work concerned with establishing a biological basis for schizophrenia. These issues are discussed fully by Bentall (1990a), but if schizophrenia is not a clearly identifiable syndrome but an umbrella term covering a range of symptoms with unclear onset, course, and outcome then it is obvious that much of the work investigating a specific biological basis will inevitably be inconclusive. So far this appears to be the case, which is not to imply that biological factors are unimportant. Obviously psychological changes have biochemical effects just as biological changes have psychological effects. The history of the search for a biological cause of schizophrenia has been overly based on the pursuit of a single abnormality leading to the variety of phenomena characteristic of schizophrenia. Such investigations have suggested either structural-neurological or biochemical abnormalities.

Structural-neurological abnormalities

Any structural abnormalities are only significant in terms of their effect on complex brain functioning and as such may help identify the processes that lead to "schizophrenic symptomatology". A number of global cortical abnormalities have been implicated using post mortem techniques (CT scans, X-ray computed tomography) or more recently magnetic resonance imaging (MRI) scans and positron emission topography (PET). Cortical atrophy, that is the degeneration of brain cells, has been found by a number of researchers (Weinberger, Powell, & Austin, 1979), as have enlarged ventricles, that is, spaces in the cortex (Andreasen, Smith, Jacoby, Dennert, & Olsen, 1982; Storey, 1966), and that these changes are progressive (Woods, Yurgelin-Todd, & Benes, 1990) in people diagnosed as schizophrenic. Other researchers have been able to discover neither cortical atrophy nor ventricular enlargement (Jernigan, Zatz, Moses, & Berger, 1982), nor found that these structural abnormalities were progressive (Nasrallah, Olsen, McCalley-Whitters, Chapman, & Jacoby, 1986). Seidman's (1984) review of the literature estimates that only 20–30% of schizophrenics suffer from gross organic impairment and others have suggested that those structural changes maybe the result of diet, institutionalisation, neuroleptic drugs, and convulsion therapy (Reveley, 1985; Trimble & Kingsley, 1978).

Murray, Lewis, Owen, and Foerster (1988) proposed a developmental model, which suggested that neurological abnormalities characterised by increased cortical atrophy and ventricular size and disordered hippocampal areas arise with the development of the brain in the foetus and during the neonatal period. This model implicates subcortical abnormalities and a number of researchers have found abnormalities in the hippocampal region and its connections with the cortex (Bogerts, Meertz, & Schonefeldt-Bausch, 1985). The hippocampal formation (part of the limbic system) plays an important role in discriminating relevant and irrelevant stimuli and could provide the physical base for the abnormalities in information processing which have been used to explain the symptoms of schizophrenia (see Psychological Models section). As Lewis (1989) and Jernigan (1992) point out, these hypotheses are still speculative but seem more fruitful than the attempts to identify specific cortical abnormalities associated with particular lobes of the brain (Jackson, 1990).

In summary, there is little conclusive, but a considerable degree of conflicting, evidence for particular structural abnormalities in people diagnosed as suffering with schizophrenia, although there are a number of relatively new and interesting lines of enquiry.

Biochemical abnormalities

Since Kraepelin's first attempts to define schizophrenia there has been a search for the biochemical "cause". It has been the feature of these investigations that shortly after a possible chemical cause is identified, a series of disconfirming studies are reported. One example of this is the transmethylation hypothesis (Osmond & Smythes, 1952) based on the fact that the chemical structure of mescaline (an hallucinogen) is similar to naturally occurring neurotransmitters known as catecholamines (e.g. dopamine and noradrenalin). These neurotransmitters are the chemicals responsible for the transmission of impulses between neurones at the synapse. The hypothesis was that schizophrenia was the result of overactivity in one of the processes of transmethylation of these amines, which leads to the production of hallucinogenic toxic by-products. This hypothesis has since been abandoned due to the lack of correspondence between the experiences induced by mescaline, LSD, and schizophrenia and the failure to replicate experiments where increasing the levels of amines lead to "schizophrenic-like" symptoms (Iversen, 1982). Many other neurochemicals have been implicated and these include serotonin, prostaglandin, GABA, and neuropeptides, but none have proved to be specifically associated with schizophrenia (Owen & Cross, 1992).

The dopamine hypothesis has been the most recent to receive widespread acceptance. The hypothesis is that there is a relative overactivity of certain tracts of neurones in which the chemical neurotransmitter is dopamine (Meltzer & Stahl, 1976). The evidence supporting this hypothesis has come from two sources. First, amphetamines stimulate the release of dopamine and other catecholamines and produces an acute psychosis similar to schizophrenia, and can produce an exacerbation of psychotic symptoms in people diagnosed as suffering with schizophrenia (Angrist, Lee, & Gershon, 1974). Second, antipsychotic drugs (for example, chlorpromazine), which are known to reduce the symptoms of at least some schizophrenics (Haracz, 1982), also inhibit the ability of the dopamine receptors at the synapse to respond to dopamine and thus reduce the activity in the dopaminergic tracts. The parts of the dopaminergic tracts particularly at risk are the mesolimbic and limbic systems which, as described earlier, appear particularly important in filtering environmental stimuli.

This original hypothesis has been elaborated as a result of research findings, which provide some support for both an increase in dopamine receptors in the basal ganglia (Hess, Bracma, Kleinman, & Creese, 1987) and super sensitivity of dopamine receptors (Bowers, 1974). There are, however, a number of studies that have produced evidence against this hypothesis. Jackson (1986) in his review points out that no consistent difference in the dopamine levels has been found between drug-free schizophrenics and normals. Also, no increase in the levels of other dopamine metabolites that would indicate greater dopamine activity has been found in schizophrenia. Jackson (1990) concludes that problems with dopamine production and receptivity are unlikely to prove the basic biochemical abnormalities underlying all forms of schizophrenia, although this may play a fundamental role in some forms.

In this brief overview, the role of a number of other neurochemicals, for example serotonin, noradrenalin, and prostaglandin have been omitted from the discussion. In general, the evidence that they play a part in the aetiology of schizophrenia is such that it does not lead to any easily stated general conclusions. Dopamine and its related pathways appear implicated in the experiences associated with schizophrenia but it is unclear whether this is a cause or effect. This inconclusiveness may, in fact, prove to be because schizophrenia includes such a wide range of symptoms that attempting to find a specific neurochemical cause will prove impossible. As Bentall (1990b) points out, perhaps, the time has come to turn to investigations concerned with specific symptoms before attempting to find the biochemical cause of schizophrenia, which could be regarded as a concept of dubious validity.

NEUROCOGNITIVE MODELS

In recent years, there has been a trend to develop models for understanding the behaviour and experiences of people with schizophrenia that integrate neurological and cognitive explanations. In such models (Shallice, 1988) the brain is assumed to work rather like a computer, which carries out a number of functions including processing and storing information, planning action, and assessing the results. The way the brain processes this complex information is assumed to be able to be broken down into a number of independent processes working in parallel. Research into understanding the cognitive difficulties experienced by people with brain damage has been highly significant in the development of these ideas (Shallice, 1988).

The understanding of the cognitive difficulties of people with schizophrenia has been pursued in attempts to identify the cognitive deficits that may underlie the disorder. There have been a number of general research findings that indicate that people with schizophrenia function with IQs on average 10 points lower than premorbid estimates of IQ (Nelson, Pantelis, Barnes, Thraser, & Bodger, 1993) and significant deficits in verbal learning and memory (Harvey, Earle-Boxer, & Levinson, 1988). There has also been a well-established finding that people with schizophrenia show a general slowness of processing over a variety of tasks (Hemsley, 1976). The studies investigating slowness have generally used reaction time tasks, although Hemsley (1976) has pointed out that schizophrenic groups perform particularly poorly if the stimulus–response link is not an obvious or natural one (i.e. uncertainty is increased). Out of these findings a number of researchers have proposed more general cognitive models about the "essential" cognitive deficit underlying schizophrenia and these are briefly described next.

McGhie and Chapman's selective attention model

McGhie and Chapman (1961) suggested that the primary disorder in schizophrenia was a decrease in the selective and inhibitory functions of attention. This proposal used Broadbent's (1958) notion of a cognitive filter that screened irrelevant stimuli. Thus, in schizophrenia a deficit in the filter meant that the individual was flooded with stimuli and therefore in a state of information overload.

Broadbent (1971) elaborated his model by proposing a second mechanism involved in selective attention, which he termed "pigeon holing", and which was more concerned with individuals' responses. Thus, when stimuli were received decisions needed to be made about which responses should be made from an infinite number of possibilities. "Pigeon holing" allowed the stimuli to be keyed in to certain categories of response without having to process all possible responses. In schizophrenia it has been argued that this function is impaired so that the individual has considerable difficulty selecting the correct response from a large range of possible responses. This deficit thus frequently leads to the schizophrenic producing inappropriate responses.

Thus, with selective attention two important processes have been suggested as being impaired in schizophrenia. Hemsley (1988) points out that the evidence for a defective filter mechanism is somewhat inconsistent. In experiments designed to test for a defective filter, schizophrenics have made more errors than normal subjects. However, when compared with psychiatric control groups the findings are less clear. The evidence for impairment in "pigeon holing", which is largely dependent on semantic cues, remains scarce (Schwartz, 1982).

Schneider and Shiffrin's controlled and automatic processing model

Schneider and Shiffrin (1977) distinguished between automatic and controlled cognitive processes. Automatic processing occurs outside conscious awareness and involves a fixed sequence of mental operations in response to a particular stimulus set. Such processes can be trained but when learned they become relatively fixed. Controlled processing is relatively slow, under conscious control, and involves temporary sequences of mental operations. Callaway and Naghoi (1982) suggest that schizophrenics have a deficit in controlled but not automatic processing. A number of authors, however (e.g. Venables, 1984), have concluded that the deficit is most likely to be in the area of automatic processing, which means that all tasks have to be subject to controlled processing. This suggestion is consistent with the findings showing slowed information processing and with Frith's cognitive model described next.

Frith's model—a failure to control consciousness

Frith (1979) proposed that a deficit in the mechanism that controls and limits the contents of consciousness caused the three principal positive symptoms of schizophrenia, that is, hallucinations, delusions, and thought disorder. Frith's model is a modification of the defective filter theory, which he argued was unable to explain delusions and hallucinations and also why, if it was such a global deficit, schizophrenics function relatively well for large proportions of their lives. Within his model a distinction is made between conscious and preconscious processes. Preconscious processes occur below the level of consciousness. They include motor outputs and cognitive operations concerned with the selection of appropriate interpretations of and responses to stimuli. Frith argues that for schizophrenics these preconscious processes are frequently conscious. Thus, auditory hallucinations are viewed as an awareness of the preconscious incorrect interpretations of auditory stimuli and therefore tend to increase in situations where there is ambiguous sensory input. Thus, with John, described in the Introduction, sounds outside the door were misinterpreted as people talking about and to him. For most people such a preconscious interpretation would be discounted before reaching conscious awareness, but not for John.

Frith (1987) revised this model and proposed a concept of "willed intention", that is, the effort required to turn perceptions of the external environment and internal thoughts and memories into appropriate action. Frith proposed that a deficit in the ability to monitor willed intention in schizophrenia means that thoughts can be considered as unintended or alien. This account has found some experimental support (Frith & Done, 1989). Frith further suggests that this deficit could be caused by damage to the neuronal pathways, which control and monitor actions.

In his latest elaboration Frith (1992) has proposed that delusions, in particular, may be caused by the inability to understand accurately the intentions of others. This cognitive deficit in understanding the social meaning of situations may arise from a dysfunctioning in the neuronal pathways between the prefrontal cortex and the septohippocampal system. Further that the problems arise from dopamine disregulation in these areas. This latest model is one that attempts to make explicit links between cognitive deficits, neurological pathways, and biochemical imbalances.

Hemsley's rapid-automatic assessment model

Hemsley (1993, p. 110) offered an alternative model, which proposed that it was "the rapid and automatic assessment of the significance of aspects of sensory input that is impaired in schizophrenia". This leads to experiencing non-relevant features of the social environment as particularly personally significant, which without this deficit would be ignored. This results in the assessing of thoughts and memories that appear strange or irrelevant to ongoing plans. This in turn can lead to these thoughts being perceived as alien and the attribution of their origin to an external source. The model proposes that the septohippocampal pathways are implicated. These probably underlie most monitoring functions, that is, checking the correspondence between events and expectations, assessing the significance of stimuli and intervening to inhibit behaviour when there is a lack of match (Gray, Feldon, Rawlins, Hemsley, & Smith, 1990). Support for this overly rapid assessment in people with schizophrenia has come from studies by Garety, Hemsley, and Wessely (1991), who found that people with schizophrenia tended to jump to firmly held conclusions on the basis of little evidence on probabilistic reasoning tasks. Again Gray et al. (1990) propose that such deficits may arise because of the disregulation of the neurotransmitter dopamine in the septohippocampal areas. This theory, although tentative, again attempts to explain some of the symptoms from a cognitive point of view as well as suggesting a possible physical basis.

In summary, a number of interesting theories have been proposed, some of which are still in an early stage of development. Their models are, however, not without their problems. The difficulty with such models is that so far they only provide explanations of some of the symptoms of schizophrenia and it remains unclear why, if the deficit is fixed, schizophrenics at times function without these symptoms and also are able to perform some tasks well (Pilling, 1988). In addition, questions about why particular misinterpretations occur and remain fixed (as with John), and why they should occur at particular times and not others, are not addressed by these models.

SYMPTOM-BASED APPROACHES TO SCHIZOPHRENIA

A major difficulty in investigating psychological factors involved in schizophrenia is the problem that the diagnostic label refers to a range of clinical experiences or symptoms. These experiences include hallucinations, delusions, thought disorder, poverty of speech, apathy, and attentional impairments. Amongst others, Bannister (1968), Bentall et al. (1988), Costello (1993), and Persons (1986) have suggested abandoning investigations into the syndrome of schizophrenia and propose instead the investigation of the experiences and symptoms. Indeed, it is now widely recognised that the most useful knowledge about schizophrenia is likely to emerge from investigations using this approach. It is perhaps helpful to briefly describe some of this work by describing the developments in the study of hallucinations and delusions. Costello (1993) provides a more comprehensive review of both the other positive (i.e. thought disorder) and negative symptoms of schizophrenia which are not discussed here.

Hallucinations

Hallucinations involve a sensory perception without the external stimulation of the relevant sensory organ. It has the sense of reality of a true perception but has a source usually external to the body but occasionally from within the body. Auditory hallucinations are by far the most common in schizophrenia (APA, 1994). In the last three decades a number of factors have been found to increase the likelihood of experiencing hallucinations (Slade, 1976); these include the experience of stress, sensory deprivation, and unpatterned stimulations (e.g. white noise). Other factors including a reduction in arousal have been linked with a decrease in hallucinations. Several models (Costello, 1993) have been put forward to account for hallucinations, although all essentially stress the misrepresentation or misperception of inner sensations (e.g. thoughts with auditory hallucinations) as deriving from an external source, the failure to check the reality of their perception, and the maintenance of these "false" perceptions as "real".

A number of researchers have contributed to the development of this view. Collicutt and Hemsley (1985) suggested that hallucinations were caused when unexpected internally generated experiences were attributed to external events, and further attempted to relate this process to a deficit in the "pigeon holing" mechanism described by Broadbent (1971). Hoffman (1986), following a somewhat similar theme, proposed that a deficit in speech production led to certain thoughts arising in an unintended fashion, which were then interpreted as alien. However, a number of attempts to offer more comprehensive theories about the development of hallucinations have been proposed (Heilbrun, 1980; Sarbin, 1967), the most evidence based of these is that of Slade and Bentall (1988). For this reason the model is outlined here without quoting the detailed supporting evidence.

Slade and Bentall (1985) proposed a five-factor theory to explain the occurrence of hallucinations. These factors included: first, the presence of stress induced arousal; second, predisposing factors; Bentall and Slade particularly emphasise importance of a deficit in the metacognition of reality testing (that is, the inferential skill of being able to discriminate between what is "real" and imaginary); third, the occurrence of particular types of external stimulation (e.g. conditions of sensory deprivation or where the stimulation is difficult to make sense of); fourth, where the hallucinations are reinforced (e.g. through anxiety reduction) and where the hallucinations are expected (e.g. when they form part of a cultural belief or part of a delusion). These factors combine and lead to the individual wrongly inferring that internal cognitive events are external "real" stimuli. There is considerable experimental evidence to support this model (Slade & Bentall, 1988), although it has been criticised because of the lack of clarity about what leads to what (Costello, 1993) and the reasons why people develop this reality-testing deficit. If some of Laing's (1965) or Heilbrun's ideas prove correct it may be that certain patterns of interaction within the family, particularly when the child is very young, mean the child fails to acquire this ability. Similarly it may be that in order to avoid painful experiences the developing child increasingly escapes into "imaginary worlds" to such an extent that in moments of crisis, or permanently if the crises are permanent, the child re-experiences those "imaginary experiences" as "real".

Delusions

Spitzer (1990, p. 391) probably provides the most succinct definition of a delusion, as "statements about external reality which are uttered like statements about a mental state, that is, with a subjective certainty and incorrigible by others". Garety and Hemsley (1994) take issue with the notion of the incorrigibility or "unshakability" of the statements in that, first, such statements are at an extreme strength of a belief continuum and therefore not categorically differently from normal reasoning processes, and, second, that they can be changed (e.g. Kuipers et al., 1997).

There have been a number of theories about possible psychological mechanisms underlying delusions and these have been thoroughly reviewed by Costello (1993), Garety and Hemsley (1994), and Winters and Neale (1983). Some investigations have suggested that they may arise out of rational descriptions of bizarre or entangled sets of events and that the delusion is a metaphorical understanding of those events (Bannister, 1968; Laing, 1965). Others have considered that delusions are rational interpretations of abnormal perceptual experiences that are fundamentally biological in nature (Maher, 1974). Indeed, the psychological theories of Frith (1979, 1992) and Hemsley (1993) described earlier have been specifically applied to delusion formation. The work of Hemsley, in particular, lends itself well to the proposal that hallucinations result from a deficit in the metacognition of "reality testing". Bentall, Kaney, and Dewey (1991) and Kaney and Bentall (1989) have investigated information processing deficits through assessing the attributional style of people with delusions. Their findings indicate that paranoid patients who tend to hold the delusional belief that others are against them attribute bad events to causes that would affect their entire lives, were beyond their control, and were caused by factors external to themselves. Thus, they showed external, global, and stable attributions for negative events. They further suggest that people with paranoid delusions also have low self-esteem, which the delusion defends against, although this notion has less empirical support.

In summary there are a number of emerging theories for the development and maintenance of delusions. This symptom-based understanding is still relatively new, although what is clear is that a complex interaction of factors is implicated in the experience and the approach has contributed to the development of innovative psychological treatment (Chadwick, Birchwood, & Trower, 1996; Fowler, Garety, & Kuipers, 1996).

PSYCHOANALYTIC IDEAS

Any discussion of psychoanalytic ideas as they relate to the experiences associated with schizophrenia needs to be prefaced with a reminder of the methods employed to gather information. Psychoanalysts have gathered data concerned with a knowledge of unconscious processes through intense contact with patients; up to five, 50-minute sessions per week. Freud developed this method and the associated theoretical ideas in order to understand the psyche of his patients. The strength of this method is the intensity and depth of understanding of the individual that can be achieved, but its weakness is the extent to which discoveries about individuals are applicable to others, that is, the generalisability of the findings.

Many psychoanalysts including Freud (1940/1964) have stated that the psychotic's problems are such that it is impossible to establish an appropriate therapeutic alliance to work using analytic methods. Although others (Fromm-Reichmann, 1950; Jackson, 1995) have disagreed with this view, Klerman (1984) and Mueser and Berenbaum (1990) in reviewing the evidence support Freud's view; namely, that intensive individual psychotherapy has proved to be a failure with schizophrenia. Tarrier (1990) has commented that there is some evidence that the overstimulation provoked by such therapeutic encounters can promote relapse. Frosch (1983) provides an impressive historical review of the development of psychoanalytic ideas about psychosis, although he, too, makes the point that although psychoanalysis has played a role in understanding the psychotic process, the extent to which this has been translated into meaningful therapy may be challenged.

In this brief chapter it is impossible to provide an overview of psychoanalytic theory as it relates to psychosis, but it is perhaps useful to mention some of the theoretical ideas. Frosch (1983) considers that the presence of psychosis hinges on the loss of the capacity to test reality. Exploration of this capacity has a long tradition in psychoanalytic writings (Ferenczi, 1913; Freud, 1911/1958; Glover, 1932; Weiss, 1950) and has interesting parallels with more recent developments in cognitive theory, which Bentall (1990a) has used to understand hallucination (that is, the metacognition of reality testing). Frosch (1983) describes how reality testing is the ability to draw logical conclusions from a series of observable phenomena, that is, to distinguish between the internal and external world. The loss of this capacity results in psychosis. The question then is how does this lack of the capacity for reality testing arise?

As with all psychoanalytic understanding the root of these difficulties is traced back to childhood experiences, although it is worthy to note that few analysts deny the impact of genetic vulnerability (Robbins, 1993). Frosch (1983) and Klein (1946/1986) propose that the core overwhelming anxiety of the baby is that of death. The baby learns how to deal with this anxiety through its interaction with its prime caregiver. The adequacy of the caregiver to help the baby with this anxiety is crucial to the infant's development of a sense of self (Winnicott, 1988) and its ability to manage its internal experiences and the outer world and to be able to distinguish between them. It is argued that through processes that include "mirroring" (Kohut, 1977) and managing constructively and containing the emotional disturbance generated by the infant (Bion, 1962; Segal, 1979), it becomes less terrorised and anxious about its own death, which allows further development of self and its relationship with the caregiver as a separate being.

Frosch (1983) and Klein (1946/1986) argue that if, through inadequate care (i.e. this could be caused by abusive traumas or the severe lack of emotional availability of the prime caregiver) these emotions are not made bearable, infants will defend their developing sense of self by splitting off these emotions and projecting them into the external world. In this way these defensive processes distort perception of reality. Fonagy and colleagues, drawing on the work of Bowlby (1973) and Main (1991), have provided some innovative and thorough research that supports the importance of early attachment experiences in forming both the basis for adult relationships but also, if such attachments are very insecure, how they appear to lead to significant psychiatric difficulties (i.e. borderline personality disorder) in adults (Fonagy et al., 1996).

It could be argued that, if individuals have developed this personal vulnerability to psychotic defences, they are most likely to be triggered when threats to their fragile sense of self occur. It is perhaps not surprising that the phase of transition from adolescence to adulthood is a period when the symptoms of schizophrenia often first become evident (APA, 1994). Thus, it is at such times that the defences of "splitting off" negative emotions and projecting them into the external world onto a person, or group in society, or even an inanimate object, occur and result in regarding that object as the source of the "badness".

When such processes are in operation, they certainly leave the individual with a depleted sense of self (Chadwick, 1993).

It is perhaps something of a tragedy that there has not been more cross-fertilisation between the ideas of psychoanalysis where attempts have been made to understand the meaning of the symptoms (Jackson, 1995), and more empirically based developments in psychology (Bentall, 1990a; Garety & Hemsley, 1994), although this is beginning to occur (Hingley, 1997). It would appear that there is a good deal to be gained for both our theoretical understanding and the development of psychological interventions to alleviate the disturbing experiences associated with schizophrenia from such crossfertilisation.

FAMILY MODELS

Even amongst strong proponents of the genetic hypothesis there is a recognition of the importance of environmental factors. In terms of environmental variables that have been linked to the aetiology and maintenance of schizophrenic symptomatology, family factors are particularly prominent (Bateson, Jackson, Haley, & Weakland, 1956; Laing, 1965; McCreadie, Williamson, Athawes, Connolly, & Tilak-Singh, 1994; Wynne & Singer, 1963). The development of early theories rested mainly on clinical observations and insights, and the quality of the empirical work designed to test these theories has been somewhat inadequate. A brief review of this early work is, however, still useful.

Bateson et al. (1956) developed the "double-bind theory" to explain the emergence of what they regarded as the schizophrenics' key problem, namely a severe difficulty in their pattern of communication. Families of schizophrenics were considered to show a particular pattern of ambiguous communication where the parent denied the contradictory nature of his/her command and also did not allow the child to point out this contradiction. There have, in fact, been few empirical investigations of this theory, although the evidence suggests that, first, it is difficult to identify double-bind messages, and, second, such messages are likely to occur in all families. It may be the case that it is not just whether such communication patterns occur but the extent to which the child is subject to such communication from birth that is important in producing the symptoms to schizophrenia in adulthood.

Wynne and Singer (1963) use the concept of "pseudomutuality" to characterise the pattern of communication in schizophrenic families. This term describes how interactions, despite superficial appearances, show a fragmented and disjointed pattern with irrational changes in focus which prevent any continuity. Underlying this disordered communication are feelings of emptiness and meaninglessness, which are taken on by the children. As the children reach adolescence and begin to enter the world beyond the family, the disordered pattern of communication prevents them fitting into this new world. Singer and Wynne (1966) produced an impressive study, which showed that it was possible to discriminate between the communication pattern of families of schizophrenics, neurotics, and adults with no psychiatric disorder on the basis of a deviance score. This deviance score was obtained by counting the number of communication defects or deviances recorded during a session in which the family were completing a projective test. Hirsch and Leff (1975) in part replicated the study and found parents of schizophrenics had significantly higher deviance scores than neurotic individuals. They explored these results in more detail and found that the differences in scores could have been accounted for by the increased verbosity observed in the schizophrenic families. Thus, Hirsch and Leff concluded that the differences in deviance scores could have been no more than an artefact of the difference in verbosity between schizophrenic and neurotic families.

Laing (1965) developed a considerably more sophisticated theory to explain the origins of schizophrenia within the family. He regarded the content of the hallucinations, delusions, and thought disorder as containing an "existential truth". Thus, the symptoms developed as both a way of coping with and communicating to others the impossibility of the familial environment. Laing published a number of thought-provoking accounts of the development of schizophrenia, which produced clear testable hypotheses. It is something of a puzzle why nobody has developed research studies to investigate these essentially clinical and theoretical writings. Perhaps the answer lies in the lack of a traditional scientific mode of investigation within the model in which Laing's ideas were embedded and the published failure of Anna to work through her psychotic experience in the way advocated by Laing (Reed, 1978). The more recent work of Lidz (1993), who describes the chaotic pattern of communication and behaviour in the families of people with schizophrenic symptoms, has clear parallels with Laing's observations.

In more recent years, research and family therapeutic work, prompted by the early studies of Brown, Carstairs, and Topping (1958) and Brown, Bone, Dalison, and Wing (1966), has focused on the concept of expressed emotion (EE) within the family. The level of expressed emotion within a family is determined by the frequency of critical comments and positive remarks and ratings of hostility, emotional over-involvement, and warmth in an audiotaped interview with a relative of the patient. The relative is rated as demonstrating high EE if he or she makes six or more critical comments and/or scores a rank of one or more on hostility and/or three or more on emotional over-involvement. The research investigating this phenomenon has revealed a consistent finding that there is a strong relationship between relapse and living with a high EE relative. This has been found in Britain (Vaughn & Leff, 1976; Tarrier et al., 1988), the United States (Moline, Singh, Morris, & Meltzer, 1985), Denmark, and India (Wig et al., 1987).

Vaughn and Leff's (1976) study, although not without its methodological problems, is perhaps of most interest because they attempted to look at the effect of medication, expressed emotion, and the amount of contact with the high EE relative. They found that in the group of patients who lived with high EE relatives, with whom they had high levels of contact (more than 35 hours a week), and who were not on medication, 92% relapsed within 9 months. Patients in a similar family but who were on medication had a 53% relapse rate. This indicated that medication provided some protection from relapse in these high EE families. However, patients who lived with a low EE relative had a 12% relapse rate if they were on medication and a 15% rate if not on medication. This indicated that in low EE families there was little change in relapse rate when medication was taken.

This work has proved extremely valuable in that it has proved possible to specify factors within the family associated with relapse in a way that leads directly to some extremely effective therapeutic interventions designed to reduce these factors (Falloon et al., 1985; Hughes, Hailwood, Abbati-Yeoman, & Budd, 1996; Lam, 1991; Leff et al., 1982; Tarrier, Barrowclough, Porceddu, & Fitzpatrick, 1994). A number of researchers have, however, pointed out some problems with the work. Tarrier (1990) criticises the early studies for their limited definition of relapse, that is, being too dependent on increases in positive symptoms without taking into account negative symptoms or social functioning. Johnstone (1993) has probably been the strongest critic of the EE work and her main points include: first, the studies generally have high refusal rates (i.e. families refuse to take up the family interventions); second, the inappropriate acceptance of medication as an adjunct to family intervention in all cases; and, third, the contradiction inherent in the message to families that although they are not to blame for schizophrenia there is evidence of a casual link between family interactions and relapse. In spite of these criticisms, the evidence is strong that these interventions reduce relapse and it remains a puzzle why these family interventions are still rarely offered in most services for people with long-term mental health problems (Lavender & Holloway, 1992; Rogers & Pilgrim, 1996). Perhaps Bentall (1990b) is right when he suggests that it is a consequence of the dominant role of biological psychiatry in the treatment of schizophrenia.

CONCLUDING REMARKS

In conclusion, it is important to say that frequently when a review such as this is written it is usual to finish by producing some overall stress-vulnerability model for schizophrenia which includes all possible factors relevant to the aetiology and maintenance of schizophrenia (Clements & Turpin, 1992; Nuechterlein, 1987; Zubin & Spring, 1977). These models include some original constitutional vulnerability (genetic) related to an organic or biochemical abnormality that interacts with particular social and familial factors to produce schizophrenia (Warner, 1994). It is tempting to repeat such as enterprise, but the evidence so far indicates that such all-encompassing models, although producing a comfort that all the factors have been taken into account, actually may be somewhat misguided in attempting to account for schizophrenia, which remains a disorder that can reasonably be argued is of dubious validity.

Researchers from all theoretical orientations (genetic/biological, cognitive, psychoanalytic, and familial), until very recently, have investigated schizophrenia as a whole and paid little attention to the particular experiences that have traditionally been described as the symptoms of schizophrenia. The fact that these distressing experiences exist, as was evident with John in the Introduction to this chapter, is not in doubt. However, whether it is useful to group these disparate experiences together and act as if they were part of a single disease or disorder clearly is at least questionable. Thus, the investigation of these separate symptoms would seem to offer an important and potentially fruitful source of information.

Perhaps a key to this integration lies in understanding the processes that lead to a disturbance in individuals' ability to reality test which seems crucial in the development of a range of psychotic symptoms, some of which are regarded as diagnostic of schizophrenia (Frosch, 1983). This has long been regarded as crucial by psychoanalysts and has also been highlighted by researchers following both cognitive (Bentall, 1990a; Hemsley, 1993) and familial (Lidz, 1993) models. Difficulties in being able to reality test occur at a perceptual and response level and probably involve different processes for each symptom. It is clearly important to investigate the nature of these difficulties in a way that allows a psychological understanding of their meaning to develop. Investigations about how these difficulties or distortions develop in the growing child and how they are related to attachment processes seem potentially interesting research areas. The development of models such as Hingley's (1997), which attempt to bring together the knowledge that has accumulated from psychoanalytic, familial, and cognitive work, is likely to prove most productive in increasing our understanding of the experiences associated with schizophrenia.

RECOMMENDED READING

Bentall, R.P. (1990). *Reconstructing schizophrenia*. London: Routledge.

Birchwood, M., & Tarrier, N. (1992). *Innovations in the psychological management of schizophrenia*. Chichester, UK: John Wiley & Sons.

Costello, C.G. (1993). *Symptoms of schizophrenia*. New York: John Wiley & Sons.

David, A.S., & Cutting, J.C. (1994). *The neuropsychology of schizophrenia*. Hove, UK: Lawrence Erlbaum Associates Ltd.

Fowler, D., Garety, P., & Kuipers, F. (1996). *Cognitive behaviour therapy for psychosis: Theory and practice*. Chichester, UK: John & Wiley & Sons.

Kavanagh, D.J. (1992). *Schizophrenia: An overview and practical handbook.* London: Chapman & Hall.

Laing, R.D. (1965). *The divided self.* London: Pelican.

Pilling, S. (1991). *Rehabilitation and community care.* London: Routledge & Kegan Paul.

Warner, R. (1994). *Recovery from schizophrenia: Psychiatry and political economy* (2nd ed.). London: Routledge & Kegan Paul.

REFERENCES

American Psychiatric Association. (1994). *Diagnostic and statistical manual of mental disorders* (4th ed.). Washington: American Psychiatric Association.

Andreasen, N.C. (1979). Thought, language and communication disorders: II. Diagnostic significance. *Archives of General Psychiatry, 36,* 1325–1330.

Andreasen, N.C., Smith, M.R., Jacoby, C.G., Dennert, J.W., & Olsen, S.A. (1982). Ventricular enlargement in schizophrenia: Definition and prevalence. *American Journal of Psychiatry, 139,* 297–301.

Angrist, B., Lee, H.K., & Gershon, S. (1974). The antagonism of amphetamine induced symptomatology by a neuroleptic. *American Journal of Psychiatry, 1131,* 817–819.

Bannister, D. (1968). The logical requirements of research into schizophrenia. *British Journal of Psychiatry, 114,* 181–188.

Bateson, G., Jackson, D., Haley, J., & Weakland, J. (1956). Towards a theory of schizophrenia. *Behavioural Science, 1,* 251–264.

Bentall, R.P. (1990a). *Reconstructing schizophrenia.* London: Routledge.

Bentall, R.P. (1990b). The illusion of reality: A review and integration of psychological research on hallucinations. *Psychological Bulletin, 107,* 82–95.

Bentall, R.P. (1993). Deconstructing the concept of schizophrenia. *Journal of Mental Health, 2*(3), 223–238.

Bentall, R.P., Jackson, H.F., & Pilgrim, D. (1988). Abandoning the concept of "schizophrenia": Some implications of validity arguments for psychological research into psychotic phenomena. *British Journal of Clinical Psychology, 27,* 303–324.

Bentall, R.P., Kaney, S., & Dewey, M.E. (1991). Paranoia and social reasoning: An attribution theory analysis. *British Journal of Clinical Psychology, 30,* 13–23.

Bentall, R.P., & Slade, P.D. (1985). Reality testing and auditory hallucination: A signal detection analysis. *British Journal of Clinical Psychology, 24,* 159–169.

Bion, W.R. (1962). The psychoanalytic theory of thinking: II. A theory of thinking. *International Journal of Psychoanalysis, 43,* 306–310.

Blashfield, K. (1984). *The classification of psychopathology: Neokraepelin and quantitative approaches.* New York: Plenum.

Bleuler, E. (1950). *Dementia praecox or the group of schizophrenics.* New York: International University Press. (Original work published in German 1911)

Bogerts, B., Meertz, E., & Schonefeldt-Bausch, R. (1985). Basal ganglia and limbic system pathology in schizophrenia. *Archives of General Psychiatry, 42,* 784–791.

Bowers, M.B. (1974). Central dopamine turnover in schizophrenic syndromes. *Archives of General Psychiatry, 31,* 50–54.

Bowlby, J. (1973). *Attachment and loss: Vol. 2. Separation anxiety and anger.* New York: Basic Books.

Boyle, M. (1994). Schizophrenia and the art of the soluble. *The Psychologist*, 399–404.

Broadbent, D.E. (1958). *Perception and communication*. London: Pergamon Press.

Broadbent, D.E. (1971). *Decision and stress*. London: Academic Press.

Brockington, J.F., Kendell, R.E., & Leff, J.P. (1978). Definitions of schizophrenia: Concordance and prediction of outcome. *Psychological Medicine, 8*, 387–398.

Brown, G.W., Bone, M., Dalison, B., & Wing, J.K. (1966). *Schizophrenia and social care*. London: Oxford University Press.

Brown, G.W., Carstairs, G., & Topping, G. (1958). Post hospital adjustment of chronic mental patients. *Lancet, ii*, 685–689.

Callaway, E., & Naghoi, S. (1982). An information processing model for schizophrenia. *Archives of General Psychiatry, 39*, 339–347.

Chadwick, P.K. (1993). The stepladder to the impossible: A first hand account of a schizo affective episode. *Journal of Mental Health, 2*, 239–250.

Chadwick, P., Birchwood, M., & Trower, P. (1996). *Cognitive therapy for delusions, voices and paranoia*. Chichester, UK: John Wiley & Sons.

Ciompi, L. (1980). The natural history of schizophrenia in the long term. *British Journal of Psychiatry, 136*, 413–420.

Ciompi, L. (1984). Is there really a schizophrenia? The long term course of psychotic phenomena. *British Journal of Psychiatry, 145*, 636–640.

Clements, K., & Turpin, G. (1992). Vulnerability models in schizophrenia. In M. Birchwood & N. Tarrier (Eds.), *Innovations in the psychological management of schizophrenia*. Chichester, UK: John Wiley & Sons.

Collicutt, J.R., & Hemsley, D.R. (1985). *Schizophrenia: The description of a stream of thought*. Unpublished manuscript.

Cooper, J.E., Kendell, R.E., Gurland, B.J., Sharp, L., Copeland, J.R.M., & Simon, R. (1972). *Psychiatric diagnosis in New York and London* (Maudsley Monograph). London: Oxford University Press.

Costello, C.G. (1993). The advantage of the symptom approach to schizophrenia. In C.G. Costello (Ed.), *Symptoms of schizophrenia*. New York: Wiley.

Falloon, I.R.H., Boyd, J.L., McGill, C.W., Williamson, M., Ranzini, J., Moss, H.D., Gilderman, A.M., & Simpson, G.M. (1985). Family management in the prevention of morbidity in schizophrenia: Clinical outcome of a two year longitudinal study. *Archives of General Psychiatry, 42*, 887–896.

Farmer, A.E., McGuffin, P., & Bebbington, P. (1988). The phenomena of schizophrenia. In P. Bebbington & P. McGuffin (Eds.), *Schizophrenia: The major issues*. Oxford, UK: Heinemann.

Ferenczi, S. (1913). Stages in the development of a sense of reality. In S. Ferenczi, *Sex in psychoanalysis*. Boston: Badger.

Fischer, M. (1973). Genetic and environmental factors in schizophrenia: A study of schizophrenic twins and their families. *Acta Psychiatrica Scandinavica, Supp, 223*, 5–157.

Fonagy, P., Leigh, T., Steele, M., Steele, H., Kennedy, R., Mattodon, G., Target, M., & Gerder, A. (1996). The relation of attachment status, psychiatric classification and response to psychotherapy. *Journal of Consulting and Clinical Psychology, 64*(1), 22–31.

Fowler, D., Garety, P., & Kuipers, E. (1996). *Cognitive behaviour therapy for psychosis: Theory and practice*. Chichester, UK: John Wiley & Sons.

Freud, S. (1958). Psycho-analytic notes on an autobiographical account of a case of paranoia (dementia paranoides). In *The Standard Edition of the complete works of Sigmund Freud* (vol. 12, pp. 3–82). London: Hogarth Press. (Original work published in 1911)

Freud, S. (1964). An outline of psychoanalysis. In *The Standard Edition of the complete works of Sigmund Freud* (vol. 23, pp. 141–208). London: Hogarth Press. (Original work published 1940)

Frith, C.D. (1979). Consciousness, information processing and schizophrenia. *British Journal of Psychiatry, 134*, 225–235.

Frith, C.D. (1987). The positive and negative symptoms of schizophrenia reflect impairment in the perception and initiation of action. *Psychological Medicine, 17*, 631–648.

Frith, C.D. (1992). *The cognitive neuropsychology of schizophrenia.* Hove, UK: Lawrence Erlbaum Associates Ltd.

Frith, C.D., & Done, D.J. (1988). Towards a neuropsychology of schizophrenia. *British Journal of Psychiatry, 153*, 437–443.

Fromm-Riechmann, F. (1950). *Principles of intensive psychotherapy.* Chicago: University of Chicago Press.

Frosch, J. (1983). *The psychotic process.* New York: International University Press.

Garety, P.A., & Hemsley, D.R. (1994). *Delusions: Investigation into the psychology of delusional reasoning* (Maudsley Monographs). London: Oxford University Press.

Garety, P.A., Hemsley, D.R., & Wessely, S. (1991). Reasoning in deluded schizophrenic and paranoid patients: Biases in performance on a probabilistic inference task. *Journal of Nervous and Mental Diseases, 179*, 194–201.

Glover, E. (1932). The relation of perversion formation to the development of reality sense. In E. Glover, *On the early development of mind.* New York: International University Press.

Gottesman, I.I. (1991). *Schizophrenia genesis: The origins of madness.* New York: Freeman.

Gottesman, I.I., & Shields, J. (1972). *Schizophrenia and genetics.* London: Academic Press.

Gottesman, I.I., & Shields, J. (1976). A critical review of recent adoption, twin and family studies. *Schizophrenia Bulletin, 2*, 360–401.

Gottesman, I.I., & Shields, J. (1982). *Schizophrenia: The epigenetic puzzle.* Cambridge, UK: Cambridge University Press.

Gray, J.A., Feldon, L., Rawlins, J.N.P., Hemsley, D.R., & Smith A.D. (1990). The neuropsychology of schizophrenia. *Behavioural and Brain Sciences, 14*, 1–84.

Haracz, J.L. (1982). The dopamine hypothesis: An overview of studies with schizophrenic patients. *Schizophrenia Bulletin, 8*, 438–469.

Harvey, P.P., Earle-Boxer, E.A., & Levinson, J.C. (1988). Cognitive deficits and thought disorder: A retest study. *Schizophrenia Bulletin, 14*, 57–66.

Heilbrun, A.R. (1980). Impaired recognition of self expressed thought in patients with auditory hallucinations. *Journal of Abnormal Psychology, 89*, 728–736.

Hemsley, D.R. (1976). Stimulus uncertainty: Response uncertainty and stimulus response compatibility as determinants of schizophrenics reaction time performance. *Bulletin of the Psychodynamic Society, 8*, 425–427.

Hemsley, D.R. (1988). Psychological models of schizophrenia. In E. Miller & A. Cooper (Eds.), *Adult abnormal psychology.* London: Churchill Livingstone.

Hemsley, D.R. (1993). Perceptual and cognitive abnormalities as the basis for schizophrenic symptoms. In A.S. David & J. Cutting (Eds.), *The neuropsychology of schizophrenia.* Hove, UK: Lawcence Erlbaum Associates Ltd.

Hess, E.J., Bracma, M.S., Kleinman, J.E., & Creese, I. (1987). Dopamine receptor subtype imbalance in schizophrenia. *Life Science, 40*, 1487–1497.

Heston, L.L. (1966). Psychiatric disorders in foster home reared children of schizophrenic mothers. *British Journal of Psychiatry, 112*, 819–825.

Hingley, S.M. (1997). Psychodynamic perspectives on psychosis and psychotherapy: I. theory. *British Journal of Medical Psychology, 70*, 301–312.

Hirsch, S.R., & Leff, J.P. (1975). *Abnormalities in the parents of schizophrenics* (Maudsley Monograph No. 22). Oxford, UK: Oxford University Press.

Hoffman, R.E. (1986). Verbal hallucination and language production in schizophrenia. *The Behavioural and Brain Sciences, 9*, 503–548.

Hughes, I., Hailwood, R., Abbati-Yeoman, J., & Budd, R. (1996). Developing a family interventions service for serious mental illness: Clinical observations and experiences. *Journal of Mental Health, 5*(2), 145–159.

Iversen, L.L. (1982). Biochemical and pharmacological studies: The dopamine hypothesis. In J.K. Wing (Ed.), *Schizophrenia: Towards a new synthesis*. London: Academic Press.

Jablensky, A. (1986). Epidemiology of schizophrenia: A European perspective. *Schizophrenia Bulletin, 12*, 52–73.

Jackson, D.D. (1960). A critique of the literature on the genetics of schizophrenia. In D.D. Jackson (Ed.), *The aetiology of schizophrenia*. New York: Basic Books.

Jackson, H.F. (1986). Is there a schizotoxin? A critique of the evidence of the major contender—dopamine. In N. Eisenberg & D. Glasgow (Eds.), *Current issues in clinical psychology* (vol. 5). Aldershot, UK: Gower.

Jackson, H.F. (1990). Biological markers in schizophrenia. In R.P. Bentall (Ed.), *Reconstructing schizophrenia*. London: Routledge.

Jackson, M. (1995). Learning to think about schizoid thinking. In J. Ellwood (Ed.), *Psychosis: Understanding and treatment*. London: Jessica Kingsley.

Jaspers, K. (1962). *General psychopathology*. Manchester, UK: Manchester University Press.

Jernigan, T.L. (1992). Neuroanatomical factors in schizophrenia. In D.J. Kavanagh (Ed.), *Schizophrenia: An overview and practical handbook*. London: Chapman & Hall.

Jernigan, T.L., Zatz, L.M., Moses, J.A., & Berger, P.A. (1982). Computed tomography in schizophrenia and normal volunteers: I. Fluid volume. *Archives of General Psychiatry, 39*, 765–770.

Johnstone, L. (1993). Family management in schizophrenia: Its assumptions and contradictions. *Journal of Mental Health, 2*(3), 255–269.

Kallman, F.J. (1946). The genetic theory of schizophrenia. *American Journal of Psychiatry, 103*, 309–322.

Kaney, S., & Bentall, R.P. (1989). Persecutory delusion and attribution style. *British Journal of Medical Psychology, 62*, 192–198.

Kendell, R.E., Brockington, I.F., & Leff, J.S. (1976). Prognostic implication of six alternative definitions of schizophrenia. *Archives of General Psychiatry, 36*, 25–31.

Kety, S.S., Rosenthal, D., Wender, P.H., & Schulsinger, F. (1968). The types and prevalence of mental illness in biological and adoptive families of adopted schizophrenics. In D. Rosenthal & S.S. Kety (Eds.), *The transmission of schizophrenia*. Oxford, UK: Pergamon.

Kety, S.S., Rosenthal, D., Wender, P.H., Schulsinger, F., & Jacobsen, B. (1975). Mental illness in the biological and adoptive families of adopted individuals who have become schizophrenic: A preliminary report based on psychiatric interviews. In R. Fieve, D. Rosenthal, & H. Brill (Eds.), *Genetic research in psychiatry*. Baltimore, MD: Johns Hopkins University Press.

Klein, M. (1986). Notes on some schizoid mechanisms. In J. Mitchell (Ed.), *The selected Melanie Klein*. Harmondsworth, UK: Penguin Books. (Original work published 1946)

Klerman, G. (1984). Ideology and science in the individual psychotherapy with schizophrenia. *Schizophrenia Bulletin, 10*, 608–612.

Kohut, H. (1977). *The restoration of the self*. New York: International University Press.

Kraepelin, E. (1905). *Lectures on clinical psychiatry*. London: Balliere Tindall.

Kringlen, E. (1967). *Heredity and environment in the functional psychoses*. London: Heinemann.

Kuipers, E., Garety, P., Fowler, D., Dunn, G., Bebbington, P., Freeman, D., & Hadley, C. (1997). London-East Anglia randomised controlled trial of cognitive-behavioural therapy for psychosis. *British Journal of Psychiatry, 171*, 319–327.

Kuriansky, J.B., Deming, W.E., & Gurland, B.J. (1974). On trends in the diagnosis of schizophrenia. *American Journal of Psychiatry, 131*, 402–407.

Laing, R.D. (1965). *The divided self*. London: Pelican.

Lam, D.H. (1991). Psychosocial family interventions in schizophrenia: A review of empirical studies. *Psychological Medicine, 21*, 423–441.

Langfeldt, G. (1937). *The prognosis in schizophrenia and the factors influencing the course of the disease*. Copenhagen, Denmark: Levin & Munksgaard.

Lavender, A., & Holloway, F. (1992). Models of continuing care. In M. Birchwood & N. Tarrier (Eds.), *Innovations in the psychological management of schizophrenia: Assessment, treatment and services*. Chichester, UK: John Wiley & Sons.

Leff, J., Kuipers, L., Berkokowitz, R., Eberlein-Fries, R., & Sturgeon, D. (1982). A controlled trial of social intervention in families of schizophrenic patients. *British Journal of Psychiatry, 148*, 727–731.

Lewis, S.W. (1989). Congenital risk factors in schizophrenia. *Psychological Medicine, 19*, 5–13.

Lidz, T. (1993). The role of chaos in the etiology and treatment of schizophrenia. In G. Benedettir & P.M. Furlan (Eds.), *The psychotherapy of schizophrenia*. Seattle, CA: Hogrefe & Huber.

Lidz, T., & Blatt, S. (1983). Critique of the Danish–American studies of the biological and adoptive relatives of adoptives who become schizophrenic. *American Journal of Psychiatry, 140*, 426–431.

Maher, B.A. (1974). Delusional thinking and perceptual disorder. *Journal of Individual Psychology, 30*, 98–113.

Main, M. (1991). Metacognitive knowledge, metacognitive monitoring and singular (coherent) vs. multiple (incoherent) models of attachment: Findings and directions for future research. In P. Harris, J. Stevenson Hinde, & C. Parkes (Eds.), *Attachment across the life cycle*. New York: Routledge & Kegan Paul.

Marshall, J.R. (1984). The genetics of schizophrenia revisited. *Bulletin of the British Psychological Society, 37*, 177–181.

Marshall, J.R. (1990). The genetics of schizophrenia. In R. Bentall (Ed.), *Reconstructing Schizophrenia*. London: Routledge.

McCreadie, R.G., Williamson, D.J., Athawes, R.W.B., Connolly, M.A., & Tilak-Singh, M. (1994). The Nithsdale schizophrenia survey XIII: Parental rearing patterns, current symptomatology and relatives expressed emotion. *British Journal of Psychiatry, 165*, 347–352.

McGhie, A., & Chapman, J. (1961). Disorders of attention and perception in early schizophrenia. *British Journal of Medical Psychology, 34*, 103–116.

McGuffin, P. (1988). Genetics of schizophrenia. In P. Bebbington & P. McGuffin (Eds.), *Schizophrenia: The major issues*. London: Heinemann.

McGuffin, P., Farmer, A.E., Gottesman, I.I., Murray, R.M., & Revely, A. (1984). Twin concordance for operationally defined schizophrenia: Confirmation, familiarity and heritability. *Archives of General Psychiatry, 41*, 541–545.

Meltzer, H.Y., & Stahl, S.M. (1976). The dopamine hypothesis of schizophrenia: A review. *Schizophrenia Bulletin, 2*, 19–76.

Moline, R.E., Singh, S., Morris, A., & Meltzer, H.Y. (1985). Family expressed emotion and relapse in schizophrenia in 24 urban American patients. *American Journal of Psychiatry, 142*, 1078–1081.

Mueser, K.T., & Berenbaum, H. (1990). Psychodynamic treatment of schizophrenia. *Psychological Medicine, 20*, 253–262.

Murray, R.M., Lewis, S.W., Owen, M.J., & Foerster, A. (1988). The neurodevelopmental origins of dementia praecox. In P. Bebbington & P. McGuffin (Eds.), *Schizophrenia: The major issues*. London: Heinemann.

Nasrallah, H.A., Olsen, S.C., McCalley-Whitters, M., Chapman, S., & Jacoby, E.C. (1986). Cerebral ventricular enlargement in schizophrenia: A preliminary follow-up study. *Archives of General Psychiatry, 43*, 157–159.

Nelson, H., Pantelis, C., Barnes, T., Thraser, S., & Bodger, S. (1993). Cognitive functioning and symptomatology in schizophrenia. In A.S. David & J. Cutting (Eds.), *The neuropsychology of schizophrenia*. Hove, UK: Lawrence Erlbaum Associates Ltd.

Nuechterlein, K.H. (1987). Vulnerability models for schizophrenia: State of the art. In H. Hafner, W.F. Gattaz, & W. Janarzik (Eds.), *Search for the causes of schizophrenia*. Berlin/Heidleberg: Springer.

Osmond, H., & Smythes, J. (1952). Schizophrenia: A new approach. *Journal of Mental Science*, *98*, 309–315.

Owen, F., & Cross, A.J. (1992). Biochemistry of schizophrenia. In D.J. Kavanagh (Ed.), *Schizophrenia: An overview and practical handbook*. London: Chapman & Hall.

Owen, M.J. (1992). Will schizophrenia become a graveyard for molecular genetics? *Psychological Medicine*, *22*, 289–293.

Persons, J. (1986). The advantages of studying psychological phenomena rather than psychiatric diagnosis. *American Psychologist*, *41*, 1252–1260.

Pilling, S. (1988). Work. In A. Lavender & F. Holloway (Eds.), *Community care in practice*. Chichester, UK: John Wiley & Sons.

Reed, D. (1978). *Anna*. London: Penguin.

Reed, T., Potter, M., & Gurling, H.M.D. (1992). The genetics of schizophrenia. In D.J. Kavanagh (Ed.), *Schizophrenia: An overview and practical handbook*. London: Chapman & Hall.

Reveley, D.A. (1985). CT scans and schizophrenia. *British Journal of Psychiatry*, *146*, 367–371.

Robbins, M.I. (1993). *Constitutional vulnerability and an epigenetic model: Experiences of schizophrenia—an integration of personal, scientific and therapeutic*. New York: Guilford Press.

Rogers, A., & Pilgrim, D. (1996). *Mental health policy in Britain: A critical introduction*. London: Croom Helm.

Rose, S., Kamin, L.T., & Lewontin, R.C. (1984). *Not in our genes*. London: Penguin.

Rosenthal, D. (1970). *Genetic theory and abnormal behaviour*. New York: McGraw-Hill.

Sarbin, P.R. (1967). The concept of hallucinations. *Journal of Personality*, *35*, 359–380.

Schiff, M., Cassou, B., & Stewart, J. (1980). *Genetics and schizophrenia: The recommendation of a consensus*. Unpublished monograph. (Original work, by B. Cassou, M. Schiff, & J. Stewart, published in French in 1980)

Schneider, K. (1959). *Clinical psychopathology* (M.W. Hamilton, Trans.). London: Grune & Stratton.

Schneider, W., & Shriffrin, R.M. (1977). Controlled and automatic human information processing: I. Detection, search and attention. *Psychological Review*, *84*, 1–66.

Schwartz, S. (1982). Is there a schizophrenic language? *Behavioural and Brain Sciences*, *5*, 175–179.

Segal, H. (1979). *Klein*. Glasgow, UK: Fontana/Collins.

Seidman, L.J. (1984). Schizophrenia and brain dysfunction: An integration of recent neurodiagnostic findings. *Psychological Bulletin*, *94*, 195–238.

Shallice, T. (1988). *From neuropsychology to mental structure*. Cambridge, UK: Cambridge University Press.

Sherrington, R., Bryn-Jolfsson, J., Petursson, H., Potter, M., Dudleston, K., Barrowclough, B., Wasmuth, J., Dodds, A., & Gurring, H. (1988). Localisation of susceptibility locus for schizophrenia on chromosome 5. *Nature*, *336*, 164–167.

Shields, J., Gottesman, I., & Slater, E. (1967). Kallmann's 1946 schizophrenic twin study in the light of new information. *Acta Psychiatrica Scandinavica*, *43*, 385–386.

Singer, M.T., & Wynne, L.C. (1966). Principles for scoring communication defects and deviances in parents of schizophrenics: Rorschach and TAT scoring manuals. *Psychiatry*, *29*, 260–288.

Slade, P.D. (1976). Towards a theory of auditory hallucinations: Outline of an hypothetical four factor model. *British Journal of Social and Clinical Psychology*, *15*, 415–423.

Slade, P.D., & Bentall, R.P. (1988). *Sensory perceptions: Towards scientific analysis of hallucinations*. London: Croom Helm.

Slade, P.D., & Cooper, K. (1979). Some conceptual difficulties with the term "schizophrenia": An alternative model. *British Journal of Social and Clinical Psychology*, *18*, 309–317.

Slater, E. (1953). *Psychotic and neurotic illnesses in twins*. London: HMSO.

Spitzer, M. (1990). On defining delusions. *Comprehensive Psychiatry*, *31*(5), 377–397.

Storey, P.B. (1966). Lumbar air encephalography in chronic schizophrenia: A controlled experiment. *British Journal of Psychiatry*, *112*, 135–144.

Strauss, J.S., & Carpenter, W.T. (1977). Predication of outcome in schizophrenia: III. Five year outcome and its predictions. *Archives of General Psychiatry, 34*, 154–163.

Tarrier, N. (1990). Family management in schizophrenia. In R.P. Bentall (Ed.), *Reconstructing schizophrenia*. London: Routledge.

Tarrier, N., Barrowclough, C., Porceddu, K., & Fitzpatrick, E. (1994). The Salford intervention project for schizophrenic relapse prevention: Five and eight year accumulating relapses. *British Journal of Psychiatry, 165*, 829–832.

Tarrier, N., Barrowclough, C., Vaughn, C., Bamrah, J.S., Porceddu, K., Watts, S., & Freeman, H.L. (1988). The community management of schizophrenia: A controlled trial of family intervention with families to reduce relapse. *British Journal of Psychiatry, 153*, 532–542.

Tienari, P. (1975). Schizophrenia in Finnish male twins. In M.H. Lader (Ed.), *Studies of schizophrenia*. Ashford, UK: Headley Brothers.

Trimble, M., & Kingsley, D. (1978). Cerebral ventricular size in chronic schizophrenia. *Lancet, i*, 278–279.

Vaughn, C.E., & Leff, J.P. (1976). The influences of family and social factors on the course of psychiatric illness: A comparison of schizophrenic and depressed neurotic patients. *British Journal of Psychiatry, 129*, 125–137.

Venables, P.H. (1984). Cerebral mechanism, automatic responsiveness and attention in schizophrenia. In W.D. Spalding & J.K. Cole (Eds.), *Theories of schizophrenia and psychosis*. Nebraska: University of Nebraska Press.

Warner, R. (1994). *Recovery from schizophrenia* (2nd ed.). London: Routledge & Kegan Paul.

Weinberger, F.N., Powell, E.G., & Austin, S.V. (1979). Cerebellar atrophy in chronic schizophrenia. *Lancet, ii*, 718–719.

Weiss, E. (1950). Sense of reality and reality testing. *Samiska, 4*, 171–180.

Wig, N., Menon, D., Bedi, J., Leff, J., Kuipers, L., Ghosh, A., Day, R., Korten, A., Ernberg, G., Sartorius, N., & Jablensky, A. (1987). Distribution of expressed emotion components among relatives of schizophrenic patients in Aarhus and Chandigarth. *British Journal of Psychiatry, 1551*, 160–165.

Wing, J.K. (1989). The measurement of social disablement: The MRC social behaviour and social performance schedules. *Psychiatry, Psychiatric Epidemiology, 25*, 2–8.

Wing, J.K., & Brown, G.W. (1970). *Institutionalism and schizophrenia*. London: Cambridge University Press.

Winnicott, D. (1988). *Human nature*. London: Free Association Books.

Winters, K.C., & Neale, J.M. (1983). Delusions and delusional thinking in psychotics: A review of the literature. *Clinical Psychology Review, 3*, 227–253.

Woods, B.T., Yurgelin-Todd, D., & Benes, F.M. (1990). Progressive ventricular enlargement in schizophrenia: Comparison to bipolar affective disorder and correlation with clinical source. *Biological Psychiatry, 27*, 341–352.

World Health Organisation. (1992). *The ICD-10 classification of mental and behavioural disorders*. Geneva, Switzerland: World Health Organisation.

Wynne, L.C., & Singer, M.T. (1963). Thought disorder and family relations. *Archives of General Psychiatry, 9*, 199–206.

Zubin, J., & Spring, B. (1977). Vulnerability: A new view of schizophrenia. *Journal of Abnormal Psychiatry, 86*, 260–266.

Author index

Subject index